Corporate Religion

Pearson Education

In an increasingly competitive world, it is quality of thinking that gives an edge. An idea that opens new doors, a technique that solves a problem, or an insight that simply helps make sense of it all.

We work with leading authors in the field of management and finance to bring cutting-edge thinking and best learning practice to a global market.

Under a range of leading imprints, including *Financial Times Prentice Hall*, we create world-class print publications and electronic products giving readers knowledge and understanding which can then be applied, whether studying or at work.

To find out more about our business and professional products, you can visit us at www.business-minds.com

For other Pearson Education publications, visit www.pearsoned.ema.com

JESPER KUNDE

Corporate Religion

*Building a strong company
through personality and
corporate soul*

An imprint of PEARSON EDUCATION

London · New York · San Francisco · Toronto · Sydney
Tokyo · Singapore · Hong Kong · Cape Town · Madrid · Amsterdam · Munich · Paris · Milan

PEARSON EDUCATION LIMITED

Head Office:
Edinburgh Gate
Harlow CM20 2JE
Tel: +44 (0)1279 623623
Fax: +44 (0)1279 431059

London Office:
128 Long Acre, London WC2E 9AN
Tel: +44 (0)171 447 2000
Fax: +44 (0)171 240 5771
Website: www.business-minds.com

First published in Great Britain in 2000
Danish edition first published in 1997
by Börsen Forlag A/S

ISBN 0 273 64380 0

British Library Cataloguing in Publication Data
A CIP catalogue record for this book can be obtained from the British Library.

10 9 8 7 6 5 4 3 2 1

Typeset by Northern Phototypesetting Co. Ltd, Bolton.
Printed and bound in Italy by Rotolito Lombarda

The Publishers' policy is to use paper manufactured from sustainable forests.

Translated by Helle Nygaard and Nigel P. Mander. Reproofed by Daz Doggett, Tim Atkins and David Sandhu.

Contents

Introduction

B J Cunningham

For the past four years I have chaired a conference in Stockholm called the New Age Event. Before you immediately close this book, the New Age Event is not about beards and crystals nor is it attended by sandal-wearing aubergine-eating soothsayers.

Instead it talks about prophets of a different kind. The kind that are derived from the careful study, proper thought and masterful communication of promises. These are the profits that interest me. The profits of effective brand marketing.

I was chosen as chairman for my irreverence. I had the audacity to raise £1.25 million in the City of London to establish the Enlightened Tobacco Company PLC, and to then market a brand of cigarettes called Death as "the honest smoke".

This act of heresy, though enormously successful with consumers, didn't go down at all well with the tobacco industry. After three years of struggle with distribution, it eventually landed me in the European Court of Justice fighting against not only every Member State of Europe (except the Spanish and Portuguese, bless 'em) but also the might of the established tobacco industry.

I lost. My scheme to effect direct distribution for Death threatened to punch a £12.5 billion hole in the Exchequer. It would have forced the Government to tax compete. The scheme used a 'loophole' called European Law to arbitrage the tax differentials between Member States by use of an agent (my company), purchasing cigarettes on behalf of over-taxed UK smokers in Luxembourg where excise is low, and then again as agent arranging for the transport of these cigarettes to the UK for personal consumption. For six months we offered cigarettes at a 40% discount turning a 25% net profit. We were riding a tobacco-filled coach and horses through Europe. Marvellous.

The ten judges in Luxembourg eventually said 'Non'. Apparently, although we were right in law, the law was never intended for us to be right: therefore we were wrong. An expensive lesson. The only health warning I missed was the most important "Justice can seriously damage your wealth."

Nonetheless Death and the European Court action gave me a certain amount of profile. This in turn meant (of course) that I became an "expert" in provocative brand marketing and hence the invitation to chair the conference in Stockholm.

The New Age Event brings together brand builders and Board Directors from the largest and most successful corporations in Scandinavia and mixes them up with leading academics and gurus from the higher echelons of the marketing world. It is Scandinavia's leading branding event, aiming to identify the key trends today and the way things will be tomorrow.

Amongst the great and the good who speak are leading lights from America and Europe who jet in to push their latest books. Also prevalent are Marketing Directors who rise to defend their brands and share their current strategies. Finally it includes the ad men who add up their latest advertising theories.

One such ad man was Jesper Kunde. His talk was entitled Corporate Religion. As a good catholic boy I was immediately riled. Religion is such a heavily loaded word. How could this man from Denmark even dare suggest that corporations should become religious? It stung of cultism, L. Ron Hubbard, brainwashing and bible bashing. The libertarian inside me cringed. In short, it wound me up.

Which is lucky, because my role as chairman is to try to shoot everyone down. To spot the bull and call it, to push the buttons that I can uncover and to generally bring the speakers down to earth (if I can).

So Jesper started talking and I started taking notes. The problem was that as I scribbled I found myself agreeing with everything he had to say. He was describing through his model exactly the philosophy I had used in establishing my brand. When Jesper talked about Corporate Religion, he meant binding a company together in a common expression.

He argued that consumers are increasingly looking behind advertising messages and brands at the companies putting them forward. They are looking for attitudes that reinforce their beliefs about that brand or message. If the company's attitudes are inconsistent or non-existent, consumers lose faith and seek a more solid attitude elsewhere.

It follows that creating a strong market position means more than creating brand awareness. It means more than focusing on the market outside. A strong market position means creating a company that delivers internally and involves consumers externally.

This is because a brand is fundamentally a promise, both rational (quantitative) and emotional (qualitative). But a promise is only valid if delivered from a sound person, a solid individual. If a person keeps changing, or the promise keeps changing, then there is no value in either.

Companies can be viewed like people. Each one of us can be seen as being made up of three separate perspectives – how we perceive ourselves, how others perceive us and how we want to be perceived. The more integrated the three separate perspectives, the stronger we are. Companies are the same. If a company perceives itself in the same way as others perceive it and as it wants to be perceived, then it is strong. How a company sees itself is its internal culture or religion. How others see it is its external market position or brand persona, its brand promise. How a company wants to be perceived is the company's mission.

Integrating the external market position of a company with the internal culture through a unifying vision, mission and system requires a consistent corporate concept that must be communicated both internally and externally. Consistent because it must secure trust and loyalty, both from within the organisation and from without amongst consumers. This requires strong leadership, clear messages and unwavering communication. It means building a Corporate Religion.

Jesper talked about brands and organisations in the holistic way in which I believe they should be considered. But most importantly, he had devised a system that could be implemented in any organisation and a visual model that made this system clear.

This unusual position of agreeing with the theory yet objecting to the language left me with no choice. I threw everything back at him. I huffed and I puffed but I could not blow his house down. In fact I had the reverse effect. By giving him such a hard time and with him answering so fluently, I actually made him look great.

Jesper was understandably delighted. I was more than a little deflated. After the conference we talked. It transpired that he had ten years ago established what is now Denmark's most successful advertising agency and had his eyes set on expansion. He very kindly pointed out that I was just about to lose my court case. Perhaps there was an opportunity.

A year and a half later I am now a joint venture partner of Kunde & Co. London. Jesper wrote this book and I have helped bring it and this agency into the English language. In this straightforward book, the message is unity and consistency. This book shows the way to a strong company and a strong brand.

So I have learnt another lesson in this life after Death, "If you can't beat them, particularly if you agree with them anyway, join them".

BJ Cunningham
Managing Partner, Kunde & Co. (London)

Preface

This book is an attempt to break away from the unimaginative thinking which today impedes many companies. They work hard, have highly qualified employees and high quality products, but they remind me of a football match where the ball is kicked around the pitch just to keep the game going, with both teams playing for a 0-0 draw. There is no change of tempo, no enthusiasm and no belief that they can score goals.

Through my work with concept development and marketing in international companies, I have seen how difficult it is to get attitudes and messages out through big organisations. I work with people at both the top and bottom of parent companies and subsidiaries alike, which gives me merciless up-to-the-minute experience of how non-homogeneous many companies are. At the same time, I have noted with alarm how many large and otherwise healthy international companies are dying of terminal administration. There are few visionary, dynamic leaders and they are most certainly the exception rather than the rule. This in spite of the known fact that companies with dynamic management are the most profitable. Those companies on the other hand which are only administered, running on the declining inertia of former greatness and growth, are already in the process of decay. It takes time before the axe eventually falls, but globally it is happening ever faster. If you want to board the train, this is your last call.

I have written this book as a constructive attempt to show another, more dynamic way, for companies to move forward. This book is not about research results, but about attitudes. Attitudes to what basically determines a company's strength or the lack of it, and how a company ought to act and organise itself. Corporate Religion is illustrated with plenty of cases from major international companies, which should ease the approach to the more theoretical part of the book.

While working on this book, I have discovered that many people crave a spiritual and goal-oriented attitude in their companies. Leaders seek ways to create it, and employees seek meaning in their workplace and the work to which they dedicate most if not all of their adult lives.

Writing this book has inspired me to practise what I preach within my own company. I hope that you too will be inspired to do the same. There is creative dynamite just waiting to be ignited and lobbed in the right direction. Boom!

Thanks to ...

So many people have contributed positively to this book that it would be impossible to mention everyone. So I will restrict myself to just a few – all the rest I shall keep in my thoughts.

First and foremost I wish to thank Casper Janns, who has been responsible for uniting all the aspects of this project, which he has skilfully controlled all the way to the goal line. Casper has not only handled the practical things, such as researching and interviewing for this book's many cases, he has also been an indispensable sparring partner for the theoretical part of the book.

I also owe special thanks to Anders Krag who during the final phase of the project has polished the text with skilled – and gentle – hands. Finally a big thank you to Helle, and to Nynne and Nanna, who have had to make do without husband and father respectively during large parts of this project.

Copenhagen, April 1999
Jesper Kunde

Corporate Religion
– the essence

*Thinking differently from the outset
often leads to the most original results*
(Henrik Ibsen)

The word religion derives from the Latin *religare* – to bind something together in a common expression. It is the defining idea of this book. Only with a strong spirit at its foundation can a company achieve a strong market position. And make no mistake, it is brand position that ultimately decides a company's success – or the lack of it.

This book is concerned with self-worth and belief. The kind of belief that enables you to succeed in business.

This book is concerned with self-worth and belief. The kind of belief that enables you to succeed in business.

The future's values will be qualitative in nature. The time has passed when technical advantages alone can sell a product. It is the attitudes to a brand and the emotional and non-material values associated with it, that create sales. The battle among brands is for positions of strength in the eyes of the consumer. This is the field on which companies will have to fight it out.

Emotional values are replacing physical attributes as the fundamental market influence. This is not something that I have invented, it's there for anyone to see. My key area of interest lies in the interpretation of this development, and the notion that you can ascribe to your products emotional values, if you have the will to do it.

I use the word religion because it means binding together in a belief. I don't think it's possible to have any meaningful vision of the future without believing in something.

To achieve strong and successful positions in the market, companies have to start thinking and acting along these lines. They need a Corporate Religion. I use the word religion because it means binding together in a belief. I don't think it's possible to have any meaningful vision of the future without believing in something. Believing in yourself, believing in your dreams.

Corporate Religion – a coherent description of the company

In the international market it is no longer products that compete, it is concepts. The company that wins is the company that holds the most lucrative market position. Against this background, the brand and its values become crucial to the company's success or failure. Companies must also be able to describe themselves – both internally and externally – because they are no longer adequately defined simply by the products they make. Customers buy the company and everything it stands for. So the company must be able to define itself in a connected and coherent way.

In many ways companies reflect the people who run them. The stronger the personalities, the more penetration they have in the outside world. They are the archangels who make a Corporate Religion a description of the company's personality. The better the personality description is, the easier it becomes for the whole company to understand it – and rally round it. A good description also makes it easier for the market to assess whether it likes the company or not.

Harmony and penetration power

In the history of psychology, Alfred Adler was a pioneering figure. In his study of the human personality, Adler concluded that it is formed by three constituent conditions which mutually interact:

Fig 1.1 The internal and external company – a total description of the company's personality

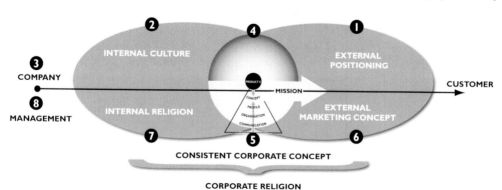

Corporate Religion is best explained using the above model, which synthesises the internal culture, external positioning and management's corporate objectives. See Figure. 4.7 for a detailed explanation of each phase.

- the you as others see you;
- the you as you see yourself;
- the you as you would like to be seen.

According to Adler, the more these three views harmonise, the stronger one's personality becomes. And with a harmonious personality, there is a corresponding diminution of inner conflicts and misunderstandings between the outside world and the individual. My contention is that exactly the same thing happens in companies. The more harmony there is between the market's view of the company and the company's view of itself – now and for the future – the stronger the company's personality will be. And the more penetration it will exert externally.

When external positioning and internal culture come into harmony, the easier it is for the company to consolidate its chosen market position. Figure 1.1 illustrates a model for a coherent description of a company. From left to right, information flows fully from the management through the entire organisation, out through the executive system to the customer, and ultimately to the total market.

The oval at the left represents the internal culture, which overlaps with the external market positioning. It is the coherent description of the company which unites internal culture and external positioning. I call this the company's Corporate Concept.

Describe your company

In the future, you must be able to describe your company in order to control it internally and externally. The purpose here is to ensure that the sole thing which accrues in the market is one single consistent value. Companies with a consistent Corporate Concept can more easily define the setting for the internal religion and creating the external marketing concept. The aim is to unite everything in a Corporate Religion: a religion that brings together the internal company and the external market in a shared, connected flow of understanding.

Think company

Corporate Religion is a completely new way of thinking about companies. Today, the product is still the main communication highway in the company. But this will soon no longer be the case. When companies make the shift to selling solutions, brands and attitudes, communicating the company's attitudes and values becomes the decisive parameter for success. And it demands that you find out who you are as a company.

Find the right formula

When top management finds a satisfactory answer to that question, it will give them the key to communicating the company internally as well externally to the market (see also chapter IV). And for managers to do this successfully in the future, they will need to be very different to the way many are today. One of the key characteristics of the new generation of leaders is that they must be skilled at communicating inside their companies and externally to the market. They will be rated by their own ability to see and describe how the market will evolve, and by their company's ability to meet that coming reality. Those who are capable of formulating and reformulating their companies will be tomorrow's winners. And the better they are at reaching into every corner and crevice of both the company and the market, the more things will flow in the same direction.

Find your hidden energy

I am prepared to bet that in almost all large international companies, half the available energy is untapped: energy that can be released to powerful effect if you can describe the company, develop a consistent company concept, formulate an internal religion – and manage the whole organisation accordingly. Do that and you will generate enough megawatts for one long and progressive sweep into the limelight.

IBM's One Voice

Louis Gerstner at IBM did just that. He described the company and communicated the result to the whole of his

Louis Gerstner's message was sent directly to all employees.

organisation in the shape of a book called "One Voice". In it, Gerstner relates how he saw the situation when he took charge as CEO in 1993. He emphasised IBM's strengths; how he viewed the future; and how he thought the employees should tackle it. Every IBM employee on the planet received a copy of the book "directly" from him.

Who doesn't believe in Microsoft?

A new kind of leader is appearing, one who is a religion leader both for their market and their company. Microsoft's Bill Gates is a prime example. He drives the market – and the biggest part of his corporation's value lies in the market's belief that he will do it even better in the future.

Gates knows how to express himself on the subject of the future. He believes in something, and has the ability to communicate it.

In the future, every leader worthy of the name will need a measure of Bill Gates' talent. To be able to express a view of the future and earnestly believe in it. This is why a Corporate Religion is decisive for managing the company and the market into the future.

Branson the Brand

Attitudes and values in the future will turn upside down a lot of things taken for granted today. Brands will become religions and some individuals, who are seen as an expression of their brands, will themselves become religions. The baseball player Michael Jordan is a case in point. In Forbes Magazine (March 22, 1999) the President of Warner Bros. Records, Phil Quartataro, stated that the real stars are the ones who can create an image above and beyond their medium, and so to speak, leverage their celebrity into brand equity. He said: "Michael Jordan is not promoting a song or a movie, he's promoting an image. That's what stardom is all about". Celebrities like Jordan cash in by building brand equity, name recognition, and then attaching that equity to many products. Michael Jordan is undoubtedly the strongest celeb-brand of all.

From 1990–98 he made more than $300 million in salary and endorsement money. According to Forbes "Top 40 Athletes" list of 1998, Jordan made $47 million in endorsement money – or off-court earnings – in 1997. This enormous world record figure illustrates the equity of the Jordan brand.

Another recent example of a religion leader who has become equivalent to his brand is Britain's Richard Branson. He personifies both the brand and brand value in Virgin. The company markets a lot of different products from air travel and bank services to fizzy drinks and cosmetics. Branson is, like Bill Gates, very conscious about his own role. And he views it from the position of the market, not the product (see page 21).

The American Way

It is probably not just for fun that the USA – one of the world's oldest democracies – has a spokesperson in the shape of the President. It is the most efficient way to lead a nation, to communicate externally to the market (the people, the world), and internally to the party faithful.

The person who the Americans choose as their President must first and foremost have the ability to act as spokesperson. Nobody these days believes that the President actually runs the country single-handed. When the Americans recognised this fact in the 80's, they gave the job to a professional communicator by choosing Ronald Reagan, a former Hollywood actor.

What do we want? Why do we want it? And how do we make it happen?

Corporate Religion is an alternative way of focusing a company's goals. It is a centralised model, which requires that management takes real responsibility and, if necessary, draws power back to the company's core. A Corporate Religion's essential purpose is to strengthen and unify a company's efforts – regardless of its market. Corporate Religion then, is a holistic concept in which the whole company chooses to be run by a "spiritual" management. Forget about bottom line exercises and internal accounting. Numbers and budgets will lead you nowhere. What takes a company to success is its philosophy, articulated by a "spiritual" management. It is a company's attitudes that make customers sit up and take notice of the qualitative, emotional values associated with its brands. The time is fast approaching when a new rule will apply – there are no rules. A company must create its own rules through its philosophy – its religion. The religion unites the company around a shared vision, mission and system.

The principles behind Corporate Religion have been employed by phenomenally successful companies. Microsoft, The Coca-Cola Company, Nike, Walt Disney and The Body Shop are conspicuous among them.

Becoming a Brand Religion

Consumers are not robots. They don't simply buy products, they buy attitudes as well. When confronted with proliferation and diversity, choice becomes increasingly informed by belief. It is belief and instinct about a brand's excellence that matters. Consumers do not get this belief out of thin air.

Today, it is about creating strong non-material values and services which together form an aura around the product and give the brand its perceived value.

They want to know who is behind the products that they buy. They want to know the company. They want to know what you think. And the better your company communicates its attitudes, the stronger you will become.

In the global market, the ultimate arbiter of success is brand position. The higher in the brand hierarchy you go, the better. And the highest position a brand can reach is when consumers regard it as a Brand Religion. Brand values – all the expressions, attitudes and abstract attributes that companies ascribe to their products beyond their functional qualities – are precisely the non-material and emotional values which give a product its brand status.

How do companies understand their brand's relationship with consumers? The keyword in this connection is consumer involvement. Take a look at Figure 1.2 – it shows the path of involvement from an ordinary product brand at bottom left to the ultimate pinnacle of Brand Religion at

Fig 1.2 Brand Religion model

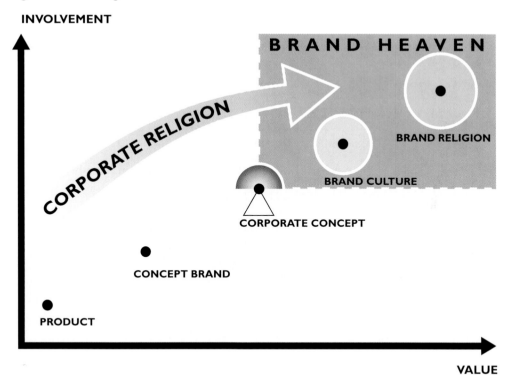

Different brands have different strengths. The stronger and more relevant the values connected to a brand, the more involved the consumers become. And greater involvement means a stronger brand and greater value for the manufacturer. A distinction is made between 5 brand types:

- Product: Products without any "added value" connected to the generic element.
- Concept Brand: Brands which are run on emotional values instead of product properties.
- Corporate Concept: Brands that fuse with a company which is seen as totally consistent.
- Brand Culture: Brands that are so strong in the eyes of consumers that they become equivalent to the function they represent.
- Brand Religion: The ultimate position for brands – to the consumer they are a must, a belief.

To reach the highest levels in the brand hierarchy, a Corporate Concept is required which binds the company and brand together in a single consistent unit. This is a difficult task, but if you succeed, the gateway to a strong market position is opened. A Corporate Religion is needed to control the process.

top right. When you reach this enviable position, the retail possibilities are limitless – as we will see in the Harley-Davidson case study. As the product itself becomes a lesser part of the brand, the demands on the company's international organisation are increased pro rata. Especially if it is geared to the practices of the past; in other words simply developing and selling products. Today, it is about creating strong non-material values and services which together form an aura around the product and give the brand its perceived value. One of the crucial demands on the company in this regard, and it's worth repeating, is that it must create a homogeneous expression internationally. Consistent visibility is the secret of the big international brands. Whether consumers encounter the brand at Charles de Gaulle airport or in the middle of the Gobi desert, the message must remain consistent.

Fig 1.3 The Value Based organisation

Only an organisation which wants the same things and goes in the same direction will be able to work sensibly with the qualitative values which differentiate brands. It is not enough to employ people just for their skills – their attitudes and values must also match those of the company.

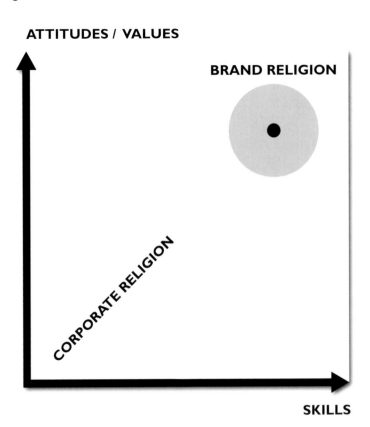

No Brand Religion without Corporate Religion

Strong brand positions are about having confidence in your own powers. And in the belief that what your company does is right – and profitable. Corporate Religion is an empowering force. It helps everybody in the company to believe in the same message.

To be able to work with the qualitative values of brands, the company must manage via a set of attitudes and values. People are usually employed for their professional skills, and of course their abilities must be the appropriate ones. But it is just as important that the employees' attitudes and values are compatible with those of the company. Only when these attitudes and values go hand in hand with skills – the whole thing being managed using a Corporate Religion – will the company be equipped to attain the ultimate position of Brand Religion.

Company growth is often the result of internationalisation. However, expansion of corporate structures can also lead to chaos. Where is the control centre? It is often no longer clear where the orders are coming from. Reaction times to changes in the marketplace steadily lengthen, and the gaps in contact between top management and customers widen day by day.

Another important point to consider here is that of market adjustment, which over the years has come to be regarded as a sort of eighth wonder of the world. But how accurate is this? The "classical" market adjustment is really a cover up for weak management, who content themselves with looking in the office guidebook to strong market positions. Of course companies must be aware of what the consumers tell them in different markets. But a strong position can only be reached if you adjust the market to the brand – and not the other way round.

If a company is going to succeed with a Corporate Religion, management must manage.

The same goes for the company's internal religion among its employees. Perhaps an employee's best qualification is their belief in the company. Once that edict is firmly in place, the company can start using time on estimating the skills of the individual. And if the company is going to succeed with a Corporate Religion, management must manage. Harley-Davidson worked this out for themselves long ago, it isn't an advertising agency or a bunch of students who go out to test the atmosphere among consumers, it's the main man, Rich Teerlink and his closest associates. Both internally and externally they send highly valuable and reliable signals by participating in Harley rallies. They get involved, they get engine oil on their clothes. There is no visible difference between Rich

Teerlink's enthusiasm and Harley-Davidson's devoted customers. That connection demonstrates the power of belief. The Virgin case history, which immediately follows the Harley-Davidson story, shows how one man's personality and "anti-convention" attitude can run an entire business empire. The Virgin story clearly illustrates how decisive a new set of values and management methods are to the modern company.

The whole truth...

Chapter 2: International chaos threatens. The signs are that international companies will tear themselves apart if they do not take the necessary precautions. There is an urgent need for a new form of management.

Chapter 3: The keywords are value, consistency and involvement. These will decide the company's success – or lack of it. Brand positioning is central. A new terminology is introduced to describe the path to the ultimate position – the Brand Religion. Four case histories illustrate the theory. During Jan Carlzon's leadership at SAS, he showed how establishing a strong consistent Corporate Concept could bring a company from crisis to success.

Worldwide Brands Inc. controls the Camel Trophy event. This relatively unknown company shows how high involvement and a strong brand position can result in massive earnings via brand extensions. Adidas and Nike fight it out over who sponsors the biggest sports stars. The case is an example of the importance of non-material values. Product quality is not enough to create differentiation. Hard Rock Café generates enormous earnings on merchandising and shows how reliable and relevant universal values open the way to rock hard profit growth.

Chapter 4: Corporate Religion, the theory. The keywords here are vision, mission, religion, system, commitment and action. Several models are presented to facilitate understanding. Don't skip Chapter 2 and 3 in your rush to get here – patience is a virtue.

Four case studies bring Corporate Religion into the real

world. Microsoft's leader Bill Gates is an example of a highly visible spiritual leader, who sets the global agenda for software. IBM is a spiritually controlled company which experienced a catastrophic decline when the management stopped paying attention to users' signals. Can Louis Gerstner now turn things around? The Danish hearing aid company Oticon escaped a deep crisis when a spiritual leader arrived to turn the organisation upside down. The Body Shop, the British "trading and caring company", is one of the strongest examples I know of how far you can get by focusing on qualitative values, both within the organisation and in communication with customers.

Chapter 5: Two elements from the central model – growth based value management, and commitment and action – will be discussed in more detail. Motivation and enthusiasm can convert belief into results. Two cases show how commitment and action can be secured through education.

Coffee chain Starbucks and burger giant McDonald's have developed elaborate educational programmes for teaching their respective Corporate Religions. A third case about Toyota shows how an efficient control system can provide a company with power steering.

Chapter 6: The consequences of implementing Corporate Religion in a traditional organisation. Central to the chapter is a discussion of organisation structure and its impact on future reality.

Chapter 7: Why leadership responsibility must return from the subsidiaries to the central top management.

Why management focus must shift from quantitative bookkeeping to qualitative value based management.

Chapter 8: A practical guide for any company that wants to change a traditional organisation into a religion driven company.

Epilogue: An optional chapter for those interested in how I have developed and implemented Corporate Religion in my own company, the marketing and advertising agency Kunde & Co.

Harley-lujah

Harley-Davidson is not only a motorbike religion, it is one of the world's strongest Brand Religions – if not the strongest.

There used to be a joke about Harleys – "If you are buying a Harley, better buy two – one for spare parts". It was a bit too close to the truth for the legendary American heavyweight. Harley quality had become very poor. Bad quality made it difficult for the motorbike's enthusiasts to cultivate Harley culture. And when the firm totally ignored the culture, the corporation came close to catastrophe and liquidation.

Harley-Davidson is an interesting case in relation to the idea behind Brand and Corporate Religion. The story of Harley-Davidson makes one thing abundantly clear: the necessity of being aware of – and taking care to build – your brand position.

Harley-Davidson was founded in 1903 by the Harley and Davidson families. After a series of competitor liquidations in the 1950s, Harley-Davidson remained the only American manufacturer of motorbikes. During the 1960's boom, the motorbike market in the USA developed with explosive power. From sales of 400,000 units in 1960 and 960,000 in 1964 to 4 million in 1971.

But Harley-Davidson didn't benefit from this growth - in fact its market share fell considerably. Why? Because Harley didn't have a countermove against Honda's lightweight machines on the American market. In 1977 Honda had 46% market share, while Harley-Davidson languished at 6%. Harley-Davidson quality was simply not good enough.

Together with 12 other members of Harley-Davidson's management team, Vaughan Beals saved the corporation. In 1981 he used $81.5 million (financed by Citicorp) to buy back Harley-Davidson from AMF, which had taken over the corporation sixteen years earlier at a time when its market share was rock bottom with just 3%.

Vaughan Beals got help at the beginning of the 1980's. From 1983-86 the US customs tariff on Japanese heavyweight motorcycles was increased by 45% – on top of the pre-existing 4.4% – a situation he understood exactly how to exploit. Taking a leaf out of the Japanese book, the company raised its quality and productivity by leaps and bounds.

Harley-Davidson: much more than a motorbike.

Harley-Davidson is closely connected to the American ideal of freedom.

*Harley-Davidson earns
large sums from
merchandising jackets ...*

beer...

and boots.

Harley-Davidson created the foundation for a sensible comeback – and in 1986 Harley-Davidson returned to pole position in the market. All over the USA, they were unrivalled in the super heavyweight class. Today Harley-Davidson commands 54% of the market for machines from 750cc upwards.

The revitalisation of production was only part of the reason for the comeback. It was also the strongly beating heart in the Harley culture which caused the new management to triumph. The Harley-Davidson myth is not only about those who actually ride the legendary motorbike – it is just as much concerned with those who know someone who rides one – and those who simply want to share the Harley spirit. To have a part in the brand values which are chiselled deep into the famous logo.

Vaughan Beals saw to it that Harley-Davidson clubs were founded, arranged Harley-Davidson rallies and special Harley-Davidson events where everyone could get their hands on Harley-Davidson merchandising. Brand values were cultivated as much as possible. And soon the latent culture was taken so seriously, that Harley-Davidson became a strong Brand Religion.

The world's biggest MC Club

Not that Harley-Davidson had ever been completely forgotten. Over the years, the company has been the object of almost unique affection and loyalty from its customers – however few of them there were. Vaughan Beals took care to found a Harley-Davidson club in 1983 with the specific purpose of cultivating customer loyalty. With 270,000 members all over the world, divided into 858 local departments, The Harley Owners Group (HOG) is today by far the biggest firm-sponsored motorcycle club in the world. HOG sends newsletters to its members and arranges rallies and special events all over the world. The worship of "USA symbolised in chromium and steel" has been enshrined in American culture.

That the corresponding Honda club rapidly fell to pieces won't surprise anyone. Not because the Japanese corporation's products don't function – they work exceedingly well and have a sensible value-for-money image. But there ain't much soul in a Honda – and without a soul you can never create a Brand Culture – much less a Brand Religion.

When Harley celebrated its 85th birthday in 1988, it happened in a way which fully demonstrates the unique relationship between the manufacturer and its customers. Every biker – including those who did not own a Harley-Davidson – was invited on locally organised runs to Harley-Davidson's hometown, Milwaukee.

As Financial World wrote in a portrait: "If Harley were a religion, Willie G. would be its God".

Willie G. makes his mark.

The admission card was a $10 contribution to the Muscular Dystrophy Association, to which the company has continuously given support. More than 40,000 bikers participated. From starting points all over the USA, different groups rode towards Milwaukee, where everyone eventually met.

Among the participants were Vaughan Beals and William G. Davidson – grandson of one of the corporation's founders, William Davidson.

Willie G. – as he is called – is worshipped as a god by many Harley disciples. The now 63 year old Willie G. has designed Harley-Davidson's bikes since 1963 and, together with his wife Nancy, is a keen participant in Harley rallies all through the summer. In his jeans and black leather jacket, the guru signs autograph books and allows himself to be photographed with bikers who are themselves of similar age. The respect is enormous.

That members of the company's management participate in rallies all over the USA is nothing exceptional. Armed with notebooks for suggestions and ideas from Harley-Davidson disciples, the present boss Rich Teerlink and the other top management figures are often out and about, cultivating the Harley religion among devotees.

When on 12 June 1993 Harley-Davidson celebrated its 90th birthday in Milwaukee, around 100,000 guests came. Every hotel within a 60 mile radius was booked solid. The countdown to the centenary celebration has already started around the world.

Merchandising

With its status as a religion, the need has naturally arisen for symbols that the many supporters of Harley-Davidson can identify with. As Vaughan Beals has said:

> *"When your company logo is number 1 in all the world's tattoo stalls, it's time to get a license which will give us a reputation in line with baseball, hot dogs and apple pie".*

"Parts and accessories" are the fastest growing part of the company.

A lot of new life has been pumped into the world-famous brand. Harley-Davidson has granted itself a merchandise collection where the fabled logo appears on everything from clothes, perfume and deodorant to jewellery and fountain pens. Then there are licence agreements, like the Harley-Davidson Café, which opened in New York in 1993. In 1994, "parts and accessories" brought in $256.5 million – making it the fastest growing part of the group. Not only is Harley-Davidson raking it in on merchandising, the purchasers themselves are walking symbols of the two-wheeled Brand Religion – and in a position to constantly influence their surroundings.

When thousands of teenage girls, who can't kick-start a moped, run around with the Harley-Davidson logo on their cycle pants, it's a signal that the Harley religion has quite some history. Who could imagine the Honda or Suzuki name exploited in the same manner? Harley-Davidson is more than a bike. Harley-Davidson means freedom in the good old fashioned sense. Brand Religion is surely not too strong a term for it.

Brand position development:

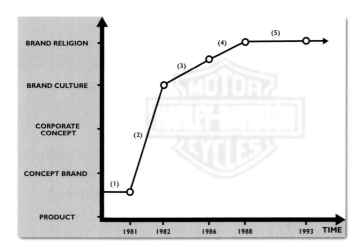

1 *Harley-Davidson's formerly strong position is weakened by poor product quality and too little attention to the brand's values. Liquidation threatens, when Vaughan Beals leads the take-over of the corporation. The renaissance begins.*

2 *The work to revitalise the illustrious brand is well under way. The Harley Owners Group is established, signalling the desire to involve consumers far more than previously. It succeeds.*

3 *Positive developments continue. Pole position in super heavyweight machines is regained in the USA. Merchandising starts to become a factor of serious importance. Turnover in "parts and accessories" reaches $44.4 million.*

4 *More than 40,000 people celebrate the corporation's 85th birthday with a special run to the corporation's hometown Milwaukee. Harley-Davidson leaders such as Vaughan Beals and William G. Davidson participate. Turnover in "parts and accessories" reaches $70.6 million.*

5 *More than 100,000 people attend the party when Harley hits the big 90. Turnover in "parts and accessories", now the fastest growing part of the group, is $199.9 million. The year after, it's up again to 256.3 million dollars.*

CASE-POINT

Harley-Davidson has shown that an old, illustrious company on its way down can be turned around by a management which understands the necessity of constantly cultivating non-material values. The establishment of HOG clubs and the management's active participation in events and rallies have been essential in bringing the brand back to the ultimate position of Brand Religion, where huge revenues can be accrued through merchandising.

The name is Bran(d)son …

Richard Branson is Virgin – and Virgin is Richard Branson. The world's greatest brand-building success has been created by consciously focusing on the real value in Virgin. And this is neither records nor air transport, but rather the owner's personal values.

When consumers buy a Virgin product, they are actually buying Richard Branson, and in this way the core of the company becomes Branson's own personal PR company, which links all Virgin products to the man and his multifarious, adventure-oriented and anti-business approach. Branson's values and the company's "David vs. Goliath" philosophy, which permeate its character in all areas of business, attracts a very large, youthful target segment – beyond which the physical products actually become irrelevant.

You never see him in a suit and tie. He crosses the Atlantic and Pacific Oceans in a hot-air balloon. He is known for having given his private telephone number to every employee and asking them to call him if they have any problems or new ideas. He has publicly stated that his ambition is to challenge the established sector – and give his customers more value for money than his competitors do. His attitude is that even financial services can be sold with a gleam in the eye. He launched a record company, signed a contract with the Sex Pistols – a group that no one else dared get involved with – and a few years later he sold Virgin Records for $1m. A transatlantic hot-air balloon crossing came close to costing him his life. These and a great many other stories abound whenever the name Branson or Virgin is mentioned. And such stories play a decisive role in the company's firmly focused strategy of building up the Virgin brand. Nothing is sacred – in fact, the more that is revealed the better. For these and similar stories provide the value that the consumer is buying.

A broad product portfolio, a tight brand

Branson did indeed sell his record company – in order to raise the capital necessary to realise his many other ideas – but with Virgin megastores he has retained his connection to music – a branch which

adds youthful dynamism to the brand. Virgin is also a travel agency (Virgin Travel Group), a fashion clothing manufacturer (Virgin Clothing), a railway company (Virgin Rail), a soft drinks company (Virgin Cola), a hotel chain (Virgin Hotels) and a great many other companies. The Virgin Group comprises over 200 companies in total. And Virgin is a universal brand that is used to an extent and in a diversity of product and service portfolios hitherto unheard of. But how is it possible to operate with a spread of activities ranging from life insurance to cola under a single brand without it becoming "watered down"?

Richard Branson is one of the world's most successful entrepreneurs, and a genius at public relations.

Virgin's success in what would be considered suicidal ventures by most other businesses stems from the fact that the Virgin brand is not rooted in a product category, as is the case with traditional brands (e.g. Coca-Cola). It has its roots in a person and in certain very abstract, qualitative values that have been elevated above product level.

The Virgin umbrella comprises over 200 companies in total. But a company can only be included if it matches Virgin's founding values and profile.

Against the establishment

A product or a service can only come under the Virgin umbrella if it matches the company's founding values and profile. Thus the focus is not directly on product specifications, but on the "linkage potential" to a range of emotional values. Virgin's policy is that new areas must, as a rule, fulfil four of the following five criteria: A Virgin product must be (1) the best quality (2) innovative (3) value for money (4) a challenge to existing alternatives, and must additionally contain (5) "a sense of fun or cheekiness".

The branch structure determines whether a product area is of interest to Virgin. Ventures into new areas of business are always approached with a "David against Goliath" mindset. Virgin identifies a new area of business that meets the majority of the criteria specified above. The new sub-brand is immediately pitted against the established market leaders – and instantly enters into the consciousness of the young, anti-authoritarian target segment. As Branson himself is on record as saying:

> "We like to use the brand to take on some very large companies, whom we believe exert too much power."

The sky's the limit: Virgin vs. BA

The best examples of this are Virgin Cola vs. Coca-Cola and Virgin Atlantic vs. British Airways. BA's long drawn out and very dirty campaign against Virgin resulted in invaluable publicity for the latter and culminated in Branson suing BA for damages. BA conceded defeat and opted to settle out of court, and on 11 December 1992 the two parties reached a settlement. BA paid £500,000 in damages to Branson personally and £110,000 to Virgin Atlantic. The money – which incidentally was divided amongst Virgin's staff – was the least important aspect of what proved to be a milestone in the history of the company. BA's accompanying apology for the false accusations levelled against Branson and Virgin Atlantic, and the damaging activities of certain BA employees towards Virgin Atlantic, were worth media gold. Virgin's victory was banner headlined in the British press ("Virgin screws BA" was The Sun's front-cover splash) and showed once and for all that mastodons can be moved aside. In 1993 Virgin Atlantic was voted "Airline of the Year".

The Sun's front cover screamer from 1993.

The Branson media phenomenon

Branson has created the youth brand of the 90's – a brand where he himself is the front runner and lifestyle guarantor. His person and his attitudes appeal directly to the selected target segment – and sympathy for Branson thus becomes the basis for the brand's strength. Richard Branson stands out as a self-made man, who in 1969 started his first business – "Student" magazine – and ever since has successfully utilised his talent, his commitment and his knack for developing business in adherence to a clearly defined set of values. With his informal approach, long hair, full beard and casual clothing, he stands out in a sea of dark suits. Indeed, the more he can upstage conventions the better. There can be no doubt that Branson is 100% aware of his actions – including those usually considered private – and their consequences for the way in which people perceive the Virgin concept, and hence the business. As Branson writes in his autobiography:

> *"When I established the airline company, I realised that I had to use my own person to strengthen Virgin Atlantic's profile and build up values in the brand name. Most companies do not acknowledge the power of the press and only have a small press office hidden away somewhere."*

Here Richard Branson hits the nail firmly on the head, for recognition of this fact plays a key role in Virgin's success.

The founder in front – and no secrets

Richard Branson is known around the world. Virtually all material from the company features Branson as the "endorser". There are no secrets about him personally – in fact, he uses every means available to get closer to the target segment. One example is the preface in the latest holiday brochure from Virgin Sun, Virgin's charter travel agency, the front page of which features Branson wearing sandals:

> *"Spain, where I regularly take my family, is a favourite but I have fond memories of the Greek islands too. Portugal I love, but it's so hard to choose which resort – good job there's the two-centre option! Turkey is a fascinating country that I just can't wait to explore. See you on board."*

All the media follow Branson's life. He often arranges and participates in extreme sports adventures and daring expeditions, and with the help of an efficient PR company his personal exploits are communicated to the target segment. All the activities which Branson undertakes in his private life appeal to his companies' target segment. Things that are conservative and traditional do not appeal to these people – they would rather take the side of the little rebel Virgin than that of the big mastodons. Although the truth of the matter is that Virgin is rarely as small as consumer consciousness tends to make it.

Awareness of the value of Branson's actions is striking. As he states in the preface to his autobiography "Losing my Virginity", this 400-page bestseller should be considered as just the first volume of the autobiography. Much more will follow in the coming years. The preface begins with a farewell letter Branson wrote to his two children, Holly and Sam, when he feared he would die during his balloon expedition in Morocco in 1997. Nothing is too personal – Branson is like a friend who shows his faith by confiding in you. And consumers do not betray such faith.

Balloon stage management

Branson has been an active balloonist for many years. Each time he lifts off he can count on ever more press coverage. Christmas 1998 saw the Virgin Global Challenger in the press spotlight. And Branson is always good for a story – or should we say a serial? First there were the three brave men who were to travel around the world, departing from Marrakech, Morocco. Then there was drama in the air over the Himalayas when the Chinese government ordered Branson to land his balloon because they were too far off course from the originally agreed air corridor – this change of course having been necessitated by the American/ British air attacks on Iraq. This whole episode

The Virgin Global Challenger Balloon – a never-ending story.

resulted in no less a person than Prime Minister Tony Blair intervening on behalf of Branson so that he could be allowed to continue his voyage. In the end Branson was forced to give up over Hawaii when lack of wind prematurely ended the expedition. All these news items were transmitted direct on CNN, the Internet and media outlets worldwide. Naturally, the focus of all this attention was on Branson – and this in turn gained exposure for the Virgin brand around the world.

And so it goes on. There are countless good stories in Richard Branson and endless opportunities for creating value in the Virgin brand. We have yet to see if it can also go the other way – Branson and Virgin receiving negative exposure in the press – with a spin-off effect on the target segment. If that were to happen, all 200 plus Virgin companies would be hit. But for now, Branson's view from the top is nothing short of fantastic.

CASE-POINT

Virgin

Virgin is a super-brand covering a great many widely differing product categories. The brand is developed and held together by Richard Branson's personal charisma, which is the real brand value. Branson is up against conventions – the values of which he transfers to the Virgin brand through deliberate extended use of the press. Hit the heights, plumb the depths… just as the entire conglomerate benefits from the goodwill Branson enjoys and creates, it will be hit equally forcefully if Branson falls into disfavour with the press and the target segment.

CHAPTER 2

International chaos

In calm waters, everyone is a good sailor
(Margaret Riis)

International companies can easily go off track.
Trends in international society will result in
companies taking themselves apart from within if
they do not change their policy. It needs
management driven by a spiritual religion to keep
the development of companies successfully on
track.

The challenge posed to companies is in international
growth. Many are emerging, and several are already
established on the international stage. Some with success,
most with moderate success, and all with the same set of
problems.

It is when internationally generated turnover and earnings achieve the greatest importance that things get difficult.

As long as the domestic market contributes the biggest
slice of turnover and earnings, it is relatively easy to
control development. It is when internationally generated
turnover and earnings achieve the greatest importance
that things get difficult. It disturbs the power balance of
the company. This does not happen from one day to the
next and it is still the headquarters that decides. But the
big international markets exert an influence proportional
to their uptake of the company's products. This new
situation creates a dilemma, with production, product
development and management on one side and the
international sales corporations on the other. The
dilemma is in management. International sales
corporations are a sprawling mass with different
management ideas and different cultures, all focusing on
different things. As long as a company has at its core a
strong ideological management with full control over the
organisation right down to the smallest subsidiary, the
problems are manageable.

But most big international companies have neither the founder nor the builder of the company in the driving seat. Instead the top management choose to give the largest influence to the subsidiary with the largest turnover. In an international company with four or five big markets it gradually gets harder to find out what the company's mission is or what it ought to be.

Market adjustment makes a virtue out of weakness

By inventing the concept of market adjustment, modern management has succeeded in making a virtue out of weakness. According to this view, decentralisation is actually seen as an advantage. But ask yourself, doesn't it simply dilute a brand and give it a weaker position, if it gets adjusted to fit different cultures in different markets? Of course it does. And that's why the concept is dying a death. In the future, it will be the market that does the adjusting to the product, not the other way round. That is the sort of market adjustment that The Coca-Cola Company believes in, and successfully operates within.

Doesn't it dilute a brand and give it a weaker position, if it gets adjusted to fit different cultures in different markets?

An international company can easily get unbalanced when the sales side starts making demands like "we've got to have a product that can match the competitors' low-priced versions". A weak management will say "yes, of course" and promptly defocus the company, without thinking about the fact that they make high-end products and that their profile is high-end.

It can be the beginning of the end. An international company may well be strong on product development, but it doesn't help much if sales and marketing can't follow. Often a company will also have different profiles in different markets, which is understandable. But when competition intensifies and product lifespans drop, then it's an absolute essential to have a focused product programme with the same profile across all markets.

The need for spiritual management

If you don't have ideas about the future, or want to be a part of it, you have already lost.

The problem for all international companies is that budgetary controls based on forecast sales are technical, dead mechanisms. Most management tools have their roots in the past, when the only interesting thing is the future.

I've heard people say, quite seriously, that there is no point in trying to predict the future. But if you don't have ideas about it, or really want to be a part of it, you have already lost. The companies that have ground to a halt are those that persist with mechanical control systems. It needs more than that to control the resources – and yet most international companies are letting this particular tail wag the dog.

There is a need for spiritual management in large international companies: to possess the will and ability to keep people on track and to lead the way, regardless of where in the company they work. Today the world's most successful companies are managed by some very charismatic personalities. In the new winner companies the guiding philosophy is so clear that everyone understands it – and contributes to it.

Companies must have a Corporate Religion

Those who manage both their company and their market with a Corporate Religion are the new winners.

Spiritual management is set to become the most important management tool of the future, because it provides the only protection against the complexity of new products and the speed of market change.

Companies need to be bold and innovative internally, to be strong externally. Otherwise there is every danger that international companies will fragment themselves from within, while management is busy looking at new products, market shares and sales Figures. It is more important to ask why the company exists and what it will be doing in five years. This is what strategic plans are supposed to address, but anyone who has tried doing this in a big corporation will know how little top management involve themselves personally in the development process. Think how many management consultant companies have laid impressive plans before top management, without them ever becoming the soul of the company.

The international companies that prosper are those in which the top management have access to reliable information, e.g. Who are the company's most important customers? Where is the company heading? These are the companies whose top management use their strength in communicating the company's values, culture and goals to the employees. These companies have – either consciously or unconsciously – created a Corporate Religion. In other words, a spiritually driven management. Those who manage both their company and their market with a Corporate Religion are the new winners.

Winner companies are focusing all their international work in one and the same direction. They have no waste, no meaningless power struggles sparked off by the clash of egos. Today one of the best examples of an effective Corporate Religion is Bill Gates' Microsoft. He manages both the company and the market via his Corporate Religion. There can be few employees at Microsoft who do not know what the company is about. It is no coincidence that Microsoft is a supremely focused and dedicated company that achieves spectacular results and earns huge sums of money.

Why is "Spiritual" Management necessary?

Trends in international society give many international company leaders the feeling of walking a tightrope between international chaos and success. Positive development depends on strong management, and I don't mean the variety that operates highly function-divided hierarchies. Strength is about having a courageous and innovative core to the company.

So let's take a close look at these trends in detail:

Fig 2.1 The 5 chaos trends

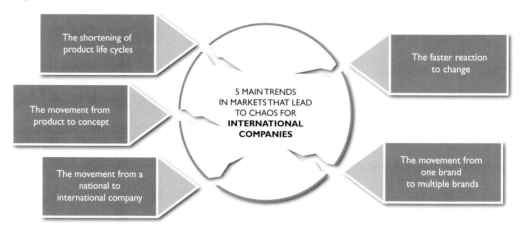

Many international companies are threatened by chaos. As the figure illustrates, 5 trends are playing a crucial role. This chapter will explore them.

Trend 1: The movement from national to international companies

Most companies start out as national companies. They are driven by the desire for greater sales – and start to export. The company's internationalisation begins, but without appropriate changes in the organisation.

What you have now created is one big parent company surrounded by a lot of independent subsidiaries. The result is an unprofitable, non-homogeneous and unhappy family. There is no shared profile and no shared soul. As I've said already, the market adjustment concept will have to be upended in the future so that the market adjusts to the company. Just think how many resources that will release for preaching the company's religion.

Figure 2.2. Shows typical phases in the internationalisation process.

1. National marketing
Corporations that operate only on the domestic market.

2. National marketing with 2–5 subsidiaries
When a company with strong domestic market presence turns to the export market, things can get messy.

Fig 2.2 The international process

INTERNATIONALISATION

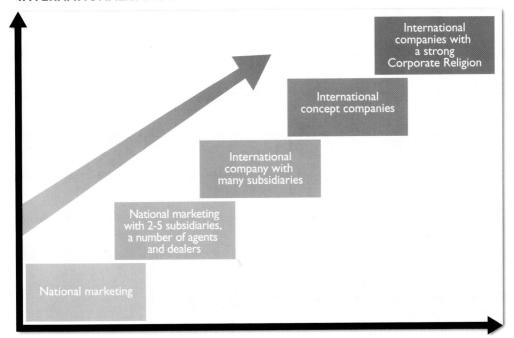

The development from national to international company is usually an evolutionary process with up to 5 steps.

In reality, it is not the same product the company is selling across all markets. Every market has their own understanding of what is right for their specific area, and that in turn affects the company's original concept. Management rarely knows how the company's profile and position varies from market to market. And very few of them dare to carry through the company's original concept against the subsidiaries' wishes. It's in this phase that business becomes unprofitable. Why? Because when market adjustments start being made, companies find that they earn too little on production. If they had a religion, they could not possibly live with that.

3. International company with many subsidiaries

The company is international and has a product with a strong position across borders. The strength of the product keeps the company on track. You could say in this case that the product is the religion. As long as they keep their position in the market, all is well. But product innovation and the erosion of trade barriers are changing the markets constantly – and these days it is simply not enough to market one product. What's really important is to market product concepts, to which new products can be added in a continuous flow. Who can remember specific model numbers of IBM computers or Sony hi-fi equipment which have been launched over recent years? Survival depends upon a strong international concept into which companies can feed new products with new numbers to satisfy the target group's appetite.

It is in this phase that most international companies get into serious difficulty, because they let their decentralised subsidiaries control development. And then all of a sudden, different customers in different markets are asking for completely different articles. No matter what they come up with, it will only satisfy half the existing customer base. Apple is a famous example. For years, Apple has been making creative computer products for a hugely diverse market – instead of focusing on key target groups.

Fig. 2.3a The non-homogeneous international company

Such companies are characterised by the fact that contact between the headquarters and the consumers is disrupted by decentralised units – i.e. the subsidiaries. The more the subsidiaries are allowed to be independent units, the worse it becomes. Individual subsidiaries end up aiming in conflicting directions, and consumer influence is dissipated. The fact that information from consumers is filtered by the decentralised companies en route to headquarters just makes a bad situation worse.

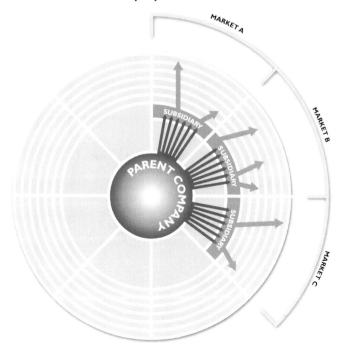

Meanwhile the competitors have also learned how to be creative. Bang goes Apples advantage. And, with no global focus, Apple loses its competitive edge, and perhaps even its foothold in the market.

4. International concept companies

Companies that have a clearly defined concept constantly evolve in line with international trends in order to keep a direct connection with the market. Typically, these are companies which talk directly to their customers. This way, they pass new knowledge all the way from central headquarters to the decentralised market – and back again.

5. International companies with a strong Corporate Religion

Good examples here are Microsoft, The Coca-Cola Co. and Harley-Davidson. They work towards the same shared goal. They do not have irrational subsidiaries – and they only use resources to advance their religion. This has a self-perpetuating effect and it keeps all employees in the right place. The result is an effective and coherent organisation, with everybody fighting for the same cause.

Fig. 2.3b   The homogeneous international company

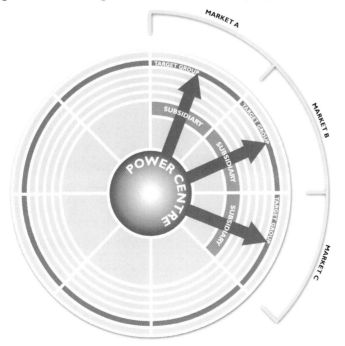

The international company is unified through a centrally controlled Corporate Religion. Power is reabsorbed into HQ and the subsidiaries are reduced to offices that carry out the mission. That way, the same target group is influenced across all markets with a consistent concept, with information flowing freely between consumers and the parent company, which becomes a power centre.

Fig 2.4a The internationalisation process comes to a halt

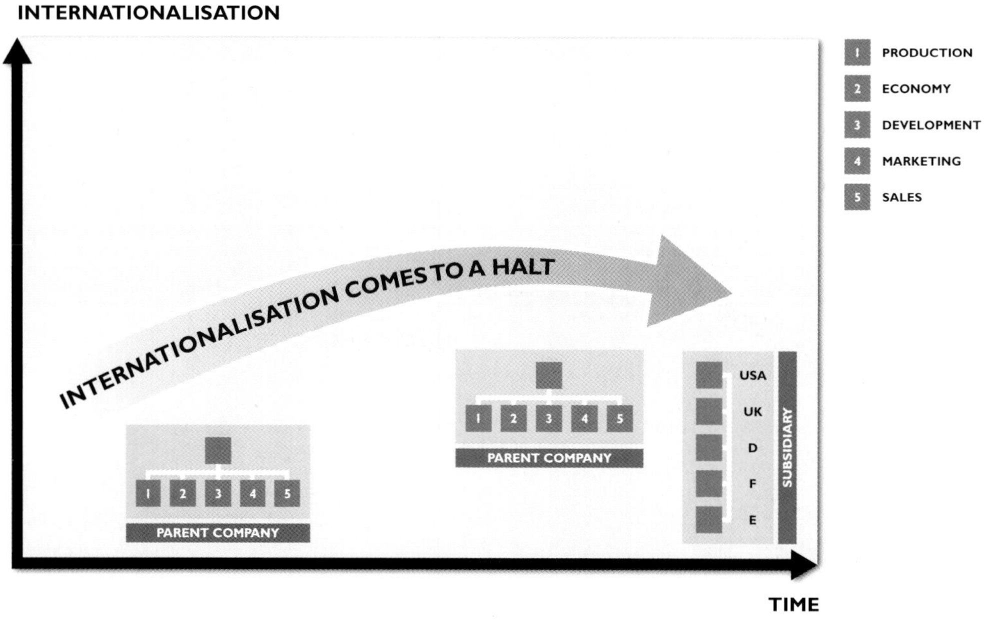

The international company's traditional organisational structure has failed. The parent company is focused on development and production. The subsidiaries are sales companies and usually report directly to top management. That means there are different companies with different goals. By separating from the parent company and going their own way, subsidiaries can bring the internationalisation process to a standstill.

Many still share the opinion that the global market doesn't exist. But no matter how many borders you cross, you keep finding the same product groups and their respective consumer groups. The same segments appear everywhere.

If anyone corners that global market, they are heading for success. Economies of scale do wonders for one's competitive edge. It also shrinks the available space in the market for international competitors who prefer to do things the old fashioned way. They take ages to respond, because they are stuck with different positions in different markets, and all the chaotic decision processes that this involves.

This is a highly vulnerable position and it can easily turn destructive if there isn't a strong management who can find a new and relevant focus. As Figure 2.3a shows, it's important for an international company to establish direct dialogue with customers: an organisation that knows the

Fig 2.4b   The internationalisation process continues

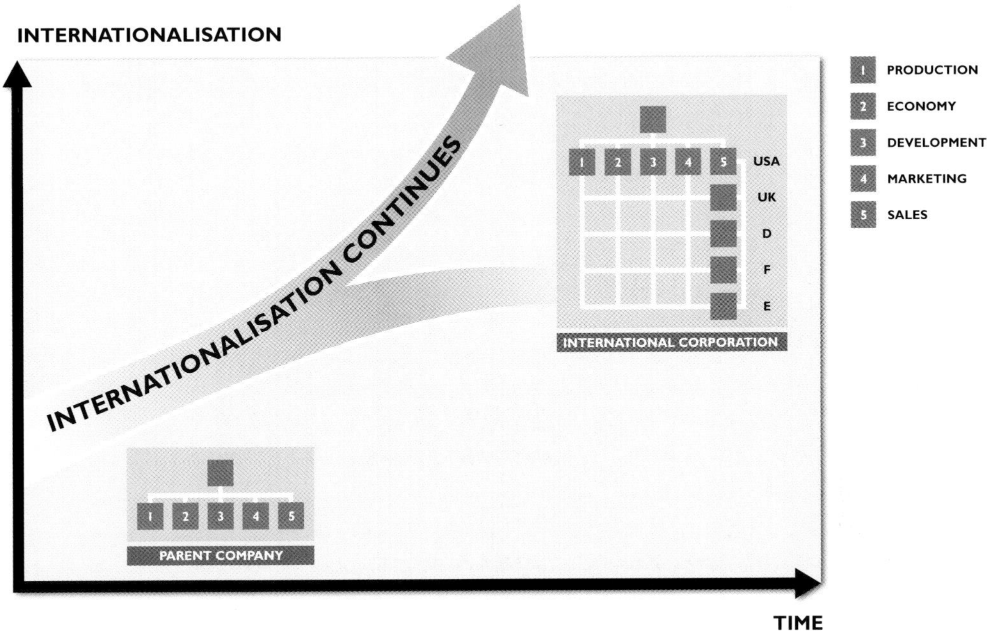

INTERNATIONALISATION

INTERNATIONALISATION CONTINUES

	PRODUCTION
1	
2	ECONOMY
3	DEVELOPMENT
4	MARKETING
5	SALES

1 2 3 4 5 USA
UK
D
F
E

INTERNATIONAL CORPORATION

1 2 3 4 5

PARENT COMPANY

TIME

For the internationalisation process to continue freely, the subsidiaries need to be brought under the wings of the parent company to create a single unit. A strong Corporate Religion makes this task easier.

way and sees the need. If information first has to pass the subjective filter of a subsidiary, management will get a confused picture that makes it impossible to get the markets pulling in the same direction.

Figure 2.3.a shows how the system normally operates in international companies. In the cause of good old market adjustment there is a built-in filter, in the shape of decentralised management, and "area management" between the headquarters and the consumers. The information needed to create new products and new marketing never arrives in the shape it's supposed to. There is no direct communication between the company and the target group for the company's products. On top of that, the traditional organisation is impeded by everyone having an opinion. It becomes a question of who is the strongest – and who gets the last word.

What they should be doing instead is concentrating their efforts into getting everyone facing in the same direction. And it's no good blaming the subsidiaries. Their problem

The traditional organisation is impeded by everyone having an opinion. It becomes a question of who is the strongest – and who gets the last word.

is that they are often locked into some "understanding" of the consumer which may not have any useful connection with where the market actually is.

Traditional subsidiaries are a thing of the past. With product lifespans dropping, the real parameter of success is how quickly a company can react to the market. To achieve this demands central management, as is shown in Figure 2.3b. The time of the small local command is over. The important task for the international company is to gather the threads again.

Figure 2.4a shows a typical course from a close-knit and homogeneous company to a non-homogeneous international company. There are two parts involved: a production and product development orientated parent company and a sales orientated subsidiary. The parent company risks ending up as an order producing company whose job is to fulfil the subsidiaries' different demands. The moment international sales surpass domestic sales, corporate strength is diverted into a power struggle between parent company and subsidiaries. Now we have two separate companies seeking very different goals, driven by equally different principles. This is the worst period for international companies and many do not make it through. Such companies settle on market shares between 10 and 25% and can easily stay there for a long time, if strong competition is absent. Because they are sales driven, they get no further. There is a natural limit to the size of market these companies can cover with their expensive sales sheets.

By contrast, successful international companies merge the parent company and subsidiaries into a single unit. It moves on the same line and in the same direction. It is not an easy task to turn the standard international organisation into a homogeneous unit. If top management is weak it can only lead to energy sapping power struggles. And the company is always the loser.

The winning formula is a strong top management with a philosophy based on direct communication links with the consumer, not on ten different sets of information squeezed through the subsidiaries' filters. And if the international company has a Corporate Religion, it makes it even easier to work in the same direction. In brief, the way to success is to create the homogeneous international company as illustrated in Figures 2.3b and 2.4b.

Trend 2: The movement from product to concept

In the past we sold products, pure and simple. Now the trend is towards selling product concepts that differentiate a brand from its competitors. By freeing a product from its generic category, more value and competitive power is added. The professional market contains many knowledge-based companies which exchange information with the market through continuous dialogue. This dialogue not only runs the market, it also runs the company that indulges in it. The process is highly demanding. Openness and speed are essential if you want to stay in front. Again, Microsoft is a good example. It listens and it gets listened to, thanks to a mass media that keeps the world informed of Bill Gates' opinions. The whole process is self-perpetuating, forming global opinion – and new products. Microsoft has reached the high ground. The company is being run by means of a Corporate Religion.

Controlling the markets via a Corporate Religion places heavy demands on the organisation. The more values that are added to the brand and the more consumers get involved, the bigger the demands on the organisation will be. Complexities increase as the brand becomes more sophisticated, while the product itself becomes a progressively smaller part of what the consumer is buying. The primary work for companies with strong brands is around brand values, rather than the physical product itself.

The "total" product requires quite another approach in terms of information, service and training. Education and control of what the international company sells all over the world is a must. And it's got to be the same all over, because the exchange of knowledge is happening globally in almost every line of business. If the product concept isn't globally consistent, the brand experience will differ from market to market.

The Coca-Cola Company and McDonald's are examples of brands which exhibit the same values no matter where in the world you encounter them. For these two corporations it is not enough to develop, produce and sell the physical product across markets. They also educate their employees and build the organisation in exactly the same way in every single country. That way, Coca-Cola and McDonald's guarantee their consistency around the globe.

There's a limit to how much knowledge you can build around a bottle of Coca-Cola. For ordinary consumer durables however, you can easily create knowledge concepts. Body Shop is one excellent example of a knowledge based company with a Corporate Religion. It sells environmental consciousness with every pack of cream, soap and eye liner. But it's in the professional product market that knowledge concepts have developed to the greatest extent. The pharmaceutical giant Smith Kline Beecham has its own internal university, for instance.

Product life cycles are shortening

Trend 3: Product life cycles are shortening

Market tradition dictates that there will always be competition on price and quality, whichever arena you happen to operate in. Unless of course, you decide to transcend the fundamental competition parameter. Plenty of companies do this, with marketing concepts and knowledge concepts that build service and financing on top of the product. Procter & Gamble is expert in building brands that occupy strong market positions.

Products with new technological and marketing advantages emerge in a continuous stream. But these days new products live shorter lives. Even for the biggest players, the pace can get uncomfortably fast. And haven't we all seen how excruciatingly slowly a new product can perform in a new market compared with its original launch by the parent company?

No matter where you are in the system, the main problem is always the same: lack of focus. Sales run subsidiaries are sluggish because new product means new knowledge and new arguments – anathema to many sales people. And there's plenty more beside this that can delay the implementation of an international strategy. Here are a few typical examples:

- A trivial thing like translations of marketing material into local languages can delay an entire product launch by six months to a year.
- Pre-launch product training is often so exhaustive that a year can easily pass before the launch gets under way.
- The adoption of the concept and product strategy can get bogged down by individual subsidiaries disagreeing during its development – a case of the "not right for our market" syndrome.
- A lack of understanding by top management that they have to lead the way and drive all the subsidiaries into the innovation. Many leaders see the company as a pipeline that just needs to be filled all the way out to the customers. They have no concept of Corporate Religion to inspire them.

Shorter product lifespans are in fact only half of another problem. Namely the back-up system, and what happens to it when international companies try to move away from the generic product – and the competitors. Soon international companies will find that a highly effective and swift production system will be crucial for the survival of the company among international competitors. And if at the same time you have an effective feedback system that monitors new tendencies among customers, you also have the key to success.

Trend 4: Quicker reaction to changes

Quicker reaction to changes

The corporate shift from simply selling products to including concept, service and knowledge in the sales process makes it difficult to monitor the market. The new ways of working involve more and more people in decision processes. It becomes ever more important to establish systems that get the right information fed back from users and buyer segments in the international markets.

Tough competition among international companies shortens the curves of product life-cycles. And when, at the same time, so much extra is being packed into the products, it's not surprising that confusion develops over managing the future. Fast, immediate response to change is essential.

Trend 5: The movement from one brand to multiple brands

By their nature, international companies need to launch new products. This enables the sales force to exploit the market position optimally. At the same time however, it has one very unfortunate consequence – it defocuses the organisation, not only in sales, but in every other department.

Over time, this activity inevitably leads to there being too many products. Primary businesses are affected if new product variations do not deliver the expected success. Even worse, what often controls development is the desire for short term cash and volume growth. Precious little attention is paid to long term considerations – such as what the company wants and what its mission is. So things jerk forward in fits and starts, and the picture that emerges is one of a very confused company. Unless the individual products are strongly defined brands with their own life, the company will not achieve a clear profile.

If a financial concern is the holding company for a lot of individual brands, the scenario hangs together, since the parent company is not projected towards the users and customers. But if a company with many different brands and products also behaves as a clear sender, then consumers get confused.

There is a very big difference between companies such as Procter & Gamble or Mars Inc. with many brands each meeting consumers as independent companies – and a company that makes all manner of products under the same name. A good example of a company brand is Canon. Colour copy machines, cameras, pocket calculators, printers or PCs – you name it – they all have the Canon logo firmly stamped on them.

Small wonder that consumers have difficulty working out

what Canon actually stands for. Canon have reduced themselves to a quality term. If that's what Canon wants, then all is well and good. But when strong competition arrives in single product areas, their advantage will be eaten away. Here I mean competition from dedicated companies that know how to create stronger involvement among consumers. That situation will force Canon to build a meaningful bridge between its many different products so that it makes clear sense to the consumers why Canon sells this huge variety of products under the same company umbrella.

The company behind the brand

When international companies seek growth there is a widespread tendency to consumer overexposure. To avoid watering themselves down, most companies split themselves up into different brands, while the company steps into the background. Companies like Procter & Gamble and General Motors have made a big success of this, but the method is problematic. It is expensive to market a brand internationally. This forces companies into choices between marketing solo brands or going back to marketing the company, which in turn is connected with the fact that today's consumers have become tired of empty marketing compaigns. They have been fooled too many times, and now they are looking for honest brands and honest products. Against this background, they are likely to return to reliable companies and assess if those companies make other things they can use.

Cars are a good example. To the customer, the manufacturer is just as important as the individual model they may be considering. No matter how attractive the model, the customer must also be able to accept the company that makes it. Skoda can make sports cars as well as anybody else, but they will never be able to sell them for more than £30,000 while jokes about their reliability continue to circulate.

Skoda has to build reliability by being good at building sports cars, while the company becomes socially accepted as a manufacturer of expensive automobiles.

Toyota knows the problem. They had a firm grip on the low and middle price segment and wanted to expand their business into the high price segment. The question was, could they remain credible as the "value for money" car in the low and middle price segment at the same time as they were selling prestige cars? To avoid blurring their healthy profile, Toyota developed a totally new brand. Lexus is a luxury car that competes with Mercedes-Benz and BMW. And Toyota does it well. But it is an expensive strategy, because Toyota has needed to create a special organisation all over the world with salespeople and mechanics who can deliver the extra service and quality that is required in the high end segment. At the same time Toyota implements a global marketing campaign for the Lexus models. They use their entire existing infrastructure for distribution and sale. In this way Toyota runs two completely separate brands outwardly – and gains extended advantages inwardly.

Those who dare to think long term ask "How can we further strengthen the brand?"

Large international companies know how tough it is to maintain consistent profiles. And it's equally hard to avoid blurring brands in the hunt for profits. "How much further can we stretch the brand?" asks the short term thinking, cash controlled management. Those who dare to think long term consider a different question, "How can we further strengthen the brand?" Think like that, and your company will be constantly that little bit ahead.

MD Foods, one of the ten biggest dairy businesses in Europe, has a brand called Høng. It started in 1920 as a camembert cheese. Over the years, Høng was extended with strong blue cheeses like Danish Blue, as well as a series of mixed blue-and-white mould culture cheeses. So the brand band went on being stretched, wider and wider. As long as there was consistency in the brand, everything went well because the different cheeses were understood as variations of the existing selection. However, that also opened up opportunities for the competitor Tholstrup. Tholstrup got a solid grip on the market with a new type of blue cheese that appealed to modern tastes – and success in that specific segment swiftly followed. At the same time, MD Foods started to use the Høng name for all sorts of cheeses – ordinary yellow Havarti-cheeses,

Emmental cheese, grated cheese and more besides. With Høng diluting its brand, Tholstrup grabbed the opportunity to take over as the experts in modern blue cheeses. And today Tholstrup is the leading supplier of mould culture cheese.

Fig 2.5 Høng brand band

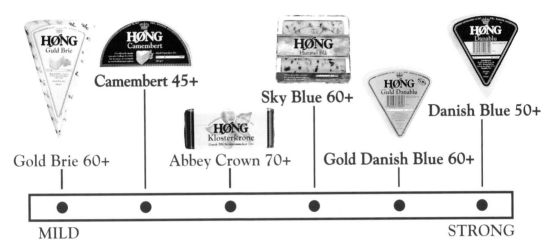

The brand band is used in a new kind of marketing that seeks to reposition Høng as the experts in mould culture cheese.

Instead of confusing consumers, MD Foods should have kept their brand band tight, and used all their resources internally and externally to take on the competition and strengthen their position on the market. Expertise and resources are things that MD Foods possess in abundance, and today they are once more deploying them to their advantage. The defocusing has stopped. They have tightened up the brand by shedding everything that is not a mould culture cheese.

MD Foods wants to be the mould culture cheese expert on the market; their know-how makes it possible. Now they market themselves to regain that position, with a mission dedicated to restoring MD Foods' former brand culture.

The whole issue of brands, Brand Culture, Brand Religion and Corporate Religion, will be taken up in the coming chapters. The Høng story is a perfect example of how a mission created a brand, and how a total loss of focus destroyed it. As soon as they recreated the religion – that elemental value, from product development to consumer – the Høng brand started working again.

CHAPTER 3

Brand Religion

The heart has its reasons …
which reason cannot fathom
(Blaise Pascal)

It is no longer enough to have brilliant products.
The crucial thing is market position, and the
highest position a company can reach is when
consumers perceive its brand as a Brand Religion.
A precondition for reaching this position is an
insight into branding mechanisms and what
increases the value of a brand.

A strong market position is the key to the future

Companies are run by their products. But it is brands that
decide the value of the company and its position in the
market. The days are gone when products held the
company together. Today, dynamic company managements
are busy moving from ordinary products towards brands;
because developments are taking place so fast that it is no
longer products that do the competing. It is a brand's
market position – not the product's – that decides if a
company achieves success. Brand positions will be the
battleground of the future. To understand the processes
involved in building a strong brand position, we need a
core model (and an associated terminology) that assigns
brands to different bands depending on consumer
involvement in the brand.

Brand Values

Brand Value can have one of several different meanings,
depending on what you're interested in. If you buy or sell
companies, it's an expression of the brand's cash value.
Another kind of value is Brand Equity, which is more
difficult to calculate. The English corporation Interbrand
specialises in a method of calculating Brand Equity from a
series of quantitative variables. This method is used in a

simplified form by the American magazine Financial World. Every year, they publish a league table of the most valuable brands. In this book however, our prime concern is not with the intricacies of Brand Equity calculation, but rather with the construction of the emotional values that play a crucial role in creating healthy brand positions in the market.

Normally, you calculate the value of a brand by using quality parameters such as knowledge, preference, market share and degree of distribution. Because the product's physical properties play a constantly diminishing role in determining brand position in the market, it is necessary to include new parameters. First and foremost among them are the non-material and emotional aspects of a brand's value. As Figure 3.1 shows, it is crucial to add emotional values to the traditional functional values in order to be able to say something about a brand's position in the

Fig 3.1 The interplay between quantitative and qualitative values

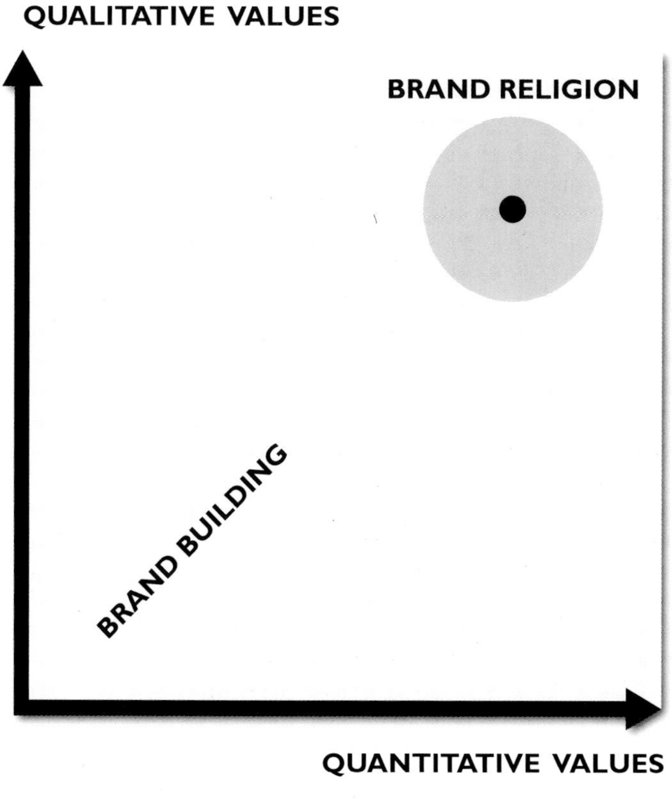

QUALITATIVE VALUES

BRAND RELIGION

BRAND BUILDING

QUANTITATIVE VALUES

It is often only the qualitative values that are utilised in the brand building process. But it is the interplay between both qualitative and quantitative values that forms the real synthesis for brand construction.

market. We all know of brands that command high awareness and preference without gaining either the sales or the big chunk of market share that are traditionally expected to follow. Of course, the reason could be that the product is just too old or simply not good enough, but usually this is not the case at all. So, there must be other variables that determine a brand's position in the market.

Figure 3.1 shows how the interplay between the quantitative and qualitative values can tell us something about a position of a brand. All the quantitative variables are measurable and are well accepted, but fewer people work with qualitative variables, which lack the same measurable frame of reference. To define an understandable and rational USP (unique selling point) for a brand is rarely sufficient. Take Coca-Cola. It's hardly the rational argument that Coca-Cola quenches one's thirst that explains Coca-Cola's monumental success. It's in Coca-Cola's ESP (emotional selling point) that the real answer lies, which equates to a laid-back American lifestyle and happy people. It's no coincidence that the Coca-Cola Company has created an emotional universe that human beings all over the world can identify with. At the same time mind you, they have worked hard with the quantitative parameter, distribution. When you can always get a Coke no matter where in the world you happen to be, it emphatically proves the point that Coca-Cola as a brand is a natural part of modern life.

Qualitative and quantitative values are working together in a 'virtual partnership' that decides the position of a brand.

That feeling commands a high rating in the emotional success stakes. Qualitative and quantitative values work together in a "virtual partnership" that decides the position of a brand. This explains why companies that win the fight for market share are those that understand how to optimise quantitative and qualitative values for their specific brand.

Several global companies have recognised how to exploit this knowledge to successfully sell many different kinds of product under the same brand. Virgin and Ralph Lauren are good examples. Of course, there are some that foul up. This is usually because they simply use the company name for a cartload of different products, at the same time failing to appreciate that it is the brand position among consumers that is decisive. Also a brand blurs out its position if it gets overloaded.

High involvement is the key to Brand Value

In connection with qualitative brand values, it is relevant to take a look at consumer involvement in a brand. Consumers may know a brand and have some sort of preference, but how interested does that really make them? That is what the high/low involvement scale seeks to express. The highest involvement a brand can reach is when the consumers understand it as a religion. And they get involved in a brand when it feels "self-relevant" – i.e. when it is not to be refused. Brands can have many meanings and levels of value, but consumers are always the final judge. In this way, the levels reflect how strongly the brand has a hold on them. High involvement then, is the key to a strong brand position – and ought to form part of any Brand Equity calculation.

Fig 3.2 The Foote, Cone & Belding involvement grid

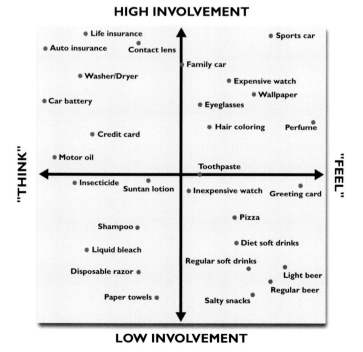

The advertising agency Foote, Cone & Belding developed a model that combines involvement with the degree of cognitive/rational ("think") versus affective/emotional ("feel") behaviour in the purchasing decision.
The FCB model is good, but it doesn't take into account specific brand involvement.
Source: William L. Wilkie: "Consumer behaviour", 2nd. edition, USA, 1990.

There's nothing new in the fact that you have to get consumers involved in a brand, if you want to build up a continuous preference – which means – value. The advertising agency Foote, Cone & Belding did it with a model which divided different articles into high and low involvement (see Figure 3.2). They used the concept in their product marketing.

The FCB model has been used as a key to the kind of things people can get highly involved in. Rice, flour and potatoes are examples of low-involvement products which were once thought impossible to get people involved in. Well, it has been disproved many times since – I need only mention Uncle Ben's Rice. The FCB model is the prevailing idea used in connection with high/low involvement products. But it needs defining. In principle, you can make anything high involvement, if you set that target for yourself – and have enough money in the bank.

In principle, you can make anything high involvement if you set that target for yourself – and have enough money in the bank.

High involvement is the password to the future – the more consumers involve themselves in your brand, the stronger your market position and the higher the value you get. But high value doesn't appear from nowhere. It has to be created. And the precondition for it is persistent effort from the company. Partly in the form of dialogue with customers about their needs. And in equal measure, the practical task of getting them involved in your brand.

Whereas the FCB model starts with categories of products, Figure 3.3 starts with brands. In the model, brands are grouped into different levels of involvement, all the way from low-involvement product brands up to Brand Religion. Explanations follow for: Product, Concept Brand, Corporate Concept, Brand Culture and Brand Religion.

Will different consumer segments understand a brand in different ways? Of course they will, and that fact must be included in your considerations.

No matter how strong the values a manufacturer feels are connected to the brand, it is the consumer's experience of a brand that decides if it will be a success. Now you might well pose the question, "Will different consumer segments understand a brand in different ways?" Of course they will, and that fact must be included in your considerations. As Figure 3.4 shows, different consumer segments can easily be involved on different levels in the

Fig 3.3 Brand involvement levels

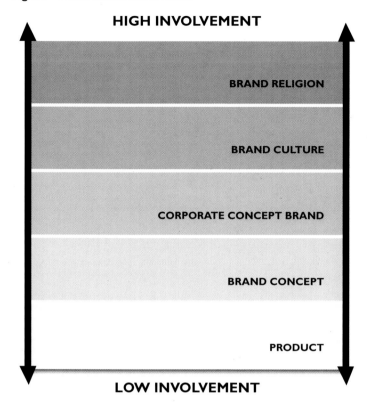

Involvement must be viewed in relation to single brands – not in relation to different categories of products. In principle, brands within all product categories can be made high involvement. The highest possible involvement is when consumers raise the brand to a Brand Religion.

same brand. Some can feel very attracted to the values of a brand. Others might not care or have negative feelings towards a brand's values, making them far less involved. Knowledge can be high across several consumer groups. The interesting thing is how consumers are dispersed between levels of involvement. Levels of involvement say something about the strength of a brand. To work optimally with a brand, you need to know exactly how consumers disperse along the involvement axis – and why.

The more involved consumers become, the more they are generally willing to pay for a brand. When a company like Colgate-Palmolive markets a whole range of different Colgate toothpastes at different prices, it is precisely to capture consumers on different involvement levels. The highest involved are willing to pay a relatively high price for the best variant, but that is far from the case for most consumers. So the company also produces cheaper

Fig 3.4   Different levels of consumer involvement in the same brand

Different consumer segments will understand the same brand differently and therefore be involved on different levels. For some consumers, the brand is just a product. For others it is a Brand Concept, a Brand Culture or a Brand Religion. The primary branding task is to push as many consumers as possible, as high up the in-volvement hierarchy as possible.

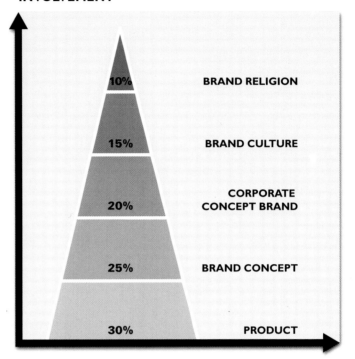

INVOLVEMENT

10%   **BRAND RELIGION**

15%   **BRAND CULTURE**

20%   **CORPORATE CONCEPT BRAND**

25%   **BRAND CONCEPT**

30%   **PRODUCT**

mainstream toothpastes for the less involved. For manufacturers that aim widely, it is vital to offer variations of essentially the same product, targeted towards consumers on different involvement levels.

Figure 3.4 shown an imaginary example where 10% of the target group is involved at Brand Religion level, 15% at Brand Culture level, 20% at Corporate Concept level, 25% at Brand Concept level, and 30% at product level.

The example illustrates that it is important to know how many customers in the target group the brand really has a hold on, and that measurements are made which enable a qualified follow-up of what has happened in individual country markets. Measurements must be based on what has actually happened among the customers – how they have been influenced, and how they see a brand's position. It is less important what the subsidiaries, customers and users think individually. Unfortunately, this is often the basis chosen by big international companies. Success in the future will depend on an efficient system of control and analysis to monitor the markets and gather valuable information. Only with this data can a company take the right action.

Brand Positions

If anything is crucial to a company, it is brand position. The frame of reference from which a corporation works is the central Figure of this chapter, Figure 3.5. In it, the different brand positions are seen in relation to each other. The position of a brand is not static. If you think of the Figure as a development model for brands, then the ultimate position is for the brand to be understood by the target group as a Brand Religion. Achievement of that position presupposes optimisation of both quantitative and qualitative values. Every brand that ascends to this position has been through several of the stages shown in the model. Let's look at each stage in detail.

Product

The lowest brand position is the product. The product has a name, but apart from that it possesses no further value. What is being sold here is just a functional quality. The prototypical example is "generics", but note that branded products can also be similarly devoid of brand values.

Concept Brand

Next come Concept Brands, which usually run on some emotional value. Branding has become the key for establishing and maintaining competitive advantages. Even traditionally generic products can be marketed using emotional values. Chiquita bananas, Nutrasweet and Intel are all subjects of intense brand orientated consumer marketing.

Intel started its branding effort in 1991 as an attempt to build customer loyalty in a business area where products are replaced several times a year. Intel started a co-operation with different PC-producers who printed an "Intel inside" icon in their advertisements.

Fig 3.5 Brand Religion model

INVOLVEMENT

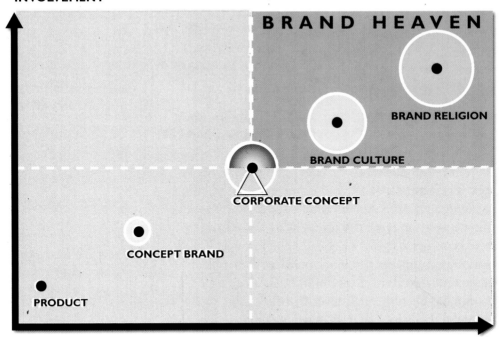

VALUE

It is when value is added to a product that consumers get involved and strong brands are created. The generic product's importance is a constant (shown in the figure as a black core). It is what surrounds it that actually differentiates brands. A consistent corporate concept is required to reach high levels of involvement which connect the brand and the company.

The effect was tangible. In just two years, awareness of Intel rose from 22% to over 80%. Benetton is another example of a brand governed by a very strong marketing concept. It isn't so much the garments that draw the consumers into the shop, it's Benetton's Concept Brand. The company has succeeded in creating involvement, a defined market position and a value, but something is missing: a Corporate Concept.

Corporate Concept

There must be consistency in everything the company does in relation to the brand.

To get further up the involvement axis requires the understanding that consumer purchasing is more than the result of accidental advertising campaigns for isolated brands. The world-wide protests over nuclear detonations in the Pacific Ocean, and the Brent Spar affair are examples of people power. In the future, consumers will go further and further in their support or dislike of the product. You could say they will be buying the company as much as the brand itself. It is for precisely this reason that there must be consistency in everything the company does in relation to the brand. Without reliability, you can forget about getting to the top of the involvement axis.

Benetton is a strong Concept Brand. But for how long? There is a thorough lack of consequence in the things the company does.

Fig 3.6 Corporate Concept

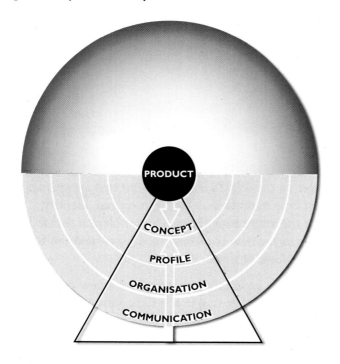

To create the necessary reliability in the different brands, they must be linked together with a Corporate Concept – which is equivalent to a clearly defined and consistent connection between product, concept, profile, organisation and communication.

The famous (some would say infamous) advertising campaigns featuring graphic images of AIDS victims, refugees, children workers and a blood spattered Bosnian T-shirt give an immediately sympathetic impression of Benetton as being a very engaged company with a reliable profile. But is that how the company is in reality? Or are they actually more interested in racing cars? After all, everyone knows that the company spends a fortune sponsoring Formula 1. If this is the case, then Benetton's

If the corporation is not consistent in everything it does, it will not be possible to reach the highest levels of involvement – at least not for long.

customers are wearing a company for whom engagement in social issues is an empty promise. If the corporation is not consistent in everything it does, it will not be possible to reach the highest levels of involvement – at least not for long.

If Benetton had a Corporate Concept, the corporation could connect company and brand together in one consistent unit. Then, just like Anita Roddick's Body Shop, they could engage in the issues raised by their advertising and create a dialogue with their consumers that is perceived as genuine.

The idea of the Corporate Concept is here to stay, if a company wants to reduce the risk of revelations in the mass media of unethical conduct. Management must remain vigilant so that what the company does as a whole is connected with what is communicated. It is also important that companies analyse their interface with the outside world and that they get their messages targeted on the brand position they desire.

It is not sufficient for management to make decisions of principle to win a Corporate Concept position. It needs real action. In the 1980's it was thought that companies could instantly manufacture a new corporate identity, whenever the whim took them. The problem was that for most of them the new corporate identity turned out to be a complete waste of time.

Managements who decided to introduce a new corporate letterhead failed to see that it was the connection between brand and company that sold the articles and not the design on their writing paper. Many companies have tried to re-profile themselves this way, but the logo and design don't do it by themselves. There must be solid foundations for a new profile, and every department of the company must agree on going in the same direction.

A Corporate Concept is characterised by the existence of a deep and reliable relationship between consumers, company and brand. To get that far is hard work. When a Corporate Concept is functioning fully, then you can really build some strong brand values and climb further up the involvement axis.

A brand must be so consistent that consumers experience it as coming from a company which has a soul and a philosophy that you can either join with or disassociate from. These elements are inextricably linked together and the core concept spreads out across all markets.

Consider the car industry. Here the qualitative and emotional values are so strong that companies don't have any problems replacing models when the brand position is first being built up. It happens even faster in the fashion industry. The life of a product is extremely short and in consequence depends even more heavily on the intrinsic strength of the brand.

A brand must be so consistent that consumers experience it as coming from a company with a soul.

If your company isn't already operating on a Corporate Concept perhaps you should get one. Corporate strengths and weaknesses must be analysed. It's essential that customers in all markets are asked their opinion before the choice of Corporate Concept is made. The profile must then express the chosen concept, so that the consumer is left with a consistent expression.

The organisation must then fit the concept, as was the case with SAS for example. SAS had to make themselves service minded in order to live up to the concept of "The

Fig 3.7 Mission controlled Corporate Concept

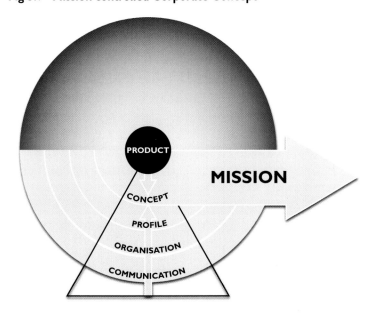

If management is mission–oriented rather than product driven, the company becomes far more dynamic.

Businessman's Airline" . The organisation was refocused accordingly.

The Corporate Concept is not a static thing. It demands a more interactive process between the market and top management. The product in Figure 3.6 can be replaced with a company mission statement. Now you have a model to manage by.

Short product life-cycles especially require a lifeline between top management and consumers. They depend on each other; besides that, a clear mission can stop any defocusing of the subsidiaries and get them tuned in.

There is no other way forward. As Figure 3.7 shows, it's the interactive process between customers in the international markets and top management that puts dynamism into the Corporate Concept and makes it a proper steering tool for the company. This is dependent, of course, on top management changing the focus from a financial to a spiritual organisation that is seriously involved with its customers. Then the corporation will be constantly ahead.

It's no mean feat for top management to plot out a genuine mission. We're talking army commanders here, not book-keepers. Big international companies are totally dependent on their organisation driving in the same direction. Someone has to point the way and streamline the company so that consumers meet the same concept wherever they go.

It is the consistent brands that win consumer involvement - and with it the market position.

It's no accident that the trend all over the business world right now is focusing – or that the idea behind the Corporate Concept has to some extent worked its way through. Ancillary brands and companies are being sold so that corporations can concentrate solely on getting their core business to hang together as a consistent whole. The big multi-brands and company brands lack synergy, and that destroys the feeling of reliability in single brands. It is the consistent brands that win consumer involvement – and with it the market position.

When an international company first reaches the homogenous stage where all the power is put to work fulfilling the mission, then it's possible to gain the kind of strength in the market that can raise a brand to a culture in its product category.

Brand Culture

So you have got yourself a strong and reliable Corporate Concept. Now you set your sights on the next level in the model – the Brand Culture. This means that a brand has gained such a strong position that in consumers' minds it becomes equivalent to the function it represents. For millions of people, Kellogg's means a healthy breakfast. Kellogg's is sitting right there at the table of breakfast culture. It doesn't just compete with other cereal brands, but also with other types of breakfast product. Another example is Colgate. But Colgate is actually more than toothpaste. It is the soul of dental hygiene.

Brand Culture means that a brand has gained such a strong position that in consumers' minds it becomes equivalent to the function it represents.

Obviously, a Brand Culture creates a very strong market position. It provides high income and also functions as a high entry-barrier. Since consumers are not all involved in exactly the same way with a brand, a brand cannot therefore be a Brand Culture for all consumers. The crucial point to appreciate is that while Kellogg's, for example, enjoys Brand Culture status with its core target group, new consumers are being recruited at the same time.

All Brand Cultures have their starting point in consumers' needs. In one way or another they have all risen above the ordinary product and concept level. That means they have added knowledge content to their concepts which makes the brand more reliable than other products in the same category. It is possible for competitors to have higher knowledge content and higher product quality, but that is still secondary to consumer opinion. How well companies communicate the total, reliable brand image is absolutely crucial.

It is possible for competitors to have higher knowledge content and higher product quality, but that is still secondary to consumer opinion.

Colgate maintains close connections with the dental profession, and constantly develops state of the art products to keep our teeth whiter than white. McDonald's is to many people the definition of fast food. The corporation does a lot to create a homogeneous product whose quality never varies. They have succeeded so well that the resistance from nutritional experts has become weaker over time. In the computer market, Microsoft has won the culture fight and taken over the mantle from IBM. Microsoft can equate its software with the "computer culture" by feeding the market with prophecies of developments in the future.

Fig 3.8 The culture fight

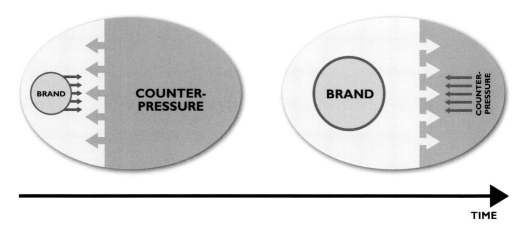

The fight between brands is a culture fight. In the beginning, the counter-pressure towards a new brand is intense, but if the task is approached in the right way, it will eventually take hold.

Within soft drinks, Coca-Cola is practically synonymous with American culture – and that view has conquered the whole world, just as Disney has solidly monopolised "family values". With the help of the Disneylands, they create a direct involvement with the main target group – children – who can experience the fairy tale coming alive. Some of these companies have succeeded to such an extent with their Brand Culture that they have risen to a Brand Religion.

Most Brand Cultures are long-haul affairs where consumers are constantly influenced in a way which makes the brand an integral part of daily life.

Most Brand Cultures are long-haul affairs where consumers are continuously influenced in a way which makes the brand an integral part of daily life.

This involves the use of extensive marketing resources. Brand Cultures are continuously marketed. The interesting thing about mega-brands is that they stick to their cultures, no matter which country they drive into. They do this even though a clash between country culture and the new Brand Culture is inevitable. Figure 3.8 shows that there is always a clash of cultures when a corporation enters a territory. In the short term it might seem a good idea to fit into another country's culture but in the long run it will harm a company, because the consistency of their position is undermined.

Brand Religion

The highest position a brand can reach is that of Brand Religion for the target group. The transition between Brand Culture and Brand Religion is fluid, but a Brand Religion is an extended, extra-strong Brand Culture. The brand is a must – a belief – for consumers. They swear by it, and are very reluctant to have other brands in the categories where a Brand Religion is present.

The brand is a must – a belief – for consumers. They swear by it.

A brand is so much more than a generic product property that gives the customers an optimal solution and ultimate self-worth. To reach the top means that you have optimised both the quantitative and qualitative variables – that is one hell of a task. But in return you get value creation on a major scale when you aspire to a Brand Religion. Now the company can sell all sorts of products underneath its unified umbrella, so long as the products stay connected to the religion. The Body Shop recognises this. The chain sells a religion based on natural ingredients and environmental concern, translated into products with a high ethical basis. The company emphasises its opposition to animal experiments, and its solidarity with third world causes.

The Body Shop's Brand Religion enables it to sell many different products within "personal care", because it is much more the attitude than the products that consumers are buying. The advantage of having such a strong brand position is that the company gains extremely loyal consumers. And The Body Shop wins them on its own premises because they control the religion themselves. In this situation, it is difficult for competitors to reach people who believe in The Body Shop, because the customer is quite indifferent to the traditional parameters of quality and price.

A Brand Religion comes naturally within the compass of a big company with large resources. One such is Coca-Cola. If proof were needed of its importance to believers, it was their awesome reaction when the legendary taste was changed towards Pepsi's in 1985. Sacrilege!

Coca-Cola had obviously taste-tested the new variant, but they failed to appreciate that not all values are of a kind that can be "tasted". Most of them can only be felt. Within a few short months, the original taste was back on the market under the name "Coca-Cola Classic". You don't change a Brand Religion just like that.

But because The Coca-Cola Company keeps on communicating its Brand Religion, it gains a better and better foothold. Every single day new "believers" join the Coca-Cola cause. Believers who help to fight off competitors and win the culture battle. And via sponsorship and communication Coca-Cola has become an integral part of universal youth culture.

This is how the soft drinks company creates their decisive reliability as "the soft drinks brand". As we saw in the first chapter, Harley-Davidson is another prime example of a Brand Religion. Harley-Davidson is the motorbike, because it is much more than a motorbike. Harley-Davidson is a religion in praise of "freedom". Figure 3.9. shows a series of Brand Religions – notice how there is always a big difference between the generic product and what is actually being sold.

Fig 3.9 Brand Religions

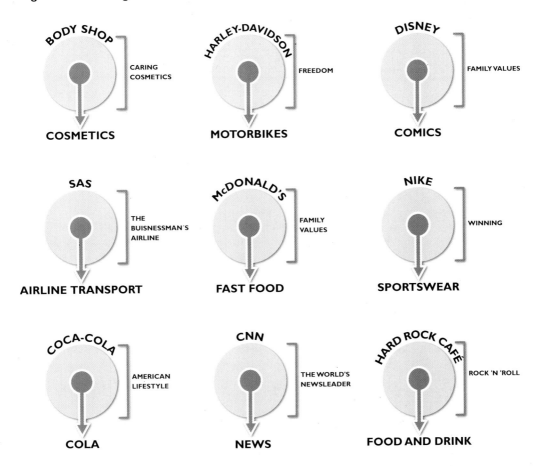

The generic product itself is only a small part of a brand, made up of a series of material and non-material benefits and associations that together form the brand. This is shown in the figure, where the difference between the brand's generic core and the whole brand is exemplified for a series of well known products. For example Harley-Davidson's generic product is motorbikes, but the Harley-Davidson brand is associated with something bigger – "freedom" itself. It is this association that gives the brand its enormous value.

Brand Religions are created by big thinking

Brand Religions are created by big thinking and big ideas. This is what consumers actually buy. To be able to work consciously towards a strong brand position, a mission must be created for the company's brand that reaches further than the product itself. The stairway to a Brand Religion ascends via a consistent Corporate Concept, which in turn requires that a brand possesses a certain mission. When we're talking international companies, it is important that the mission is attuned to the international markets and is rooted in the interplay between consumers and the company.

The mission is a framework that ensures dynamic brand development. By moving away from static product qualities and forcing the company into a mission that contains plenty of qualitative values, it becomes possible to add value to a brand. It involves a shift from a product definition of the product to a value definition, where the brand's mission controls the company. After that, the major task is to pull everything around the brand and get the company to follow the mission. McDonald's can only say that they want to be the ultimate family restaurant if they have control of the entire organisation; and construct marketing concepts and shops; and educate personnel to deliver the same article; and most important, create the same experience – every time. In other words, there must be a system that can communicate the religion in every single market. What does this mean? It means management must start thinking in a new way, because with a Brand Religion, the company is led by values – not by product qualities and product sales. A Corporate Religion is necessary for driving the company up to the ultimate position of Brand Religion.

The following case concerns SAS, and exemplifies the thinking which underlies the Corporate Concept as a starting point for brand building.

The businessman's airline

Jan Carlzon turned the Scandinavian airline SAS into a gigantic success. He did it with a strong Corporate Religion based on the businessman's needs.

SAS (Scandinavian Airlines System) is owned, uniquely among the world's airline companies, by three countries. The corporation was established in 1946 as a consortium between national airline companies in Sweden (ABA), Norway (DNL) and Denmark (DDL). The shares are equally divided between private shareholders and the three nation states, of which Sweden owns 3/7 and Norway and Denmark 2/7 each. In the whole chequered career of SAS, there was nothing to match the state of the corporation when the Swede Jan Carlzon was employed as leader for the flight division. Carlzon arrived from Linjeflyg which he had made into a low price profiled airline, and became one of four administrative managers under the overall leadership of Carl-Olov Munkbjerg. Two years before his accession SAS had spiralled into deficit, after a period of 17 years in the black. On top of that, the corporation was awash with dissatisfied customers and unmotivated employees. Something had to change. Together with other key people, Carlzon started to analyse the situation. The result was a proposal for a strategy that put primary focus on the income side.

SAS should aim, it said, at business travellers – those who could afford to pay a higher price for their tickets. In March 1981 the concept "The Businessman's Airline" was presented to the board. One presentation later, the board decided to offer Carlzon the job of heading up the whole SAS organisation. He accepted.

A new concept

Jan Carlzon had realised that it was necessary to add value to the corporation, besides those things that had to do with transport itself. With a concept focused on the needs of the businessman, they could make a start. The goal was to make SAS "the best airline for the businessman who travels frequently". The task was to fit the company to the concept. Everything that could contribute to giving the businessman the most pleasant journey possible was investigated.

SAS Corporate Concept

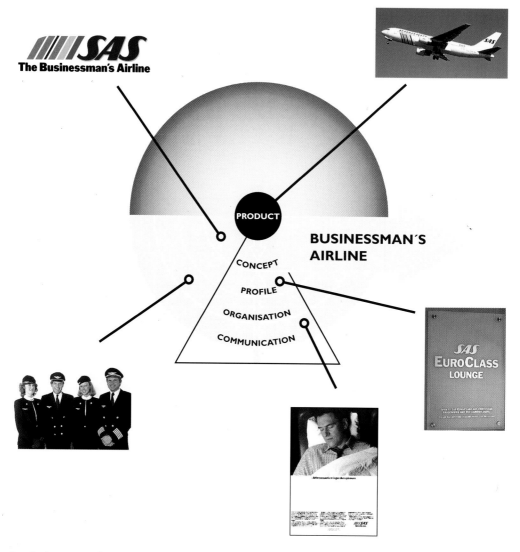

Jan Carlzon created a wonderful Corporate Concept with a clear connection between all the elements. The starting point was the concept "The Businessman's Airline", which placed a series of demands on the product. Smaller, smarter airplanes were introduced. There were more departures, and punctuality was razor sharp. The profile was clear: The whole SAS organisation was determined to do something for the business traveller. Euro-Class Lounges in the airports were just one example of the service profile. The organisation was trained to give the best service possible. The desk personnel were given new uniforms designed by Calvin Klein. The "new" SAS was communicated in a stylish way through advertisements that focused clearly on the businessman's needs, but the essential communication Carlzon handled himself. The press loved him and he was more than willing to act as his own personal PR!

High priority was placed on departure frequency and punctuality. It required massive organisational changes which were in fact rejected at the outset, but further investigations showed that they were possible.

It was critical that everyone could see why it was important to implement change, and so a guidebook was created which explained the reasons in detail. Carlzon raised the concept to a Corporate Religion that embraced marketing, profile, service, personnel, flights, departures; the lot. If the concept had been created by a marketing department and run as an advertising campaign, it would never have become such a huge success.

It was crucial for customers to realise that SAS were serious, and that there was consistency in all the initiatives taken to make travel more pleasant for the businessman. SAS was more than a brand – it was a whole company that functioned with one and the same way of thinking.

Charismatic Carlzon

Jan Carlzon's charisma and magnetism had a lot to do with the success of the corporation's development. The religion was marketed outwardly and preached inwardly by a strong spiritual management. They succeeded beyond all their expectations in creating a company culture founded on a better service for business people. Employees were sent on charm school courses and new management methods were implemented. Everything they did showed that SAS really meant what they said about better service. Jan Carlzon communicated to his organisation through the media – rather like Bill Gates does with Microsoft. It was strong because when the new management theory was quoted in the media, it raised everyone's belief in its validity.

Airline of the Year

The strategy worked. Smaller planes taking off more frequently – and on time – plus a perceptibly improved service. SAS' answer to Business Class was called EuroClass, a brand in itself, and it was offered to everyone who paid full price for their tickets. Instead of building special cabins for EuroClass passengers, all SAS planes were equipped with a curtain that could be moved to separate the two classes of passenger. That gave considerable flexibility, which was mirrored in the result. Before long, SAS were stratospheric in both senses. In 1982 SAS had already become Europe's most punctual airline, a position the corporation maintained for 9 consecutive years.

Carlzon had little red books produced for distribution to all employees. They were written in an easy style that everyone could understand. At SAS, no one was in any doubt about the strategy they were pursuing.

The enthusiasm was unstoppable when Carlzon held celebrations with his employees. To his left is Vice President Frede Ahlgreen Eriksen, to his right the Norwegian Deputy Director Helge Lindbergh.

In 1985 they passed the hundred million pound profit mark for the first time. Among the outstanding highlights was the American Airline of the Year award in 1984. The relatively unimportant prize handed out by the magazine Air Transport World was not normally one which commanded much attention. When Swissair had won it the previous year, a few newspapers carried small notices. That was the measure of the award's perceived value. Carlzon was not satisfied with that. Surrounded by a host of Press, he went to New York and received the prize. Following that he hosted a celebration party in one of New York's most exclusive discotheques. The whole thing was transformed into a huge PR-show that profiled the corporation and its success. Receiving the prize was characteristic of Carlzon's way of promoting the corporation.

Even internally, they were amazed at the amount of positive PR that Carlzon was able to squeeze out of the media. It reached a pinnacle when he hosted a press gathering to present a teaspoon that could fold in half to fit inside SAS passenger cups.

Hoopla in the hangars

It is always fun to share in a success, but at SAS the employees felt something closer to euphoria. It was seen at its best with a colossal party which Carlzon and the personnel held for each other – not forgetting the Press of course.

The celebrations were conducted at full pelt in the hangars at Oslo, Stockholm and Copenhagen. This was a party to end all parties and Carlzon was the master of ceremonies. At one point, he even took over the lead guitar of a top Danish rock band who were booked for the occasion. Everyone got carried away. This was Corporate Religion in the largest sense of the words. Carlzon was also able to apply his strong Corporate Religion to the customers, so that in a short time SAS became a very potent Brand Culture for business people. With SAS' positioning, success bred success. Businessmen appreciate a winner. That strengthened the position within SAS' target group – and the company religion soon became their religion too; if you were a real businessman, you flew SAS.

The religion was created by an amazing level of engagement at the very top of the company – by spiritual management, in other words. It shows how quickly and efficiently you can lead your company in the right direction if you play your best cards.

Carlzon was also able to apply his strong Corporate Religion to the customers, so that in a short time SAS became a very potent Brand Culture for business people.

The crash landing

For a long time all went well for Jan Carlzon and SAS. But eventually the picture started to change. It became difficult to maintain focus on service, partly because SAS' level of ambition had overstretched their resources. By this stage SAS were servicing the businessman's needs with a "door to door" concept, which included hotels and credit card associations (Diners Club was incorporated into the SAS group in 1986).

Carlzon's ambitions were also being expressed in another way. By the start of the 1980s he had already formed ideas about how the liberalisation of the traffic would lead to radical changes in the European Market. Carlzon had the opinion that there would be parallels to the developments in the USA, where only the most cost-effective corporations had survived the transition to free competition on price. Carlzon pursued a vision of SAS being "One of five in 1995" – one of five remaining major airlines in Europe by that date. He figured that only British Airways, Lufthansa and Air France, plus a couple of other corporations would survive. On the basis of that vision, they steered SAS towards being one of these corporations by buying, merging and/or making cartels.

In November 1993 a merger between Swissair, Austrian Airlines, KLM and SAS was very close to becoming a reality. But KLM pulled out. Perhaps Carlzon had misjudged the situation, or maybe he was just ahead of his time. The 22 European airlines that existed in 1985 all made it through to 1995. This failure of vision resulted in Jan Carlzon being forced to leave the corporation, which yet again had plunged into financial difficulties. Just as success had spawned more success, so failure brought on more failure.

When you aspire to a religion, you can also become vulnerable, especially when your consumers (in this case, businessmen) expect to see success. Internally, Jan Carlzon had not sold his idea about merging. In the SAS 50th anniversary book it says:

> "This time, Jan Carlzon did not get his organisation to follow. He seems to have let down his own religion. A common feeling of the management not really having their heart in their daily work, was spreading in the company".

It seemed that it was Carlzon himself more than the organisation who needed a new vision.

It seemed that it was Carlzon himself more than the organisation who needed a new vision. A strong administrator who could act as a counterbalance to the management might have kept the corporation on track. But in spite of this, Jan Carlzon, who after his 12 year stint at the top was the longest reigning SAS manager, could leave the corporation with his head held high.

He remains the most progressive leader the corporation has had. Precisely because he understood the importance of spiritual management and how it operates both inside the organisation and out in the market. SAS still retains a firm hold on the business segment. Perhaps SAS is no longer a religion for the target group, but it certainly still has a Brand Culture status in the market, which the corporation can choose to build on or let die.

The development of the SAS brand position

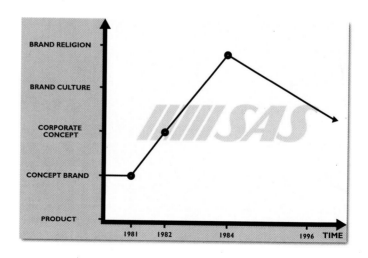

1. Until 1981 SAS sells transport by air. It was at its best in 1978/79, when profits exceed £10 million. In the two following years there is loss.

2. *Jan Carlzon arrives in 1981. A strong and consistent Corporate Concept is created. Everything is adapted in order for SAS to become "The Businessman's Airline". The results show immediately.*

3. *Sweet success: The best period in the history of the corporation.*

   In 1988 profits top £30 million.

4. *A new vision shifts the focus away from the core concept. The merger plan fails. Carlzon quits SAS. The spirit leaks away.*

CASE-POINT

SAS

The establishment of a strong Corporate Concept, built around "The Businessman's Airline", was the starting point for the tremendous success that SAS achieved under Jan Carlzon in the 1980's. He redefined the product and through his highly visible, press conscious leadership created commitment for his Corporate Religion both internally and externally. This is how SAS winged its way to Brand Religion status.

Brand building

The reason why it is so difficult to work with brands is that their values are based in the subjective understanding and opinions of human beings. Blindfold tests can be highly misleading. Who says it's the taste which makes consumers prefer one brand to another? It's not enough that a brand has high awareness and preference. It must also fit the individual's needs, purse and willingness to spend their money on exactly this product. That willingness will only be there if the personality of the brand fits the individual consumer. That obviously includes the basic need that the product is designed to satisfy. The quality must be equal to expectations of the product, and that must happen every single time.

In brand building it is crucial to add value to the product, so that consumers involve themselves. The more they do it, the more value accrues to the brand.

There are many factors that determine a brand's value to consumers, and all these factors have different weightings. Added to that is a bewildering array of methods for assessing them; among the more popular being knowledge-percentage and top-of-mind preference measurements. In recent years concepts such as liking and disliking have arrived. These look at the subjective values around the product concepts with which consumers establish contact. In brand building it is crucial to add value to the product, so that consumers involve themselves. The more they do it, the more value accrues to the brand. The model in Figure 3.10 shows that both the soft qualitative values as well as hard quantitative values must be worked with at the same time to climb the involvement axis and build a stronger brand.

Since there is such a wide range of factors which give a brand its value, as much exact knowledge as possible should be collected to form the basis for brand building and involvement. To give an example: Coca-Cola gives progressively more value to its customers, the more they encounter it out in the world.

When a brand is socially acceptable and has high prestige, it rubs off on the rational price/quality relationship. A high price is the proof of a prestige brand. The rational and the emotional values are inextricably linked in a "virtual partnership" that gives value to the brand.

Fig 3.10 Factors that give a brand its value

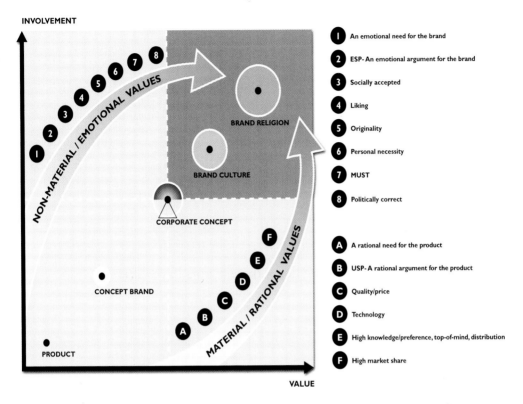

INVOLVEMENT

BRAND RELIGION

BRAND CULTURE

CORPORATE CONCEPT

CONCEPT BRAND

PRODUCT

NON-MATERIAL / EMOTIONAL VALUES

MATERIAL / RATIONAL VALUES

VALUE

1 An emotional need for the brand

2 ESP- An emotional argument for the brand

3 Socially accepted

4 Liking

5 Originality

6 Personal necessity

7 MUST

8 Politically correct

A A rational need for the product

B USP- A rational argument for the product

C Quality/price

D Technology

E High knowledge/preference, top-of-mind, distribution

F High market share

It is the interplay between quantitative and qualitative values that creates brand position. The quantitative parameters on the x-axis are well known, while the qualitative parameters on the y-axis are somewhat more difficult to measure. But that should not keep companies from trying to set up some measurable values for qualitative assessments of the brand. The moment you succeed in making it measurable, you have created a strong way to differentiate yourself from your competitors. The higher the consumers ascend the y-axis, the more involved they become in the brand. As a support for an USP, which usually builds on rational product advantages, an ESP is also ascribed to it – an emotional reason for choosing the brand. Point 3 is reached if the brand fits into the consumer's personal attitude to life and the social status being aspired to. Point 6 is reached when the brand becomes viewed as a personal necessity. At point 7 we reach Brand Religion status, where the brand is a must. The ultimate rank is when a brand soars to such a height that it is seen as being politically correct. This last factor will become increasingly important in the future.

Show business

WORLDWIDE BRANDS, INC

Worldwide Brands Inc. (WBI) was created to strengthen and extend the Camel brand. Starting with the world's biggest and most spectacular 4WD endurance event, the Camel Trophy, the little corporation has built up a power-brand in the most remarkable way. It involves consumers all over the world.

*WBI asked that the term "brand diversification" be used to describe the company's activities. This request has been complied with, though the description used elsewhere in this book is "brand extension" – a concept which WBI claims does not apply to their activities.

WBI has realised that soft, non-material values are decisive for differentiation of brands, and form an essential part in the brand building process. WBI was established in 1981 as part of the RJR Nabisco Group which owns the illustrious Camel cigarette brand. The corporation's task was to work with some of the parent company's brands, primarily Camel, and exploit it in a diversification-related* manner to create more profits from extending not only the brands themselves but also brand value. In addition to the normal practical work with diversification, WBI placed added focus on Brand management and brand building. Brand diversification is defined by WBI as a commercial exploitation of the inherent goodwill in a brand for diversification purposes.

WBI has created high involvement through the Camel Trophy. Starting from the values that have made Camel Trophy so relevant for so many, WBI has brand diversified to a whole series of products and secured a position in Brand Heaven.

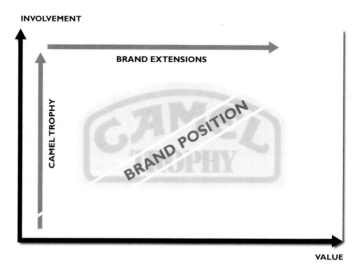

WBI has its headquarters in Cologne, Germany. Today, it is a single organisation with around 85 employees (among them several former participants in the Camel Trophy) and more than 20 management offices around the world. Their job is exclusively concerned with one essential: the brand.

All production is carried out on licence. The germinal point for WBI was the Camel Trophy adventure expedition, inaugurated in Brazil in 1980.

Camel Trophy

Since its inception in 1980, the Camel Trophy has been an annual event. It is arranged by WBI in co-operation with the Global Event Management corporation (also a member of RJR Nabisco Group). The Camel Trophy is a hybrid between a Land Rover rally (Land Rover is co-sponsor) and a traditional adventure expedition, with a stack of tasks to complete along the way. It has now been staged 17 times across four continents, in some of the most exciting and challenging terrain on the planet. The latest Camel Trophy was run from Santiago in Chile to Ushuaia in Argentina, the 3,000 miles trip lasting 3 weeks. The Camel Trophy is strictly for amateurs, professional soldiers cannot participate. So it is "ordinary" consumers that are given the opportunity to enter into the spirit of the brand. There are two competitors from each designated country or area (Scandinavia is regarded as one geographical area). By ensuring there are competitors from many countries, WBI is sure of creating massive media interest. National media are of course always most interested in their own national competitors.

The Camel Trophy has an official logo.

Before the actual event there is a long selection process. This is necessary because of the enormous interest there is among potential participants. Every year, more than a million would-be competitors fight to become one of the 40 that make it to the final. WBI does not hide the fact that personal magnetism and ability to communicate with the press play a role in the selection process. This is business – the investment must generate its own return. This starts through coverage – usually the most reliable and strongest resource for building brands. Naturally all participants must sign a contract, giving the organiser unlimited right to use the participant's name, picture and biography for advertising the Camel Trophy and Camel Trophy products.

Camel Trophy bag.

All participants are equipped with Camel Trophy Adventure equipment. This has two purposes. Firstly, all new products can be tested by the participants before they are introduced on the market. This has proved to be valuable, and there are examples of equipment that has been adjusted on the recommendations of the participants. The products' reliability thus gains from a serious connection with the event. The second purpose of giving competitors the equipment is

There are plenty of opportunities for shooting spectacular press and promotion pictures during the Camel Trophy.

Press coverage of the religion

WBI calculates how many people are exposed to Camel Trophy every year through the enormous media interest.
As the figure shows, publicity has practically exploded in recent years.

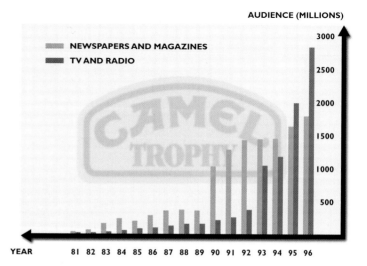

AUDIENCE (MILLIONS)

NEWSPAPERS AND MAGAZINES

TV AND RADIO

3000
2500
2000
1500
1000
500

YEAR 81 82 83 84 85 86 87 88 89 90 91 92 93 94 95 96

that it provides a unique source of product exposure to the press. All the promotion pictures and film are of course from the Camel Trophy. This way of involving the consumers in the brand universe works. The first million are already highly involved in Camel Trophy, simply because they have participated. Millions more are involved by the connected brand values (nature and masculinity first and foremost), the reliability and the consistency that is created around all aspects of the brand. The Camel Trophy makes the brand come alive for consumers. The PR work is the trump card behind the trophy.

The participants are used actively in the marketing.

Press coverage

Press coverage means everything to the financial success of the Camel Trophy. PR work is therefore something that is taken very seriously by WBI. The regional offices handle contact with PR agencies and journalists in their individual markets. 300 journalists from all over the world are invited to accompany the expedition. The treatment they get has a guaranteed effect – namely they would all like to come again! The interest generated has almost Olympic dimensions (see Figure showing how interest has increased over the years). CNN, MTV and Eurosport are among those that feature The Camel Trophy. Media which are not on location can also cover the event from the daily press releases they receive. Nothing is left to chance when it comes to spreading the Camel Trophy religion.

Land Rover is co-sponsor.

Diversifications

WBI earns a lot of money. In 1995 the corporation had a turnover of 430 million dollars. These earnings come from diversifications of the Camel brand which are all manufactured on licence. There are two essential components to this – Camel and Camel Trophy. The former focuses mainly on traditional clothing. The latter includes Camel Trophy Adventure Boots, Camel Trophy Adventure Wear and Camel Trophy Watches, plus the non-material value universe that surrounds this enormous event. Production is handled for WBI by a range of different companies: shoes and boots by Salamander, watches by Melco, bags by Michael Belheim International. Clothes are by Bültel Worldwide Fashion, Dornbusch & Co., Como Sport and Outdoor Sportsartikel. The shared parameter for all products is that they fit into the value universe surrounding the Camel Trophy. Nothing is allowed to destroy the religion. It can prove a good investment to push a brand up the involvement axis like this with the aid of non-material values created through big events; events which in reality are big shows put on for the honour of potential customers. This is pure "show business".

WBI earns money on different products. There are three Camel Trophy lines: Adventure Wear...

WBI´s retail sales

Adventure Watches...

and Adventure Footwear.

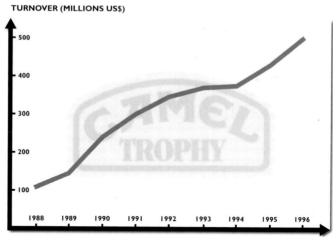

TURNOVER (MILLIONS US$)

500
400
300
200
100

1988 1989 1990 1991 1992 1993 1994 1995 1996

VALUE

As the brand position has improved and involvement increased, WBI's turnover has followed suit.

CASE-POINT

WBI
Worldwide Brands Inc. is a model example of how you can create a high consumer involvement in an unconventional way. The Camel Trophy, which directly involves more than 1 million participants and achieves phenomenal media attention every year, has been the starting point for a series of brand diversifications based on the same values which have created the involvement. They have translated consumer involvement directly into earnings.

The brand band

A brand can contain a number of different products, depending on the strength of the brand. The brand band illustrates how far a brand can be extended. It is interesting to us because it is crucial to get as much as possible out of our investments in single brands. The big question is how many products and product categories you can sell under a brand.

The big question is how many products and product categories you can sell under a brand.

Many international companies load more and more different products into a brand because of the scale of their marketing investment in it. They simply can't afford to run several brands. An international brand requires incredible marketing budgets. That's why major international companies now employ big brand umbrellas using the company's name for a mass of products. It is an attempt to optimise the brand of course, but in most cases stretches things too far. It's hard to create a sense of reliability when you appear to be making everything under the sun. The brand ends up as little more than a quality stamp. If there is a dedicated competitor, the brand will never become the best in any special category.

These days, many companies are blurring their brands because they do not appreciate the importance of irrational soft brand values for the future. I have witnessed however, that after a period of extensive diversification, companies often return to their core business for single brands simply because there is no synergy or structure in the other route.

The challenge in the future will be to develop brands with rational and irrational values that can get as many products as possible beneath it without eating into the brand values or bursting the brand band. It is important to create brand involvement in order to extend the brand band.

It is important to create brand involvement in order to extend the brand band.

A product brand is closely tied to the product's physical qualities and so it is impossible to have several products under the band. Where a concept has been established, you can usually fit up to five products within the brand band. It requires a Brand Culture where the products are united by the brand's values, to add further products but there's a proviso. In Brand Cultures and Brand Religions

Fig 3.11 The stronger the brand, the wider the brand band

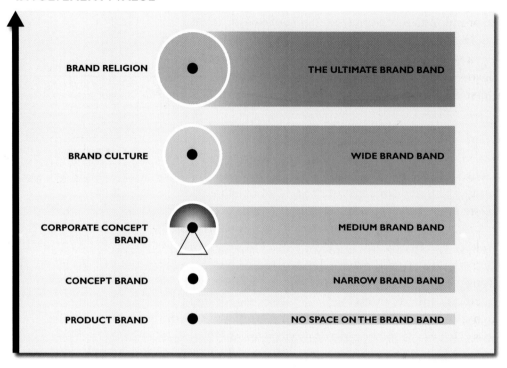

There is a close connection between brand position and the number of variants a brand band can tolerate. The higher up in the hierarchy, the less the brand is tied to the generic product and the more products the brand band can contain.

the brands are so strong that you have to be careful what products you put under them.

A Coca-Cola orange drink for example would undermine the brand. But accessories such as sportswear, towels, cool bags and sunshades all hang naturally together with the values in the brand. The same is the case with Harley-Davidson. It can support anything from leather jackets to aftershave, as long as the product is clearly connected with the brand's basic positioning and values.

When concept line extensions and brand extensions are produced indiscriminately, the connections are often misunderstood. Most so-called line extensions are harmless, but for some products they could be catastrophic, e.g., a Coca-Cola orange drink. Perhaps it's time to stop treating line extensions as a game and start thinking about what the extension adds to the brand. Ask yourself, what kind of things can contribute to building a stronger brand and higher involvement? Later on, the widening of the brand band will become possible. It might seem a round-about way, but it's only building on ideas which take the brand's consumer reliability into account. Too many product managers have destroyed solid brands through a continuous drip feed of so-called line extensions. Over the course of time, consumers become confused and the brand is undermined.

It's time to stop treating line extensions as a game and start thinking about what the extension adds to the brand.

Never permit a line or brand extension that lies outside the brand band, or fails to contribute to brand strengthening. Every brand band has its limits, and the company that ignores this fact does so at its peril.

Star Wars

When sports stars compete, it isn't only the fans who are cheering them on. For the large sports clothing companies that sponsor them, victory = market share = money. Consumers want to be associated with winners and so give preference to the brands which sponsor their idols. When Adidas released their hold, Nike took over with a pre-eminent Brand Religion. Adidas however is now on its way back into the fray. The common weapon is sponsorship.

Adidas – the Olympic way

Horst Dassler was a great asset to Adidas.

It was Adidas that first saw the potential of sponsorship. In 1920 the shoemaker Adolf ("Adi") Dassler invented a sports shoe that formed the basis of what today is a 14 thousand million dollar market. A calculation made by the trade journal Sporting Goods Intelligence shows that in the sports shoe market Nike takes the gold, Reebok the silver, and Adidas the bronze.

It hasn't always been like this – far from it in fact. It was Adolf's eldest son Horst Dassler, with his insight into business mechanisms and operational methods, who won the game and created the sport clothes religion. Dassler was the first to manage his business empire on the correct assumption that sponsoring sports stars was the path to sales success.

The first time Adidas was worn at the Olympic games was in 1928. However it was not until Melbourne in 1956, where Horst himself was present, that sports marketing started to achieve serious significance. Two years earlier, West Germany had won the World Cup in football wearing revolutionary new Adidas boots – an event which captivated the country en masse.

By providing help with a number of sporting events, Horst Dassler became a conspicuous man behind the scenes with principal sports organisations like the International Olympic Committee (IOC), the International Athletics Union and FIFA. Via his influential contacts, Dassler engineered a unique position from which he could control the major sporting events.Because his company had world control, Adidas became a world religion. In a presentation book on the history of the corporation, Adidas calls itself "a natural partner of the International Olympic Committee, National Olympic Committees, Sports Federations and individual athletes". Sports stars are aptly described as "Adidas partners in the world of sports". Stars like Jesse Owens, Bob Beamon, Edwin Moses, Daley Thomson, Franz Beckenbauer, Michel Platini, David Beckham and Steffi Graf have contributed immeasurably to the growth of the Adidas religion. Adidas was the winner's brand. For a period of time it seemed almost impossible to win anything major in anything else but Adidas. Dassler was really the man who brought sport and commercial interests together in a shared success story. In 1984 he was presented with the Olympic decoration by the IOC President Samaranch, with whom he had particularly close contacts.

Gradually, as competitive corporations opened their eyes to the possibilities that lay in sponsorship, the Adidas position was challenged. But it was only when Dassler died in 1987 at the age of 51, that the German giant got into serious trouble.

The personal contacts which had paved the corporation's way to conquering the stars died with Horst Dassler. The power of Adidas gradually diminished, and the corporation was not geared to handle this situation. Nike, already in an advantageous position on the American market, struck with new designs and intensified their efforts in the exploding sponsorship market. A market, I should add, where the sporting idols had not been slow in learning their value.

Brand position trends

The chart below illustrates the brand position trends for Adidas and Nike.

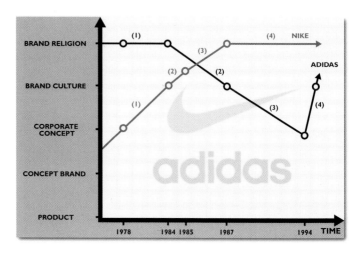

Adidas 1: Adidas dominates all the big sports events in Europe, largely due to Horst Dassler's massive efforts to get Adidas connected with major sports arrangements such as the Olympic Games and the World Cup in football.

Adidas 2: The monopoly is challenged by strong pressure from Nike, which increasingly gains a foothold. You can actually win in equipment other than Adidas!

Adidas 3: When Horst Dassler dies in 1987, Adidas starts to get into serious difficulty. Personal contacts are lost, and Nike proves impossible to hold back. Adidas goes quickly downhill.

Adidas 4: Robert Louis-Dreyfus takes over the control of the company. Everything apart from marketing is cut back. Several big sport stars come on board. After posting a deficit of £53 million in 1993, a surplus of £85 million the next year shows that the ship has headed round. In 1995 the surplus is £40 million.

Nike 1: Nike signs a contract with John McEnroe in 1978 and starts to sell outside the American home market.

Nike 2: Nike's position becomes stronger each year – also as a result of a series of product developments. At the 1984 Olympic Games, 58 athletes sponsored by Nike collect 65 medals. The greatest of them all is Carl Lewis who wins four gold medals.

Nike 3: Nike signs a contract with Michael Jordan of Chicago Bulls in 1985. A part of the contract states that Jordan has his own Nike collection – Air Jordan.

Nike 4: Nike is a Brand Religion. The 1994 football World Cup demonstrates that the corporation has an iron grip on this major sport, which earlier was completely dominated by Adidas. Ten players in the winning Brazilian team – among them Romario and Bebeto – play in Nike boots. Nike controls all the big sports.

"You don't win silver. You lose gold"

Nike is the name of the Greek goddess of victory. It is a symbol that connects perfectly with the company and its success in dominating primary markets.

Nike was started in 1964 by Phillip Knight and Bill Bowermann under the name Blue Ribbon Sports Company (BRS). From the mid-eighties the corporation has dominated sports clothing, especially running shoes, tennis shoes and basketball boots. This is because of a thoroughly global marketing strategy with its main emphasis on worthwhile sponsorships. They seek to establish the company's products as identity-creating culture components. The means to this end has been the creation of sports hero myths. They are portrayed as having dependence on Nike products for their achievements, in campaigns that often have the status of a mantra.

Nike tempted Michael Jordan away from Adidas with his own Jordan collection.

The best example of this is Michael Jordan (Phillip Knight's recipe for a "fantastic super hero myth"), who in the mid-eighties came into the Nike family despite the fact that he at that time preferred Adidas. Besides the money, Jordan was persuaded to join Nike by the promise of his own Jordan collection and personal influence upon

At the Olympic Games in Atlanta, Nike ran this advertisement which in a few words describes the soul of the whole corporation.

the design of the shoes. Nike has exploited the sponsorship of Jordan so well that they have actually succeeded in building the image of the star as an ideal type of a human being. He has become a hero in the old-fashioned mould, with a rare "larger than life" ability to present the grandiose in a pure form. Jordan symbolises something clean and unambiguous. Jordan is an absolute winner with an almost godlike status. He is worshipped in sports centres and supported through the purchase of equipment from his collection – whereby the fabulous deity comes that little bit closer to the ordinary mortal. The recipe is identical every time. Winners use Nike. And thus, like Adidas before them, Nike builds up its image as "the winner's brand".

Nike has realised the importance of the fact that people do not invest their emotions in generic products (no one cheers a product); and that building non-material benefits are a basis for creating brand specific involvement on the consumer side.

Dreams are woven around stars like Jordan, dreams in which you acquire a personal share by purchasing Nike products. The following quotation from Donald Katz's book, "Nike – Just do it", specifically referring to the main US target group – boys from 13–18 years, illustrates how the products (shoes in this case) get their own life through the value added to them.

> "The shoes were beauty. The shoes were sublime. The shoes were how the boys felt about life and they had been magically ingrained with their secret aspirations."

Nike uses a fan analogy with the customers as fans. This applies to practically all the product areas in which Nike is engaged. The corporation's TV commercials, produced by the Oregon based advertising agency Weiden & Kennedy for all markets, are often purely shows of world stars dressed in Nike equipment.

John McEnroe was – and is – Nike man, just like Pete Sampras and André Agassi. In the soccer market, which is very small on the home front and where Nike has traditionally been in a weak position, they have seriously entered the fray by sponsoring stars like the Brazilians Ronaldo, Romario and Bebeto, and the Italian Maldini. Nike conscientiously works on cornering the top stars in the highest profile sports. The corporation has been nicely helped on its way by the media explosion within the sports world. One which has made the Olympic Games perhaps the biggest media event in the whole world. Where else could a sponsor be sure of getting its message out to the whole world for three weeks in a row? Nike has been exceptional in the way it has been able to connect the awesome media coverage to their products – worn by the idols of track and field in full view of countless millions of captivated consumers. Nike is in the spotlight at all times, which is what the strategy demands. Only in this way can you achieve the riches of a religious status.

Corporate Concept

The Nike Corporate Concept can be summarised as follows:

The product
Began with sports shoes. After the brand had gained strength, it spread out to include clothes and other sports articles.

The concept
To make the best sports shoes in the world; and later, the world's best sports equipment. The mission that controls it is a winner concept where Nike will always be the best. This is expressed in everything: the best products, connections with the best sports practitioners etc. Product development is a high priority in order to ensure the company remains at the forefront in materials and design.

The profile
Nike has built their profile on the big stars they have attracted to their stable. With the marketing profile "Just do it" there is a profound connection made between the big stars and the individual consumer. You feel like a winner just by wearing Nike equipment.

The organisation
Nike is to a large extent controlled by the big sports event where the stars present the products. All Nike's outlets are sport shops or in-store sport departments, where the shop assistants are young, sports oriented people who always wear the same shoes that the sports gods are currently wearing. The sell-in of new products is effectively done via sports coverage on television. All Nike has to do is time the product introductions in relation to the essential sports events and ensure that the products are available in the shops.

The religion imbues the organisation

It is crucial that the winner ideology is not only communicated externally as Brand Religion, but is also firmly rooted in the organisation as a Corporate Religion. Phillip Knight has created a robust and remarkable business culture based on Nike as a winner religion. Connected to the stars via sponsorships, their commitment to being in the forefront of development is clearly understood. You can formulate Nike's Corporate Religion in a more figurative way: Sports gods wear Nike products in what the target group sees as the high temples of sport. They ensure commitment and action in the organisation because the employees throughout the whole distribution chain can see for themselves which products the stars are wearing. It is not necessary to convince anyone about the product's outstanding qualities. The fact that Carl Lewis has won Olympic gold in Nike shoes is argument enough for all the shops to stock them. The shop assistants need no motivating to sell them. Everyone wants to be connected with the sports gods.

Sponsorships are therefore the external information carrier of Brand Religion, at the same time creating and communicating an internal Corporate Religion.

Nike does the missionary work – others produce the goods

Just like The Coca-Cola Company, Nike has focused its strength on spreading the religion, rather than expending unnecessary energy on production systems. Nike uses outsourcing to a great extent, functioning as a centre for design, production, co-ordination and marketing. The key tasks are innovation, product development and co-ordinating the dealers. Production itself is left to others. The corporation operates with three types of "production partners", categorised by their ability to handle products at different levels of sophistication: "developed partners", "volume producers" and "developing sources". Besides having major cost advantages, it also focuses core competence on what is really decisive – the missionary work of the Nike religion.

Keeping up with consumers

It is important for Nike to constantly monitor which types of sport their consumers are most interested in and which get the biggest global media coverage. So the corporation keeps pace with the consumer and makes sure it always has the most interesting stars in its fold.

Nike concentrates on the big American sports and global events, especially the Olympic Games. The Tour de France, with its enormous media exposure in Europe, is the latest in a row of events that are now being sponsored. By focusing their effort on specific types of sport, it is inevitable that Nike's strength will vary from country to country depending on the sporting culture.

Instead of adjusting to each country and involving themselves in the main national sports, they focus on the global, media driven sport and against that background discount other markets. This strategy optimises the use of their resources and ensures that the company is not defocused because certain parts of the market have special interests.

Adidas' comeback

The star wars have recently entered a new phase. Just when you thought Adidas were finished, the corporation has mounted a remarkable comeback under the new leadership of Robert Louis-Dreyfus, previously a manager with Saatchi & Saatchi (now Cordiant plc). He took control in 1993 – just as the corporation recorded a loss of £53 million. Dreyfus cut down on everything except marketing. The results have been fantastic. In 1994 profits soared to £40 million and in 1995 to £85 million. Capturing the absolute top stars is an essential part of the marketing: athletes in the second-best category are no longer seen as particularly interesting. Winners are all that matter, if Nike's position is to be seriously threatened. At a press conference, Nike's Phil Knight said: "It is a natural development in the shoe and clothes business to divide the world into their sports people and ours". Actually, the battlefield has been extended, because sports clothes are no longer worn just for sport. Placement advertising is used ever more frequently. Tom Hanks wore Nike in the film Forest Gump, while John Travolta and Christian Slater sported Adidas in Broken Arrow. Adidas has also claimed a bevy of actors in well known series such as Baywatch and Melrose Place. The culture fight between the different sports brands has entered a new phase, with action on several fronts. The future will show us who is best at getting their religion through, and whether Nike can be pushed off its gold pedestal.

CASE-POINT

Nike & Adidas
In the sportswear market it is crucial to be associated with the winners, which is why sponsorship of the biggest sports stars has become the way to involve the consumers. The battle between Adidas and Nike has proven one fact beyond dispute – the company which has the stars, has the success.

adidas

"Waiter, a T-shirt, please!"

The Hard Rock Café chain has relatively few restaurants but a very valuable trade mark, with the illustrious aura of Rock'n'roll. The adroit use of the brand has made Hard Rock's Brand Religion known and worshipped all over the globe.

It was two Americans longing for a burger, that lead to the opening of the first Hard Rock Café in London on 14 June 1971. Newcomers Peter Morton and Isaac Tigritt created a café with a relaxed atmosphere, serving traditional American diner food. The café was characterised early on by an eco-conscious "Save the planet" way of thinking, which today remains one of the foundation stones for the way the chain is run. In a similar way, "Love all, serve all", summarises another part of the business concept – that everyone should feel welcome no matter what your race, social status or creed.

The original Hard Rock Café in London in its opening year 1971.

The central factor for success that Morton and Tigritt latched onto was the rock music which they wanted to give English youth the opportunity of experiencing. Hard Rock became a Mecca for musicians. One day, Eric Clapton came in with one of his old guitars which he suggested Tigritt could hang up on the wall. Tigritt duly obliged. When Pete Townsend saw Clapton's guitar he was not slow in delivering one of his own guitars to the café. Up on the wall it went, together with a small sign which read: "Mine is as good as his". The idea of a living rock museum thus came into being. The total collection, the world's most valuable collection of rock trophies, today consists of more than 25,000 objects. They are all registered at the head office in Orlando, where their authenticity is confirmed before they are exhibited in the cafés. Around one third of the collection has been donated by rock musicians themselves, while the rest has been bought in auctions.

Hard Rock Café's success grew and grew. The product was food and drink, but the concept was Rock'n'roll – a universal culture. It is still like that. Young people all over the world can gather around rock music, and Hard Rock Café was and still is the gathering place. Nevertheless it was as recently as 1983 that Hard Rock Café No.2 opened in New York. However the expansion then proceeded at a rapid pace. In 1985 Tigritt and Morton divided the rights to Hard Rock Café between them geographically.

Rank International took over Tigritt's part of the corporation in 1988, and Tigritt then started the chain "House of Blues". In June 1996, Rank also succeeded in buying Morton out for the equivalent of around a hundred million pounds. Hard Rock Café is now one corporation with 64 restaurants with several more on the way.

The expansion has, among many other things, resulted in the Hard Rock Hotel & Casino in Las Vegas.

The merchandising explosion

At one time, Tigritt and Morton had some T-shirts made with the famous logo designed by artist Alan Aldrige, who had also done some work for The Beatles. These T-shirts were kept under the counter to sell to those interested. There was no shortage of takers! As Hard Rock Café has expanded all over the world, so the interest in Hard Rock merchandise has increased. Today Hard Rock Café sells jackets, backpacks, bean bags, shades, badges, peaked caps and teddy bears. These products are, as most of you will know, printed with the name of the town they are sold in.

The equipment has developed into a trendy form of souvenir all over the world. The products, especially the thousands of different Hard Rock badges, have become collector's items to the extent that they are now pirated on a grand scale.

The sale of merchandise is conducted from special shops inside the restaurants. It makes up around half of the chain's turnover. Actually, it has become quite common for the merchandising shop to open before the restaurant itself. Which is not that odd when you think

In October 1990 Hard Rock Café started selling T-shirts designed by artists with a special connection to rock culture. A portion of the profits from this "signature series" goes to charitable organisations. Here is Elton John's contribution.

Don Henley has also contributed to the "signature series".

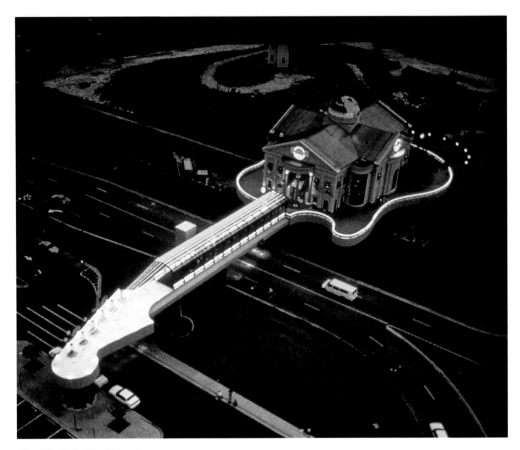

Hard Rock Café in Orlando: a manifestation of Hard Rock religion.

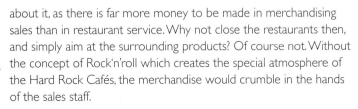

about it, as there is far more money to be made in merchandising sales than in restaurant service. Why not close the restaurants then, and simply aim at the surrounding products? Of course not. Without the concept of Rock'n'roll which creates the special atmosphere of the Hard Rock Cafés, the merchandise would crumble in the hands of the sales staff.

The present concept has involved so many in the yellow & brown logo, that it has made Hard Rock Café into a Brand Religion. It is worshipped by consumers all over the world who like to be associated with rock music. It's a marketing manager's dream.

Small wonder that Hard Rock Café's concept has been copied by several others. Most notably by Planet Hollywood (with Arnold Schwarzenegger, Bruce Willis, Demi Moore and Sylvester Stallone as minority shareholders), which was started by Robert Earl who jumped ship from the Hard Rock Café Corporation. Concept restaurants like Harley-Davidson Café and Robert de Niro's Tribeca Grill also have special "shops-in-restaurant", where merchandise is sold.

The Hard Rock logo contains so much value that many happily pay for the privilege of advertising the chain.

Used in the right way, merchandise can create synergies between the brand's generic core (the restaurant in this case) and the merchandising equipment. The restaurant causes the consumer to buy merchandise and the merchandise promotes the restaurant. Merchandising can play a useful part in lifting a brand up into Brand Heaven if the basic concept is strong, as the Hard Rock Café's was from the very beginning.

The children's T-shirt is as good for business...

CASE-POINT

Hard Rock Café
Hard Rock Café has been able to build a reliable, genuine position as the bastion of this musical religion. Sales of Hard Rock merchandise, which makes up half the chain's turnover and even more of the profits, proves it. So why don't they concentrate on merchandising and forget about the restaurants? Because it is on this bedrock that their unshakeable reputation rests.

...as the grown-ups version.

CHAPTER 4

Corporate Religion

Nothing great was ever achieved
without enthusiasm
(Ralph Waldo Emerson)

Strong market positions do not come out of the blue. This chapter explains why and how companies can be driven by spiritual leaders and Corporate Religion.

A strong brand requires a strong organisation

How does a company set about enlarging and strengthening its market position? As was stressed in the previous chapter, it must include qualitative, emotional and non-material parameters in building better brands. If a company hopes to reach the ultimate brand position – Brand Religion – it must also upgrade the qualitative aspects of management.

If a company hopes to reach the ultimate brand position – Brand Religion – it must also upgrade the qualitative aspects of management.

Large international companies have many people of differing rank, many systems and above all many opinions, attitudes and value. As Figure 4.1 shows, advantageous brand positions do not spring into existence by themselves. As its dominant management tool, the company needs a spiritual focus. This is Corporate Religion.

A Corporate Religion ensures that all employees in a company share the same qualitative values. This is important because it is rarely the quantitative variables, like skills and efficiency, that give companies problems.

The problems arise over qualitative variables, opinions and values. Hardworking, capable employees are also capable of wasting their energy fighting over the latter two especially. Most of the misunderstandings stem from conflicts over what different people believe to be true.

We are all individuals. Through work, we can seek our *raison d'être* in a wider context. Nevertheless, the vast

Fig. 4.1. Corporate Religion

INVOLVEMENT

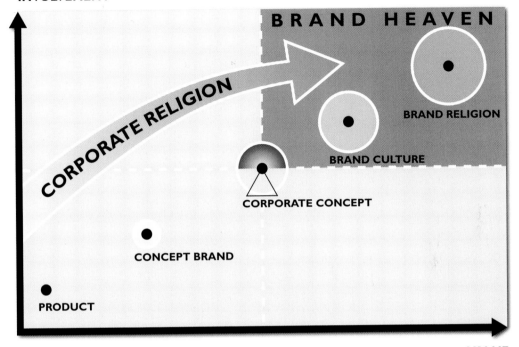

Companies with a Corporate Religion have the best chance of making it to Brand Heaven because all the employees have the same spiritual focus.

majority of top managers fail to motivate or focus the company's most important motor. It is not easy, I admit, but market differentiation demands more than marketing strong brands.

A management which is able to transfer intelligence to its employees becomes a greater company than one in which only the boss manifests the IQ. Every competitive leader can be assumed to meet that basic criterion. This is why the concept of 'emotional intelligence' will become so important in the future. There is an important distinction between normal IQ and emotional intelligence – the latter being connected with the ability to inspire others.

Many of the leaders described in the case studies presented in this book have exactly this ability. They may not have achieved better exam results than everyone else, but they have all been able to cut through to the core, to focus the whole company and transfer their thoughts and ideas to everyone in the organisation.

It is not capable employees that companies usually lack – rather it is the ability of leaders to lead them in the right direction.

It is their qualitative energy in the form of spiritual leadership that has moved the company. First and foremost, they have created a set of values for the company – instead of letting ordinary skills control its progress. It is not capable employees that companies usually lack – rather it is the ability of leaders to lead them in the right direction.

You can choose to lead your company with measurable facts, numbers and techniques. The effect on personnel of promising year-end figures and upward share price movements is understandable enough. Nevertheless the organisation must have spiritual sustenance in order to optimise productivity.

You don't get belief out of a slot machine

In many companies, employees tend to get nervy when they are addressed on the subject of company attitudes and values. As I mentioned at the outset, religion derives from the Latin religare – to bind something together in a common expression. A religion is a way to give a group of people a set of attitudes and values. Everyone can see what kind of products a company manufactures and sells. But why they do it, what the next product will be, what the company's mission is – that is something management may not know much about. If a company uses the word religion to describe their overriding management tool, then there's no doubt about what management wants, what the company stands for, where it is going and how it will get there. Corporate Religion is a question of belief.

It is no longer enough to employ people for their skills – their attitudes and values must also be compatible with those of the company. Only when these attitudes and values go hand in hand with skills – the whole thing being managed using a Corporate Religion – will the company be equipped to attain the ultimate position of Brand Religion.

Fig 4.2 The value based organisation

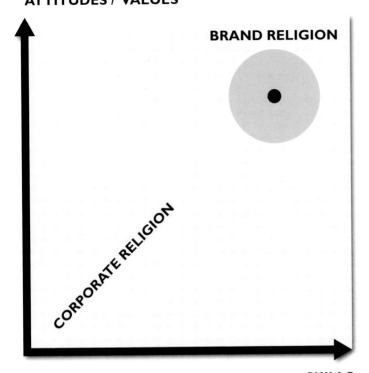

Only an organisation which wants the same things and goes in the same direction will be able to work sensibly with the qualitative values which differentiate brands. It is not enough to employ people just for their skills – their attitudes and values must also match those of the company.

You don't get belief out of a slot machine. Top management has to believe. When the employees sense that the leaders are fighting for a cause, it rubs off. When the leaders' fire is burning brightly, the next step is a 'bible' which describes the nature of the belief, the set of values and the rules of conduct which apply to all who live in this particular community. This bible is the most valuable management tool of all.

Top management has to believe. When the employees sense that the leaders are fighting for a cause, it rubs off.

Spiritual management

How do I get an overview of my company, and how do I make my company coherent and homogeneous throughout the international system? Many companies prefer to avoid the question altogether, satisfied that their rich human resources will follow the same unified spirit through a kind of default process. The focus tends to be on product development, sales and market shares. The international company system is seen as little more than an aggregate which channels products out to the customers. What often gets completely overlooked is that the same system which delivers the product also channels valuable information back to the company's management. But ignorance is bliss, and the system is considered to be perfect until the day when sales start to collapse. By this time, the company is usually well on its way out over the precipice.

Very few international companies use their full resources to give their whole organisation a higher level of understanding of the company's shared goal so everything comes properly into focus. Even fewer keep tabs on end-users around the world and take care to gather in unfiltered information. In the name of market adjustment, most content themselves with subjective reports from their subsidiaries. When such reports get as many biases as the number of conflicting egos operating behind them, the organisation very soon loses its balance. Corporate Religion is a strong focusing tool for counteracting organisational turbulence. Traditionally the subsidiaries are independent units that do things their own way. But as product lifespans have decreased, it has become vital to be able to act quickly in all markets to ensure success. This damages the subsidiaries because there is simply not enough time for anything to be done in more than one way. The subsidiaries must climb back into the central organisation, so that the company shares the same values and attitudes – no matter where in the world they have their office address. Things will then look as in Figure 4.3b.

When the company has a Corporate Religion, it is the company's vision of the future which is really being presented in the new product brochure. The product itself is just a small part of it. It is by communicating the company's spirit, attitudes and values that you extend your market position in an already well-defined segment.

Everything requires careful preparation and education. How you set about the sales process, and who you are marketing to, demands a lot of effort for each and every target group. Then comes more work on how to

Fig 4.3a The non-homogeneous international company

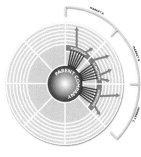

See Figure 2.3.a in Chapter 2 for explanation.

Fig 4.3b The homogeneous international company

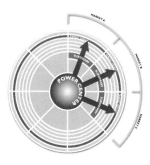

See Figure 2.3b in Chapter 2 for explanation.

implement the strategy. This isn't about presenting a handful of colourful overheads, it's about a great deal of deep thinking being implemented with scrupulous thoroughness. It might sound totalitarian, but with a clearly defined Corporate Religion, there is nobody who will have problems on the course because everybody's job is connected to the company's Corporate Religion – the first criterion for being employed. When your company is conscious about focus and feels a responsibility for it, work becomes efficient.

The company which has complete control of – and keeps in step with – its international organisation can control both the organisation and the market with the aid of a strong Corporate Religion. A company's success depends simply on direction. Nike is a shining example of how big a success you can become by raising the whole company to the status of a religion. Through sensible sponsorship contracts the corporation has captured the sports gods – at the world's biggest sporting events Nike is everywhere you look. The connection between the gods and their millions of fans has been beautifully encapsulated in the concept "Just do it". Perhaps the most obvious examples of companies spearheaded by charismatic leaders are The Body Shop, personified by Anita Roddick , and Microsoft – whose guiding light is the subject of our next case.

The code word for international success is control and if you can get the star role in the market, your company only goes one way: towards success.

Religious leadership

Microsoft®

Bill Gates uses his own personality to incredible effect in his running of Microsoft. As a spiritual leader he shows the way forward and communicates both with his organisation and the market.

The story of Microsoft is a tale of two nerds. And a vision of the computer revolution. What started as a very modest enterprise has developed into a gigantic business with more than 17,000 employees and a turnover of 6,000 million dollars.

Microsoft originated from some computing lessons at Lakeside School towards the end of the 60s, where Paul Allen and Bill Gates had a vision of a totally new world. Later – in the spring of 1975 – Bill Gates left his studies at Harvard to start up his now legendary software company together with Paul Allen. Gates was then 19 years old. Eight years later, Paul Allen was to give up his part in the company because of Hodgkin's disease. However, the partnership was already 60-40 in Gates' favour, because he had played a bigger part in the development of the company's first product, Microsoft BASIC. The businessman in Gates showed itself at an early stage.

Bill Gates is a unique combination of hyper-intelligent technician and hard-nosed businessman whose eyes are firmly directed towards the bottom line. This has been one of the keys to realising the vision of "A computer on every desk, and in every home" and "Microsoft in every computer". Another, equally important key to global success is Bill Gates' ability to use Bill Gates in his leadership, both internally and externally; often at the same time.

Bill Gates is the American dream personified, and that makes him interesting material for the media. He has exploited this magnificently in his efforts to run what started as a company religion and progressed to a whole market religion. It is Bill Gates who travels the world and holds conferences for preaching the Microsoft religion; it is Bill Gates who leads the market in the right direction. Wherever he goes, the reception he is accorded is usually on a par with that reserved for a major statesman.

Bill Gates gets undreamed of amounts of press coverage. Here courtesy of Time. Photo: Gregory Heisler

Better than anyone else, he has been able to establish himself as a visible guru in the world picture of computer and information technology, and there is money in that status. Bill Gates writes articles, participates in talk shows – how many other company managers could you see as a guest on the David Letterman show? Gates has a unique platform as both the symbol and the mouthpiece of Microsoft, and because he is a guru he sets the agenda for the whole business. It is Bill Gates' opinions the Press prefers to devote column space to; and the man answers, even when he is not being asked. His 1995 book "The Road Ahead" is just one example of how Gates appeals to his followers – and wins new ones.

In the book, Gates uses several pages to describe in fine detail the building of his palatial new residence, an already long running worldwide media event. The house – all 4,500 square metres of it – is a tourist attraction at Lake Washington in Seattle. It is a shop window for future information technology in the home. At Gates' place, there are 24 large video screens on the wall. The idea is that the pictures

The Economist *has also covered the subject of Gates & Microsoft.*

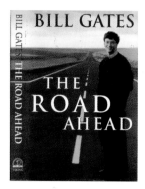

Bill Gates wrote "The Road Ahead" *in 1995.*

you see on the screen change continuously according to the present situation. By making a virtue out of showing us the technology in his futuristic home, Gates is not so much parading his wealth as maintaining the impression that he and Microsoft are constantly at the forefront of technological development.

His status as a guru enables him to communicate his vision to Microsoft employees through external channels. The amount of focus that Gates commands in the Press ensures that his message reaches every corner. Every single employee knows what the company's goal is, and what the company's culture is. Microsoft is no hierarchic jacket & tie outfit, it is a company for employees who think. That makes it easier to attract the right new recruits. Microsoft is run by a Corporate Religion where Gates is, if not God, then certainly a religious leader. The result has been fantastic both in terms of growth and profits, created by the rapid expansion made possible by the company's greater focus and higher vision.

When Bill Gates visited Denmark in connection with the launch of Windows 95, the presentation itself was just one part of the show. Interviews and meetings with Danish Finance Minister Mogens Lykketoft among others, made up the full picture.

CASE-POINT

Microsoft

Bill Gates is an outstanding example of a spiritual leader who uses the media to control both his company and the business area in which Microsoft operates. In spite of many critics, Bill Gates has taken over the computer market's guru position from IBM, and sets the future agenda for software.

Corporate Religion – Value-based growth management

It is much easier to show a model of how you can lead your company with a Corporate Religion than to invent the actual religion itself. But models have their uses, and Figure 4.4 shows the different steps which lead to value-based growth management. The starting point is the company's Corporate Concept as described in Chapter 3.

Fig 4.4   Value-based growth management – a development model

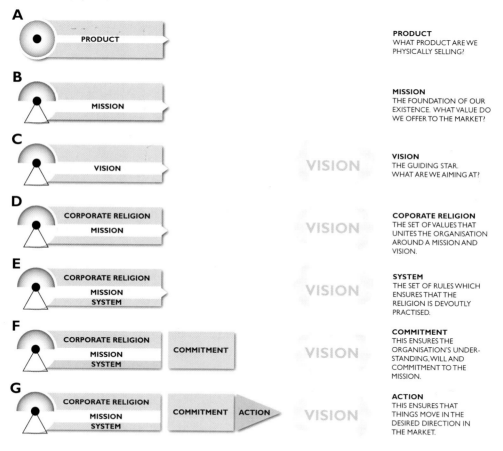

Value based management might seem an abstract notion, but it can easily be made tangible. The above shows how a company which wishes to move ahead along the lines I am advocating must build up its value-based growth management successively. In most companies, the product is the starting point. This must be replaced with a mission – your business foundation. Directly connected to the mission is the company's vision – to go somewhere you must have a goal. Your mission statement and vision statement will however remain empty words if the company is not united around a set of values – the Corporate Religion. The preaching of the religion must be ensured via a system which operates through a set of routines that apply to every employee. Finally, commitment and action is required if the whole thing is going to generate concrete results.

A Product

Product: what product are we physically selling?

Almost every company starts with products. Since day one the products have been in control, we imagine. Their competitiveness has dictated growth and everything going on around them. But as I have pointed out in the preceding chapters, this state of affairs is not good enough for survival, because global competition, differentiation and value give the product's physical properties a progressively smaller role in the brand's joint value as it is perceived by the consumer.

The product in itself and its physical properties are of course important in the face of stiff competition. But when you are leading your company towards a stronger market position, you have to focus on other aspects and values which surround the product. Today, virtually anyone can make a good product. But quality is not a goal in itself. Quality must have a soul. Even companies that have fared brilliantly with a unique product still get competitors. So they are forced to ask why their company exists. Why is it that they want to make a unique and brilliant product for their customers? What customer needs do they want to satisfy? In other words: What is the company's mission?

Quality is not a goal in itself. Quality must have a soul.

B Mission

Mission: the foundation of our existence. What value do we offer to the market?

Gradually, as brands become differentiated by qualitative parameters, companies are forced to look towards something other than the product to assure their future. They must have a mission – their foundation for existence. The mission must express what the company wants to do for its customers, and why.

The mission focuses on qualitative values because it is these which create high involvement among consumers. So when you define the mission – the idea foundation – of your company, you must concentrate on what it is about your company that can create high involvement, because consumers are inexorably drawn towards companies and brands with real attitudes and real values. The company can express its mission to its customers, in language which is both precise and easy to understand. If your mission statement consists of pronouncements on turnover, profits and market shares, it's likely to be off track.

When Jan Carlzon created a mission for SAS, he called the company "The Businessman's Airline". In that formulation there was a precise promise to the target group of what kind of airline SAS was determined to be. Carlzon's mission said that real business people travel with SAS, and at the same time it sent a clear signal to the whole company about what everyone had to concentrate on. Out of concentration comes focus, and so a clear mission will provide the control – of everything from product development and marketing to how the employee should greet a customer. The mission doesn't have to be condensed into three words – the essential thing is that everyone clearly understands the message.

It's important not to confuse a mission with a marketing concept or a slogan.

It's important not to confuse a mission with a marketing concept or a slogan. But the closer the mission and marketing are to each other, the more efficient the company's communication becomes – both externally and internally. The SAS mission had a highly positive effect on attitude among the employees. They felt special because they worked for SAS, and that feeling rubbed off on the customers, creating an atmosphere of high involvement. With a strong mission, you can aim high when you formulate the company's vision.

Vision: the guiding star, what are we aiming for?

C Vision

Vision is where you want to be. The vision may be value-based in an economic sense, but it doesn't have to be. A concrete goal like "we want to achieve a turnover of 1 million" can become "we want to have the biggest market share in our line of business". The vision must contribute to creating motivation in the whole organisation, so it is crucial that the vision is framed in such a way that everyone can feel inspired by it. You can safely forget visions which only appeal to the earning potential of top management.

There's a good reason for placing the mission before the vision. A vision can only have intrinsic value if there is a realistic connection between what you are capable of and what you are aiming to achieve. It's when you have first nailed down what you want to create for your customers that it becomes relevant to discuss the goals to aim at.

The vision is a guiding star – which must be realistic, but can also be highly ambitious. Ted Turner's CNN is a case in point. He aimed straight for the top as 'The World's Newsleader' and demonstrated at the same time that his concept was based on sound reasoning. He would create a TV station that only broadcast news. The more specific you are, the more differentiation you achieve. Make it easy to understand and you create high involvement among the users, and therefore more value. Thanks to Ted Turner's courage, CNN has become synonymous with news.

The vision is a guiding star – which must be realistic, but can also be highly ambitious.

The tricky thing about developing the right mission and the right vision is that it involves doing the apparently impossible: accurately predicting the future by foreseeing with clarity how the world and the market will develop. But that is top management's most important task – if they want to lead the company and not the other way round.

D Corporate Religion

In Figure 4.4. I exchanged the product with the mission – the value the company offers the market. Following on from that I included the vision as the guiding star for the work of the company. So where does Corporate Religion fit into the picture? Corporate Religion is the set of values which unites the organisation around the mission and the vision. It is the spirit of the company – a series of values and attitudes upon which the organisation is founded. These are the qualities which truly inspire, because they are shared by everyone.

Corporate religion: is the set of values that unites the organisation around a mission and vision.

Corporate Religion is about consensus, about uniting many minds in a common purpose. It is crucial for success that everyone has the same attitudes – and goes along the same shared path to create more value. A company which is governed by a Corporate Religion only has jobs for believers.

Companies with strong cultures are not the easiest places to work in. Powerful religions polarise opinions – people either love it or hate it. I see that as positive, because a strong spirit controls focus and efficiency. It's been suggested in some quarters that strong company cultures kill initiative. Frankly, that's nonsense. Within the frame of a well-defined Corporate Religion there can be plenty of space for individualism and creativity. The difference is that creativity and individualism can now be used constructively whereas before, vociferous individuals with their own personal agenda could defocus the organisation.

Corporate Religion is about agreed guidelines. Nobody changes the product or the accounting system in an international company just because they feel like it; so why should corporate attitudes and values be viewed any differently? Yet this is exactly what so many subsidiaries indulge in.

The real problem, however, doesn't start there, but with the management. You can't blame someone for not having the same set of values if they are not given a clear set of guidelines.

It is about thinking of the company in relation to mission, vision and human beings.

How do you set about developing a Corporate Religion? Try for a while to forget all about quantitative values and concentrate your mind exclusively on qualitative values. It is a very rewarding exercise, because it raises a lot of fundamental questions for the company and its leaders, who usually let the market run both themselves and the organisation. So instead of busying yourself around all those day to day problems, take a little time to look at product development, construct some budgets and follow the money through to the end result. This exercise is purely about creativity. It is about thinking of the company in relation to mission, vision and human beings. Start with a thorough analysis of existing values in the company and the attitudes that have engendered them. Against this background, it's a whole lot easier to see if these attitudes fit with the mission.

The way management normally proceeds is to arrange big meetings for the whole company and bring in external consultants to mediate the process. That's fine, so long as it is the management who decides what the religion is going to be – expressed in clear and simple terms so that everyone can understand it. When that task has been accomplished, the management must then work out the guidelines for operating the religion. When Jan Carlzon at SAS defined the mission 'to be the Businessman's Airline' it became a religion the moment he issued guidelines showing how his employees were going to meet it.

That was why Carlzon produced the 'little red book'. A company cannot practise its Corporate Religion until every employee in the organisation has understood the message and focused their efforts accordingly.

Company leaders should ponder the following company questions: Why do we exist? Where are we going? How do we get there? What attitudes do we expect our employees to possess? What values do we protect in our company? What behaviours do we think express that attitude? What are the rules of conduct enshrined in our religion?

A company cannot practise its Corporate Religion until every employee in the organisation has understood the message and focused their efforts accordingly.

Wrestling with issues like these is the substance of spiritual leadership and it requires effort. Top management must find out how the religion can be made visible, and that first occurs when the whole organisation can communicate the religion unambiguously. A key success criterion of a Corporate Religion is that the organisation experiences it as genuine. There must be a visible "religious leader" who takes care of communicating the company's seminal message and who acts as the company's mouthpiece, both to the employees and the marketplace.

Two of the best Corporate Religion driven companies are The Coca-Cola Company and The Walt Disney Company. In both cases, they have been able to make the religion such a deeply woven part of the company's fabric that they are not so dependent on a highly visible leader. That must be the ultimate goal for all aspiring companies.

Development of a Corporate Religion

When a company wants to develop a Corporate Religion, the management has to look at both the internal culture and the external positioning. It is the harmony between these two sides of the same coin which creates the strong company.

A company is rather like a human being; it needs a strong personality to manage it. The stronger the personality the greater the penetration power. But what is it that creates a strong personality? In 1927 Alfred Adler, one of the founders of modern psychology, made some revolutionary assertions about the nature of the human mind. In essence, Adler's thesis was that three things must be in balance for a human being to possess a strong personality:

- the way the individual sees himself
- the way the individual would like to be seen
- the way the individual is seen by others.

The more these three views harmonise, the stronger the personality will become. This idea is shown in simplified form in Figure 4.5.

Corporate Religion is about people and how you get them to work together in a unified spirit of purpose and direction. I will permit myself the liberty of applying Alfred Adler's thoughts to the company, in order to give a clear and simple picture of what Corporate Religion is primarily about.

Your company's personality

To apply Alfred Adler's thesis to companies, you must first make a complete description of the company, which focuses on the company's personality. The strong company is characterised by a balance between the following three conditions:

- the way the company sees itself;
- the way the company would like to be seen in the future;
- the way the market sees the company.

Fig 4.5 An individual's personality is determined by...

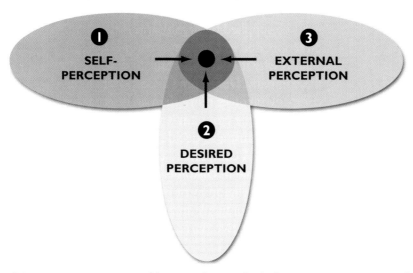

Three conditions must come into mutual harmony for an individual to possess a strong personality.

The greater the balance in the company, the stronger its personality will be – and the more powerful its market penetration (see Figure 4.6).

Fig 4.6 A company's personality is determined by...

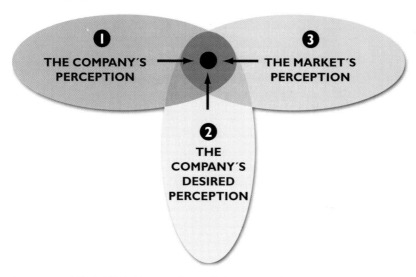

In an analogous way, Alfred Adler's ideas can be applied to companies.

More than an internal practice

It is well recognised that a strong market position is the key to a company's future prosperity. The task is to build that position and consolidate it. The future will not be about products so much as brands and brand values. Those values must be supplied by organisations which move in the same direction, and in harmony with the values of the brand. That is why it is so important to describe the personality of the company. Developing a Corporate Religion for a company involves more than an internal practice of uncovering the company's values. In isolation it makes no sense. You must also decide on your external positioning to the market. A company is a living organism which must reveal its value to customers every day. Therefore, a Corporate Religion must describe the connection between the internal company and the outside world. The bridge between these two parts is absolutely essential.

The positive spiral

Experience shows that the better the company's internal organisation understands how customers see the company – and what they are really buying from the company, the more motivated the employees will be to deliver the right values.

SAS speaks a clear language

SAS employees were highly motivated to attend internal service courses because they understood the objective – that SAS should be the businessman's favourite airline. And that implied of course that SAS was the best. When the internal and external culture are connected, the company gains harmony, consistency, a stronger personality, stronger growth and a stronger market position. That is the positive spiral, and it is important to get into it.

Political consumers

Corporate Religion is therefore a coherent description of the whole company, as shown in Figure 4.7. It is a comprehensive endeavour – and very rewarding too, especially for bigger international companies which still define themselves in terms of their product, when customers are actually buying something else from them, for example a solution or a brand. Many companies run on their own inertia, and in most cases it is external forces that cause them to halt and redefine themselves. It may be a crisis brought on by strong competition, or by political consumers who force companies to take a standpoint on difficult issues – questions which they do not themselves connect with their product. The reason why they get caught in this position is because they define their product too narrowly, while customers take a much wider view. The political consumer is an up and coming breed to be ignored at your peril. Shell's handling of Brent Spar and the revelation of Nike's use of child labour are just the beginning. Things are going to get a lot hotter in the political kitchen.

Fig 4.7 The internal and external company – a total description of the company's personality

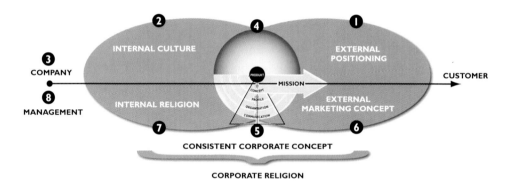

These are the sequential steps a company must take in order to achieve consistency all the way from the inner core to the furthest horizons:

1. *How does the outside world view the company? The company's external positioning is discovered.*

2. *How does the company see itself from the inside? The internal culture is described, based primarily on the company's history and the actual values which have made the company what it is today.*

3. *How does the company see itself in the future? The management's corporate aims are defined.*

4. *On the basis of these three descriptions, the company's Corporate Concept is formulated. A Corporate Concept is a consistent and clearly defined connection between product, concept, profile, organisation and communication. See Chapter 3 for a detailed explanation.*

5. *The validity of the Corporate Concept must be tested both internally and externally before implementation to ensure mutual understanding. As the main communicator of the company's new description, management must feel that it fully expresses the company's personality. It is advisable to develop a concept bible (not to be confused with a design manual) that accurately describes the Corporate Concept.*

6. *A marketing concept is developed which can communicate the Corporate Concept, and thus enable the company to attain the desired market position.*

7. *The internal religion is developed and described. The aim is to manage the company in a way that delivers a consistent brand to the market.*

8. *The company's management must take charge and clearly communicate the new message so that everybody understands the direction in which the company wants to go.*

How does the outside world view the company?

1. External positioning

Companies take up a lot of space in the consumer's daily life. When consumers buy the brand they buy the company – warts and all. For this reason they demand that the company is more "right" than it actually can be. Many companies – and especially their leaders – are not at all equipped to meet that idea. They grope about in a world where the boundaries between the consumer's and the company's understanding of morals are becoming less and less distinct.

When the brand and the company fuse into one consistent unit, customers cease to distinguish the one from the other. So you must unite the internal culture with the external positioning, and the company's future intentions. Figure 4.7 describes the course of this development. The first step is to investigate how the market and the customers view the company – from the outside.

This process concerns the whole company, so you must investigate the position among consumers in a representative number of markets. You can use psychographic methods to get under the skin of the interviewees – and keep the questions mainly qualitative. It's a good idea beforehand to have a number of hypotheses that you can test on the customers – otherwise you don't force customers to come to a decision. Often you have to search very thoroughly to find a consistent picture of the company – things which serve as common denominators. Maybe there will be one or more markets which don't fit under that description, in which case you face the difficult question of whether to work them into a shared picture – or dispense with them. These are necessary choices, which help to create a consistent picture of where the company actually stands.

How does the company see itself from the inside?

2 Internal culture

The internal description of the company is the most difficult task. Here, the aim is to get down to the heart and soul. It is essential to use psychographic methods in order to uncover the qualitative aspects of the company. The crucial thing is to find the positive power in the company – don't set your focus on diagnosing corporate diseases. When you find the positive elements which have carried the company forward, you can accelerate them so that they push the negative elements aside.

The internal concept is developed in the same way as you describe the company to customers by means of an external concept. Uncover the history of the company; find out where the company has come from, and what has moulded it into its current shape. History will usually explain where the internal values come from, so it is important to get the company's 'true core' identified. Use those employees who have the culture in their bones to uncover it. This 'culture group' should be composed of people from across the company, so that the total organisation is fairly represented. This will ensure that everybody understands the description you ultimately reach.

Putting the company into a historical perspective gives you a clear view of the point when the company moved forward decisively in the market. What did the employees do in concrete terms? Which values were predominant? If you can isolate the success factors, and view them in relation to where the market and customers are today – you have a good foundation for assessing where they will move in the future. All this information can prove very useful for recognising the need to adjust the company.

3. The company

To get the full picture of the company, yet another layer of information is needed. It is the answer to the simple question: What does the management want to do with the company in the future? No matter how difficult it is for a top manager to answer that question, it is nonetheless crucial that he or she does so. Otherwise the company just runs on inertia, unable to keep pace with the changes happening everywhere in the global society. The manager must move right to the front line, and know where the market and the customers are moving – or which direction they should be steered in. It places heavy demands on the top manager, and ought to be the most important qualification for being in that position in the first place. By uncovering management attitudes on where the company is heading for the future, you have all the necessary building blocks to complete the description.

How does the company see itself in the future?

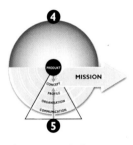

The company's Corporate Concept is formulated and tested.

4. and 5. Corporate Concept

With an external description of the market, an internal description and the management's attitude to the future, you have the three necessary building blocks for a complete description of the company – a Corporate Concept, defined earlier in Figure 3.7. By defining the mission for the company you get a guide to the future, the direction which everything else relates to – product, concept, profile, organisation and communication. This total description of the company must be gone over many times between management and the internal culture group. It also helps to do the same with the markets via a task force group set up for the purpose. The most important thing is that you test the 'new company description' against the market, to see if you are in line with the market and the customers. It does not matter if you are a bit ahead of the customers. The internal and external test phase usually involves several adjustments before you find the right Corporate Concept. You have to take this task seriously – it is the company's most important problem – and you ought to monitor your company at least every second year to see that it also stays consistently on the right track – externally and internally.

A marketing concept which communicates the Corporate Concept is established.

6. External marketing concept

Once you have developed and tested your Corporate Concept, it must be confirmed and a total description made from it. It is the total description of the company which forms the basis for the development of the external marketing concept – and it is that concept which must communicate the company's values to the market and the customers. When you view the company using a total religion model, the external marketing concept is no longer a detached activity where a subdepartment does the advertising and selling of the company's products. It becomes a total concept to which the entire company is committed – and which makes bigger demands on the external concept. You can't let any subdepartment run the external concept independently of what is otherwise going on in the company. Unfortunately, that is just what is happening in so many companies today.

7. Internal religion

As if that isn't hard enough, the company must also develop an internal religion to help keep the company on the right track, because it is the religion which explains and communicates the values you have found relevant and important to the company.

The internal religion is developed and described.

In developing the religion, you must include history to be able to understand the company. Where has it come from? What have been its defining moments? Where does it stand today? What does it want to be in the future? That knowledge belongs to the company. You can choose to write it down and hand it out to new employees – or you can hold courses for them where you recount history, and describe the company's total concept. It is not sufficient to do this just once. It must be continuously updated (where is the company right now and where is it going?).

When Jan Carlzon was in charge at SAS, he continuously sent out small, easy to read leaflets to all the employees, in which he explained his thoughts – a strong way to communicate consistent information. In large hierarchies information often loses its value because people tend to distort information as they pass it on. The more direct the communication the better. It is important to keep the path as short as possible, so everybody knows where they are, and what they must do. Seminars and open meetings are strong rallying points for the organisation. Everybody needs to understand the message and the formulation of the company – and what the formulation means to the individual. The internal religion must be formulated at a level which gives individuals an understanding of the whole company, and of the factors and values that are important to the company – a level where you explain what the company's mission means to the individual, and how the company's values and objectives are translated into daily work. If you can relate the company's assessment and human resource development system to the religion, you have a great opportunity to create a strong and homogeneous company culture in harmony with the company's external system.

8

MANAGEMENT

*The company's manage-
ment clearly communicates
the new message.*

8. Management

The total description of the company must in this way be communicated to the entire organisation. The management must take care to send the information directly to each employee – just as Carlzon did. Louis Gerstner from IBM did the same when he turned round the giant supertanker. In a book called 'One Voice' he presented his view of the market, IBM's situation and what he thought were the strengths of IBM. Then he went on to describe how the market would develop, and how IBM should tackle the future. He sent the book directly to every single IBM employee.

A question of involvement

The management must involve themselves and not leave the work to external advertising agencies which come up with isolated ideas to create attention out in the market. It is an equally high priority to communicate the inner culture – what the company stands for, and what it wants to stand for. This demands consistency in external communication – a big problem for most companies today, which are often divided into many different departments.

In most companies, external communication gets to the market from a variety of internal sources. The management sends out signals to the market via interviews in the press and the annual report and accounts. Some of the information is targeted on the financial markets. Some of it is extracted under pressure when companies face demands to reveal their attitudes on different issues. They often feel that such things lie in the borderlands of what is relevant to the company, but in fact it is exactly those regions which interest customers/users and the outside world in general.

The political consumer has become a sort of evil spirit for many company leaders. Like it or not, they are going to get plenty of fighting practice in the future, as companies become bigger and take up more space in our consciousness. Companies will almost become states within the state – and consumers will demand greater responsibility from them. A responsibility that will become just as important for assessing the company as their products.

Tomorrow's confused managers

All this confuses many top managers because they think it is illogical. I disagree. Not from a traditional product point of view, but from a brand point of view it makes good sense. You have to know who you are as a company to be able to control the information flow – and most companies' information departments have primarily been geared to control financial information, and to help out in crisis situations. Information departments are rarely prepared for the new building task. Perhaps because this information task lies between the traditional marketing department and the PR department, and in reality between top management and the product and sales departments. There is a need for total communication, because consistency is the only thing which really counts with the consumer.

Just look at Internet communication

Today, internet communication is managed very differently from company to company. It all depends on who has taken the lead – internally. It may be the information department, or the marketing department or even the data processing department. The information sent out on the Internet might be financial or product related, or perhaps campaign and brand news.

It might act as a service function – or a sales tool. Obviously, all this makes massive demands on coordination, given the traditional way that most companies are built. So who manages the home page? Who decides how it looks – and how you communicate?

When the sales department is big brother

The highly product-driven company furnishes another interesting example of outgoing communication. In this case, product concept and design lies in the technical department of the organisation – which often generates a large part of the company's total communication to the market; and it is usually a development manager who runs the whole show. Then there is the company whose sales system is an important part of the company's external communication – this is often the case when solutions are sold to customers. Sales and distribution become very large units in many international companies. If they are not bound tightly to the company concept, they deliver the value they think the market wants. This is not a bad idea in itself. However, the drawback of this approach is that the company cannot steer the market or the customers in the direction it wants them to go. Nor can it supply customers with a level of value which is more than they expect. The traditional marketing department can also be added to the list. It often develops into a pure communication department, creating advertising which takes the consumer as its starting point.

All these examples have been included to illustrate that there are in fact many different departments which handle a company's external communication. It is extremely important that all departments are fully aware of what the company concept is – and that everyone knows their role in the whole process. To strengthen the connection internally in what is communicated externally, it can be useful to develop a concept bible in which the management defines how the different departments contribute to the coherent company concept. Later in the book we will see how McDonald's provides a clear example – see page 173.

Spreading the word

A concept bible should not be mistaken for a design manual. It is not about brochure formats, font sizes and advertisement layouts. The concept bible is a manual which explains why the brand has been developed in this particular way, and how it relates to every parameter from product, concept, marketing, design, Internet, sales and the PR function. It also explains how the company's management and organisation must tackle the outside world when they meet it. The concept bible is a value bible. It defines those values, and explains how they must be communicated to the market. It also gives you the necessary guidance for approaching any task, whether it is product, design, advertising or a press conference. After the concept bible, it is of course important that you also make a design manual to ensure consistent expression in the market.

Fig 4.8 The total concept department becomes the nerve centre of the company

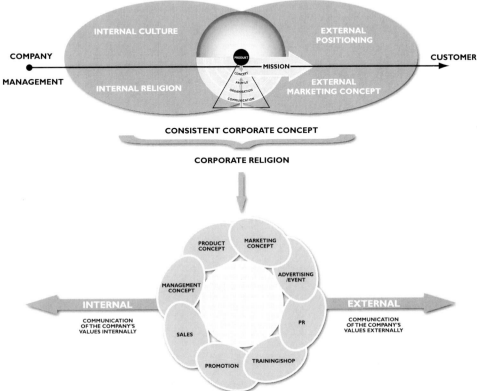

To implement a total company concept, the organisation needs to be rearranged accordingly. It must be simplified, and all departments which influence the company's communication with the outside world must be united in a single total concept department.

Dynamic design manuals

The design manual of the future will be more comprehensive than the traditional design manual, and will include every aspect of external communication. It must not be too rigid on technical specifications otherwise it will soon go out of date. Then you will need to renew it together with the business concept every second year. Don't view concept bibles and design manuals as static things. They are dynamic tools which develop continuously as the company and the market change.

Waiting for Godot

In most companies, change is something that prefers not to happen. Some may make an effort every 5th or 10th year to try out a new look. Others just carry on with an outdated look. Neither are attractive. It is vital to monitor the market continuously – and make sure that the entire company keeps up in one consistent movement. The best solution is to have a department which unites and manages all outgoing and incoming information. For most companies, this will entail a complete rearrangement of the organisation. Today PR, concept, advertising, promotion and product design are staff functions in the main organisation, but each of them has a major influence on external communication. The more important the brand and the market position becomes, the higher they move up in the organisation. What is really needed is a total concept department reporting directly to top management, and preferably led by the company's chief spokesperson (see Figure 4.8). Here everything is united: product marketing, advertising, PR, sales, sales training, value marketing (events, education), Internet, shops, analyses, product and concept development, human resources and recruitment.

You can't stop the future

Figures 7.2.b and 8.8 show how the total concept department is responsible for channelling all incoming and outgoing communication to the market. The department is also responsible for internal communication (see Figure 4.8). The traditional organisation obstructs the total Brand and Corporate Religion way of thinking – and the army of external advisers and suppliers will only pull the company in the wrong direction. External advisers are typically consultant companies which specialise separately in strategy, concept development, design development, advertising, PR advising, promotion, human resource development, Total Quality Management .... the list is endless. All they succeed in doing is to increase the company's problems, with different advisers working on different levels in different places within the organisation. As individuals, these specialists are no doubt good at what they do. But that does not mean they will necessarily do

Fig 4.9 The fully integrated communication company of the future

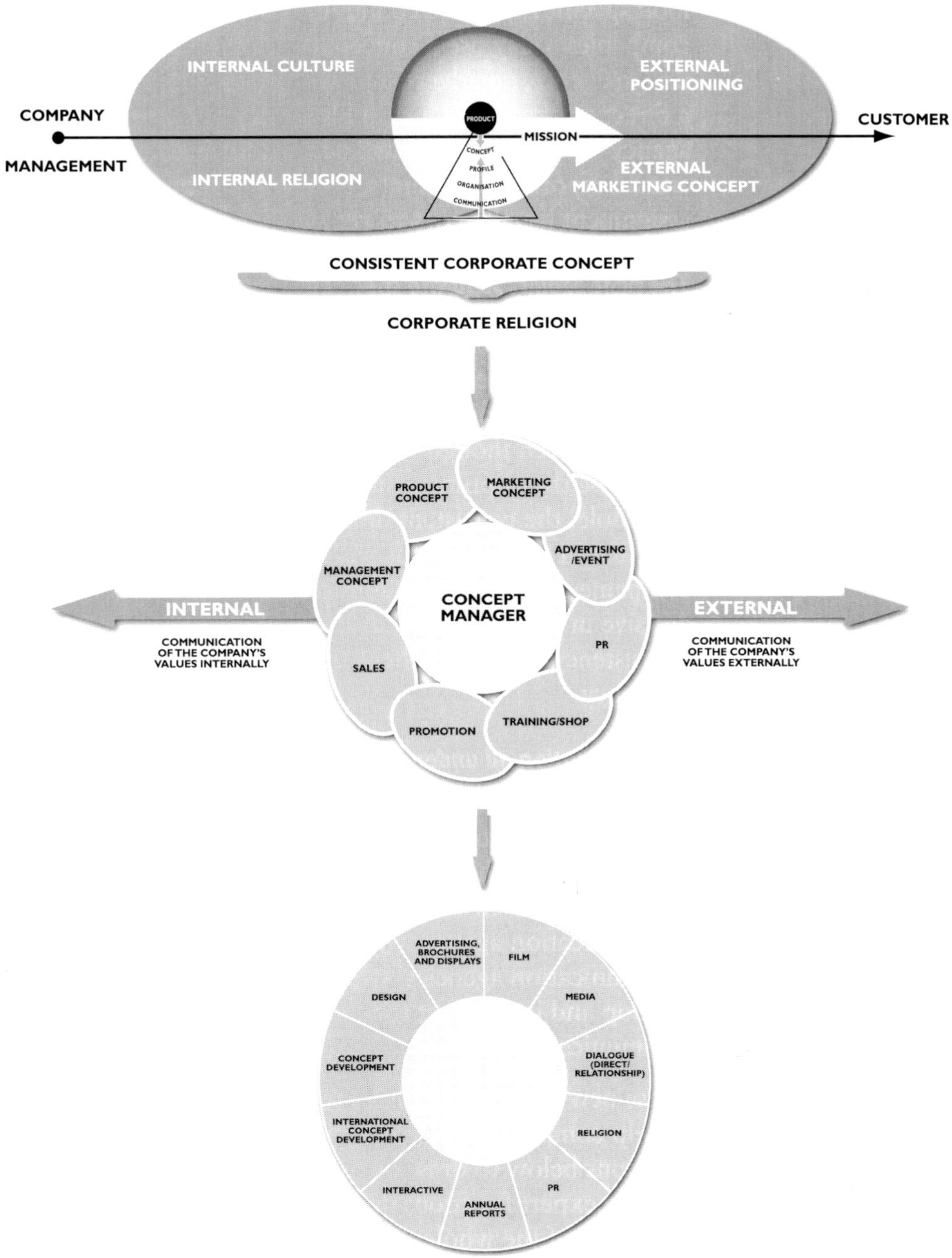

Companies that organise themselves around a total company concept will experience problems with external consultants, who are the dominant force at present. There is a tendency for such people to carve out their own specialist niches in advertising, direct marketing, PR, design or whatever. And all these experts will each try to lead the company in a preferred direction. What the company really needs is a communication company that can help to develop and implement a total integrated communication with the market, so that seamless consistency can be achieved in practice.

any good for the total consistency of the company. If we look specifically at the communication sector, most large companies today use a concept development agency, a design agency, an advertising agency, a promotion agency, a direct marketing agency, a PR agency and an interactive agency – none of whom will be used for making their annual report and accounts. For some obscure reason, that assignment usually goes to yet another agency.

The fight against separate specialities

Every specialist company tries to be creative and optimise their speciality area to the best of their ability, but it will certainly lead to different profiles and content for the company, even though they follow a design manual. That is because they optimise their speciality at the expense of the whole, the consistent description of the company. I am sure that in the future this will be a growing problem for companies because it is a consistent profile which will be decisive in the customers' assessment of the company. Consistency also strengthens the company's internal efficiency.

Communication all under one umbrella

The communication sector has tried to adjust by buying up the different specialities, but they operate as separate entities without the unified co-ordination and consistency that is required. In the future, new forms of communication agency will come into being – 'integrated communication agencies' which will enable clients to develop and implement total and coherent communication.

These new agencies will have total communication experts to help companies at the overall level, with expert functions below to draw on as needed. This will ensure that the expert functions don't veer off at a tangent to the detriment of the whole. Figure 4.9 shows an example of a total integrated communication company. Chapter 9 examines the evolution of Kunde & Co. from a marketing agency to a total integrated communication agency.

Parallel with the work on this book – it has lasted three years – I have come to realise that the total integrated communication agency is the one and only way ahead. The question is, where will they come from? From the traditional advertising agencies? From PR agencies? Design or concept agencies? The answer is that they can come from any or all of them. And from management and human resource companies; because they all overlap. That said, none of these companies is ready for the task in reality. They have each cultivated a narrow segment of the future working task. Only the largest companies with the resources to build up competencies on every speciality level can become total integrated communication companies. The bigger they are, the more difficult it will be to cross-coordinate. So competence will be crucial – the ability to understand the totality and recognise that value is created on the bridge between the external positioning, the internal culture and the total description of the company.

Fig 4.10   Corporate Religion description in relation to the individual employee

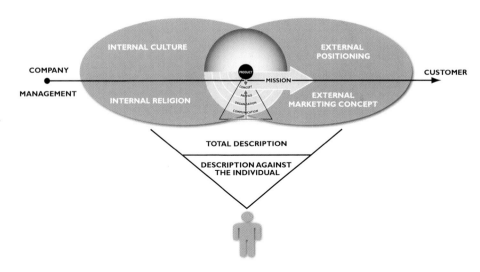

The whole organisation must be included if a Corporate Religion is to be implemented. Certain professional groups can have difficulties relating concretely to a Corporate Religion. But it cannot be tangible unless everyone is involved. It's important that the religion is presented in an easily comprehensible way so that every single employee understands what it actually means to him or her in their daily work. A link between the total description and the individual job function must be firmly established.

The end of the line for structuropaths

As conventional boundaries disappear, companies with traditional management will fail if they don't start digging into the market and company. They will fail if they don't stop their obsession with structure. It is in distinctiveness and values that you will find your future. The great challenge is to turn the normal organisation on its head – and create a total way of thinking. This applies especially to external consultants, who need to redefine themselves and think in totalities without losing their expert knowledge. The winners will be the few who can overview the many complicated connections and weave them into a consistent and developing movement for which there will be a demand in the future. The top few international managers who have created rapid and efficient successes will be the ones who are capable of analysing the situation, redefining it, and setting the whole company efficiently and effectively into the new context. People who can laser beam into every corner, both internally and externally as shown in Figure 4.10. It is important that the religion is presented in an easily comprehensible way, so that every single employee understands what it actually means to him or her in their daily work.

The soul and the belief in harmony

Companies need to put more focus on soul and belief and less on products, packaging and logistics. Many companies work with fragments of this thinking, but very few are capable of creating a coherent Corporate Religion, which binds the entire company together in a value related and spiritual communion with the market.

Many companies have strong internal cultures and self-perception abilities, which do not necessarily tally with the market's understanding of the company. It may be expedient to have different cultures in the company depending on whether it is production or the executive parts of the company that interface with the market. You just have to make clear who it is that understands the market and develops new products and solutions for the future. It's no use having an inward-looking production culture running the company if the product you actually sell is a solution or a concept which is more than the product itself. You might get away with it today, but this kind of disharmony will kill companies off in the future.

Fig 4.11 Corporate Religion – a total description of the company

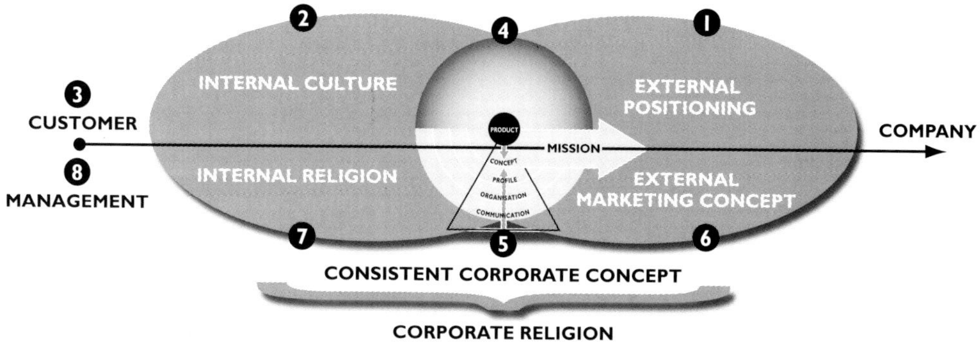

A balance must exist between the internal and external perceptions of the company. See the legend for a detailed explanation of the model.

Play the right role

In the future, companies will need a total understanding of their market position, will need to know how to constantly keep that vital step ahead, and recognise what consistent values the different parts of the company must deliver. Any disharmony between the internal and external positioning will be highly destructive; but if the management have described the company properly, disharmonies are unlikely to occur. It's like staging a play in a large theatre. Everyone has different roles, and they must know them inside out in order to achieve a great result. But first the play itself must be written. It needs a good story, a good director, and a blend of audacity and commitment that will involve the audience.

E System

System: the set of rules which ensures that the religion is devoutly practised.

A common characteristic of the world's Corporate Religions is that they construct systems for extending their belief. For the religion to become an integrated part of the company you must systematise it – otherwise it's just words. The system is the set of rules which ensures that the religion is devoutly practised.

For McDonald's to be 'The Family Restaurant' in every country, they have to make sure that consumers get the same experience every single time, no matter which McDonald's they visit. The burger itself is just a part of it.

The restaurant, the surroundings, the service, the speed of that service and the activities for children are equally important. It requires a massive system to control all these activities and ensure that the whole thing stays a consistent and homogeneous product. McDonald's system comprises a mix of training procedures and rule books through which the religion is communicated. The hamburger religion can give thanks to its system for seeing to it that the McDonald's spirit has maintained its strength.

Disney is a successful religion because the company protects its 'family values' – not least through a huge business in selling promotions. Disney never breaks the rules governing the attitudes and values which permeate the organisation, so Disney products have total constancy in their mode of expression and every product greets the consumer with the same values. This happens because Disney employees have a very visible religion to follow.

Figure 4.4 shows the importance of the system in defining Corporate Religion, which has to reach all corners of the world to exert its proper effect your task is to set up a system that makes the religion an integrated part of the company.

The next chapter describes how international companies can set their religion into a system. It often involves a mixture of education, training and tight control, and always requires a clear set of rules. In every case, these rules have their starting point in the religion, which in turn has its starting point in the mission, which aims to give the consumers more value.

Commitment: this ensures the organisation's understanding, will and commitment to the mission.

F Commitment

When the company's mission and vision are in place below the religion, it is important to create commitment in the organisation for the goals and the values which must be adhered to. We're talking about engagement and obligation, and it's important that they reach into every corner of the organisation – and after that out into the market. It's amazing how many companies have carefully defined their objectives, formulated clear rules of conduct, and then forgotten to ensure commitment in the organisation. Too often, top leaders avoid setting limits for fear that it will take away personal initiative. It is a misguided friendliness – and managements who think that way are doing their people a bad turn. Nor will they succeed in finding the soul of the company – that which gives every employee their sense of belonging, as well as their motivating force.

What must we demand of our people? What attitudes and values must we constantly cultivate in our organisation?

A Corporate Religion can make an organisation into a united movement which moves towards a shared goal. It is formed from the attitudes and values which will take the company there. So far, I have concentrated on the descriptive aspects – now we must start addressing the task of adopting the religion into the organisation for real. The big questions which management should ask themselves are: What kind of commitment must we ensure throughout the company so that we fulfil our mission? What must we demand of our people? What attitudes and values must we constantly cultivate in our organisation?

Focus on commitment means focus on attitudes and values rather than skills. It is difficult and demands a lot from the management, but it's essential.

G Action

Action: this ensures that things move in the desired direction in the market.

The last element in the model is the action required in the individual markets to fulfil the company's mission. In Figure 4.4 action is shown as an arrow to illustrate that the only thing that counts is what reaches the market.

Companies can have the best of intentions, but it is only the things that reach the consumer which really matter. Too many international companies use too much of their resources on product development, educational material and marketing material, while leaving the subsidiaries to handle the action. Because of the ubiquitous power struggles between parent companies and their subsidiaries over who decides, things are rarely carried out as planned.

Companies can have the best of intentions, but it is only the things that reach the consumer which really matter.

Since most companies don't follow up properly on how the activities are being carried out, it's not surprising that gaps start opening up between market intentions and market reality. It is especially important to monitor the qualitative variables, which are decisive in creating differentiation and thereby a stronger market position. A strong hand here prevents local attempts to control the brand's values.

Lack of planning is one of the primary reasons for action failing to reach out to the individual markets. The speed with which things happen in the global market makes it extremely important to plan your activities in the correct way. Getting it wrong affects homogeneity and penetration power. If local markets can't rely on what they get from headquarters, they will develop their own communication. Then the game starts and the big loser is always the company. That's why you must have a system which ensures consistent, focused action. You must also be practical – it is better to concentrate a few strong initiatives and implement them everywhere, than go after everything at once and risk mistakes. It's a common failing of many companies that they start up too many activities in relation to what the market can really grasp. It wastes a lot of money and even worse – it has an adverse effect on focus. Planning is about foresight, and the value of the Corporate Religion model as a management tool is that it gives you a telescopic view.

Paradise regained – perhaps (IBM)

IBM lost the lead in the computer business through a lack of focus on – and empathy with the end user. Louis Gerstner put the giant back on its feet again.

IBM has been through the whole gamut of feelings and emotions, from small national producer to international company with a selling concept – and back again. It was in 1924 that visionary manager Thomas J. Watson Sr. changed the company's name from 'Computing Tabulating Recording Company' to 'International Business Machines Corporation'. At that time the corporation was a fairly ordinary company with 52 salespeople, which primarily sold timepieces and weights. As the change of name indicates, Thomas J. Watson wanted something more – namely that International Business Machines Corporation should be a big international company, and he expected his employees to want the same. So Watson introduced the rule that the sales staff should wear sober suits, he forbade alcohol, and he asked his unmarried employees to get married. Why? Because he thought that married men would be more loyal if they had a family to provide for. These rules formed just a small part of an extensive code of conduct for the IBM employee. The corporation's three basic values were formulated thus: "The pursuit of excellence", "the best customer service" and "respect for employees". IBM was to be the best of the dealers in their line of business and the employees were expected to live up to the name. In return for their efforts and their loyalty to IBM values, job security was ensured.

You were employed – or rather incorporated into the IBM family – for life. Already by the 1930s, the education and indoctrination of employees was so ingrained in the system, that an IBM school was established for the company's salaried employees of the future. It was absolutely necessary for employees to be true disciples of the ideology – or Corporate Religion. In the 1985 edition of "The 100 Best Companies to Work For", IBM was described as a company which has "institutionalised its convictions in the same way as a church would do it".

IBM was known for its hard central control, where everyone towed the HQ line, from education, marketing, how to sell things and prioritise segments, to building and training the organisation in the right spirit. In the 1960s and 1970s, things really started hotting up. In employee training centres all over the world, IBM preached their gospel. The whole organisation was continuously schooled in the right way of thinking. In this way, the company built a strong Corporate Concept with a well defined mission. IBM invested substantial resources in getting their Corporate Religion to function, to gain commitment and ensure action. The whole thing was centrally controlled by a rock solid management – no one in IBM could have any doubt about what IBM wanted. Watson Sr. established "The Open Door Concept", which meant that any employee could go directly to him – or write directly to him – and expect an answer. In addition, IBM devised a system of ensuring that every voice was heard. Once a year, all employees were asked to reply anonymously to a questionnaire on the operation of the corporation. In this way, valuable information went directly to the top. With no filters.

The same atmosphere permeated the market, so that by the beginning of the 80's IBM had established a strong Brand Culture. By the mid-80's, IBM was a market religion. Nobody did anything without first gazing heavenwards at IBM. The corporation was the fountain of all knowledge about administrative systems for any large or middle-sized company in the market.

Why did it go wrong?

IBM was everything that characterises the true international company. Everything fitted Thomas J. Watson's dream, but at the same time IBM also acquired all the diseases to which international companies are vulnerable.

In 1980 the corporation had a turnover of 40 billion dollars; nothing could stop the growth, it seemed. If development continued the way management was counting on, turnover would reach 100 billion dollars by 1990. The top management of the day, headed by John Opel, decided to prepare the corporation for its anticipated future. Expansion was accelerated. New factories were built and more than 100,000 new employees were recruited. By 1986, the IBM family boasted 407,000 members. Everything was coming into place, and by 1990 IBM stood equipped and ready for a turnover of 100 billion dollars. But a "slight problem" arose. The turnover was only 50 billion. The PC revolution floored IBM. On previous occasions, the corporation had been overtaken on the inside by sudden leaps in technology, but that was not the problem this time. IBM had the technology. They came onto the track hot on the heels of Apple, which was the first to exploit the commercial advantage of the micro-computer. IBM's first personal computers were a huge success and the corporation immediately took the lead with a market share of 26%. But the success didn't last.

It was the organisation's lack of commitment to the PC market which proved the decisive factor. IBM was simply not geared for the change from large mainframe systems with a high margin of earnings to small personal computers with small margins.

The company held on stubbornly to mainframes as its primary aim. Product development departments steadfastly continued to make bigger systems, while neglecting to gather information from the market which could have told management what was happening. They forgot the golden rule – stay close to your end users. IBM was sitting solidly on a customer base – but they were data processing managers of companies, who were ill-informed about other user wishes and needs. Users wanted computers that were more flexible and simpler to use – it was "the solution" that was important now, not the machine in itself.

IBM was weakened by a market that on the customer side had taken the power away from the data processing managers and given it to the ordinary user. To the latter, it meant nothing that IBM was a Brand Religion among the former. The situation worsened as IBM acquired a reputation for being arrogant and non-user-friendly. This negativity rubbed off in turn on the enthusiasm of the otherwise highly committed employees, who could only watch as their beloved giant sank to its knees.

Decentralisation increases

IBM started to deviate from some of its basic rules, for example that of central control. Regional centres were established, which became progressively more autonomous and even started to market themselves differently. That sowed the seed of the corporation's fall from grace as a homogeneous international company.

As the company hastened to decentralise, so it sped further away from its customers. Thomas J. Watson Jr. (son of the founder, who took over from his father) had already lit the warning lamps in an internal memo back in 1961:

> "With our decentralisation, it's very easy to become so concerned with our own immediate responsibility, that we may forget we are all working for the IBM company …"

(quoted in D. Quinn Mills & G. Bruce Friesen: Broken Promises – An Unconventional View of What Went Wrong at IBM). Those words took on even greater significance during the 1980s and the beginning of the 1990s.

The brakes go on

In 1991, the corporation lost 2.9 billion dollars, then 5 billion in 1992 and 8.1 billion in 1993 – the second biggest loss ever recorded for an American business. When the crisis was at its height in 1993, IBM changed its management. The new leader was Louis Gerstner – a former chairman of RJR Nabisco. He soon identified the problem:

"I believe that IBM fell into a classic trap. It was so successful over a decade that it tried to catapult its success into a set of systems. Then it wound up managing those systems, which is a fatal mistake. You need to manage the marketplace, not the systems that happen to work at any given time, to be successful."

(Scanorama, February 1996).

Louis Gerstner prevented IBM from being split into smaller units and has since resurrected the giant.

Gerstner wanted to get back into close contact with the market – and control it. He halved the global IBM organisation from 400,000 employees to 200,000. In that way he cut away most of the decentralised power. By 1994 IBM was already back in black with a surplus of 3 billion dollars. Before Gerstner joined IBM, there were plans to split IBM up into lots of small Baby Blue units. The company had a weak management and an unclear mission. Only a few individuals retained any overview. If the fragmentation had been carried through, IBM would probably have been finished as a superpower. But Gerstner did the exact opposite. He stopped the decentralisation which was about to take the company apart. He set up a unifying mission and created a new Corporate Religion. At the same time he has placed the focus on the users. Gerstner uses around 40% of his time to talk to customers. It was a strong Corporate Religion which realised Thomas J. Watson's dream about a worldwide IBM, and it is Gerstner's new Corporate Religion that is giving back to the company the leader role it lost.

IBM Brand Position Development

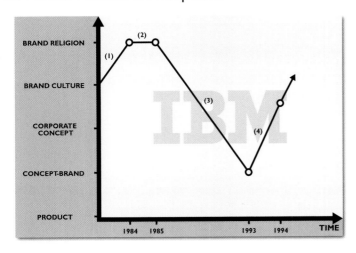

1. Over a period of years, IBM has worked its way up to a commanding position as the absolute culture within their business area. Nothing seems to be able to stop them from marching on.

2. The corporation has never occupied such a strong position. 1984 is a fantastic year. IBM is a Brand Religion.

3. The PC revolution is in full swing. IBM starts having difficulties keeping up with it. The fall is dramatic. But it is only in 1991 that the corporation starts recording losses. The 1993 loss of 8.1 billion dollars comes close to breaking all records. Louis Gerstner is employed as a new manager.

4. Gerstner quickly shows what he is worth. The organisation is tightened up and the brakes go on the decentralisation process. A surplus of 3 billion dollars speaks for itself. IBM is on its way back.

CASE-POINT

IBM

Once a Brand Religion, always a Brand Religion? No way. IBM's religion lost the power over its EDP customers because the corporation lost its feeling for what the users wanted. At the same time, the decentralisation process was literally taking the company apart. That it's possible to stage a comeback has been proved by Louis Gerstner, who stands at the forefront in the battle to keep IBM as a united company which takes the end user seriously.

Corporate Religion can focus all types of companies

The Brand Involvement model, Figure 4.2, shows a collection of companies I have chosen – subjectively divided into involvement levels with a special focus on companies which have attained Brand Heaven. The Figure shows that there are many international companies driven by a strong Corporate Religion, and that very different types of companies have become cultures, each in their own market.

Fig 4.12   Brand involvement levels

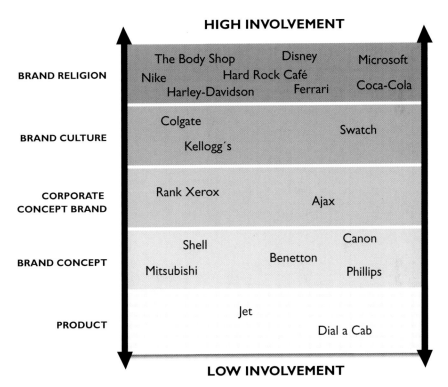

Involvement has to be seen in relation to individual brands, and not different categories of product. In principle, brands within all product categories can have high involvement. The highest possible involvement occurs when consumers raise it to the level of Brand Religion.

In the professional segment, it is knowledge and education which run the religion and create the position on the international market; while it is non-material and emotional brand values which run the religion on the domestic consumer market. The best consumer-oriented companies are those which understand how to build high qualitative values into the brand. It may not be possible to build a reliable religion on advertising alone, which is why events and PR become so important in this connection. Swatch is a good example of a brand which to a large extent has been built with the aid of events which have supported the youthful, trendy value universe.

The same goes for retail chains where, besides the marketing, physical location is a decisive factor. McDonald's is an example of a retail chain and a brand all in one, where the extension in itself also creates brand values which become manifested as a culture. For McDonald's the extensive use of Disney Figures in their children's menus plays a very important role in building the religion as "the family restaurant". You could say that both companies benefit from the co-operation, because their religions are based on the same essential family values. Disney provides McDonald's with the best family entertainment there is, while in return McDonald's gives Disney incredible amounts of promotion for their latest film.

Corporate religion in business-to-business companies

Professional companies which exert control through a Corporate Religion are usually driven by product development and education of the organisation and the market.

The most progressive companies run the religion via knowledge concepts, where they function as a knowledge bank for customers through open dialogue with the market. At the same time they also maintain extensive contacts with leading researchers. This is particularly so in the case of the pharmaceutical industry. Companies in this field carry the knowledge and educate the doctors, because the industry is so far ahead as a result of co-operation with the top researchers. The pharmaceutical industry's commercial interest in spreading knowledge as quickly as possible – and thereby the products – has equipped them to deliver information much faster than in the doctors' own world. These companies are constantly vying to be the innovators with new treatments – they get the status of knowledge carriers via knowledge concepts. Those who understand how to exploit that position can attain Brand Culture status within a given field – or even become a religion.

Within the field of psycho-active drugs, Eli Lilly is a good example. With Prozac they have gained the lion's share of the market for anti-depressants. They are pioneers in this area and have taught general practitioners that they can easily treat milder forms of depression. Within diabetes, Novo Nordisk has set new standards of treatment by pioneering the development of the insulin pen which is far easier for patients to handle than conventional syringes and vials. The Swedish pharmaceutical company Astra has used large scale education programmes in an attempt to monopolise the market for treating gastric ulcers.

Corporate Religion based companies in the business-to-business market usually become seen as the experts within their area. IBM was for years the expert in building data processing and administration systems in companies and in so doing, became an integral part of the customer. IBM was not only a supplier of hardware, it was also a supplier of vital knowledge. This shows the advantage of being a Brand Religion – when customers place a high value on what they receive, the price becomes a much smaller influence.

Music to the ears

oticon

**The Danish hearing aid manufacturer Oticon was
stagnating when a new manager, complete with
Corporate Religion, took over at the controls. Lars
Kolind's spiritual leadership propelled the
company to startling success.**

In the 1940s and 50s Oticon started educating the hearing aid
business and gained recognition as the most knowledgeable company
in their line of business. It meant that you always went to Oticon
when you were dealing with the most acute cases of hearing loss. The
business area steadily developed, and certain suppliers did sterling
work on cosmetic solutions (hiding the hearing aid inside the ear
canal). To begin with, this innovation provided auditory solutions that
were in fact worse. It prompted Oticon not to go the same way but
that decision, taken in the 1970s and 1980s, turned out to be the
wrong one.

The market for "in-the-ear-solutions" exploded, driven chiefly by the
American supplier Starkey which had a very strong Corporate
Religion. Their credo was that they could do something for any kind of
hearing loss with hearing aids as discreet as humanly possible to make.
Accordingly, they built their business around individual customer
solutions. The new religion created a big new market in the USA,
where Starkey has 25-30% of the market. Since the USA makes up
half of the world market for hearing aids, it had major consequences
for Oticon. The Danish company experienced stagnation and decline
while during the same period Starkey enjoyed phenomenal growth.
From being the leading supplier – almost a Brand Culture – for severe
hearing loss solutions, Oticon had been reduced to a run-of-the-mill
hearing aid producer. The company lost both its self-confidence and its
focus. Along with the defocusing came international company death
syndrome, where power is divided between the subsidiaries and the
parent company, and between sales and development. Oticon lost its
overview and had no mission. The company pursued a zigzag course
according to whichever subsidiary was shouting the loudest. Everyone
wanted the same things as their competitors already had. Oticon had
descended to the level of market follower. Profits followed suit – and
by 1988 the company was in deep crisis.

Lars Kolind focuses the organisation

In 1988 Oticon changed its management and employed Lars Kolind. He bought a minority shareholding and thereby demonstrated that he was strongly interested in the company's survival. Kolind soon realised that Oticon had acquired the very bad habit of following the market leaders. He had to give new focus to the organisation and stoke up product development. Kolind focused from the beginning on values. A natural consequence of this was that Oticon's new Corporate Religion was founded on the human values which lie behind what the company does. Lars Kolind redefined these values as follows:

■ *The attitude to the customers* – it's not just about improving hearing, but improving people's lives.

Lars Kolind - the innovative religion leader.

DigiFocus is a result of the sharp focus which Kolind set.

- *The attitude to having reduced hearing and the wish to hear better* – not a handicap, but a natural development in the course of life – just like getting glasses for impaired vision.

- *The attitude to hearing clinics and dealers* – not customers in the traditional sense, but partners who wish to do good work and to achieve success.

- *The attitude to the employees* – the term personnel is not used. Instead you talk about co-workers, people who work with each other rather than against each other.

- *The attitude to the workplace and how it is arranged* – not an organisation divided into departmental boxes, but a free room with the minimum of organisation necessary to solve the tasks.

DigiFocus - the world's first digital hearing aid.

The last of these especially has made Oticon famous. Lars Kolind let the employees work in project groups instead of fixed departments. Development engineers, marketing people, researchers, constructors and sales people, all working together in groups to reduce project development times. Every employee was equipped with a 'box on wheels' for transporting all their things from group to group, depending on which projects they were working on.

At the same time Kolind formulated a mission for the company which would serve as guidance for all development work: "Oticon should make the best devices in the world, measured by the extent to which they enable people to hear better". It meant that standards had to be raised.

Recreating self-assurance

The revolution, the mission and the new Corporate Religion: all on a grand scale and inspired by a strong spiritual leader, turned Oticon's situation around.

From a fumbling, self-effacing company, Oticon has developed into a self-assured and strong organisation which has launched a range of new, improved hearing aids onto the world market in the last four years. It culminated in 1995 with the first completely digital hearing aid – a revolution in the industry. Since Lars Kolind started driving Oticon forward with a clear mission and a strong Corporate Religion, the value of the company has increased tenfold, profits are up around 15% of turnover and its market position has been profoundly strengthened. Oticon is working on becoming a Brand Culture in its business area, and its higher target is to become a religion in the market for hearing aids. Oticon has led the battle with Starkey back to its original starting point. The fight is now about improving hearing – not whether the solution sits behind the ear or in it.

CASE-POINT

Oticon

Oticon is a good example of how the right spiritual manager can lead an ailing company back onto the path to success. Lars Kolind focused the company and put major emphasis on the values which would bind the organisation together in their endeavour to fulfil a shared mission. It has resulted in a strong Corporate Religion based company which also delivers results to its shareholders.

Corporate religion in consumer-oriented companies

While it is pretty clear that knowledge and education are going to be the prerequisites for becoming a culture or a religion in the professional market, it is more difficult to foresee what will create a Brand Culture or Brand Religion in the consumer market. But even so, plenty of consumer durable brands do make it as Brand Cultures and Brand Religions. Coca-Cola, Nike, Disney, The Body Shop and Harley-Davidson are among the most outstanding, but there are many other companies, big and small, which also belong in this category.

It must be possible however, to measure consumer involvement in a brand. By standardising measurements, you can determine where your company lies in relation to the consumer. The advertising agency Young & Rubicam's so-called 'Brand Asset Valuator' is a step in the right direction. The marketing methods used to date have tended to concentrate on quantifying parameters such as knowledge and preference. With these you can get a fast fix on the situation, but they do not tell you anything about how deeply seated the brand values are, or what the limits of their practical use may be. The future lies in consumer involvement, and connecting brand values to actual buying behaviour. Many people will gladly tell you how good they think a brand is, even if they can't afford it. It is important to relate to the whole interface where the brand meets the consumers: marketing, packaging, outlets, personnel, coverage, direct and indirect information sources.

The best brands have consistent Corporate Concepts, and when they reach Brand Culture status they become part of the consumer's daily life. The more powerful the brand's involvement with the consumer, the more important it becomes not to dilute it. A company that takes this seriously is The Body Shop, which in record time has built up both a strong Corporate Religion and Brand Religion.

The Body Shop creed

In a remarkably short time, The Body Shop has established itself as a global Brand Religion. Its founder Anita Roddick has inculcated a unique Corporate Religion whose theme is 'Trade And Care'. This combination of trade and care is imbued into everything that the organisation does – creating a synergy between the company's internal and external components. A synergy which has resulted in spectacular growth.

The Body Shop is an unusual company with an unusual Corporate and Brand Religion. It is The Body Shop that originated the concept of the 'Caring Cosmetic'. The corporation is both a manufacturer and retailer within the cosmetics industry and at the time of writing has nearly 1,500 shops in 46 countries. 199 of them are owned by the corporation, the rest are franchises. If The Body Shop's 'Caring Cosmetic' is one phenomenon, the corporation's high profile involvement in social activities is certainly another. It campaigns vigorously with grass-roots movements like Greenpeace, Friends of the Earth and Amnesty International. The Body Shop has developed a synergy between business and social understanding, where its abhorrence of animal testing, high regard for the environment, and vigilance over third world trade connections go hand in hand with continuous attempts to encourage employee involvement in social issues.

The clash with conventional cosmetics

Anita Roddick was born in 1942. She opened the first The Body Shop in Brighton in 1976 to enable her to provide for her two daughters during husband Gordon's two year absence on an extended journey in the Americas. When Gordon returned home (a year earlier than planned), his wife already had two shops, but owned only half the company. Anita had sold the other half for £4,000 to the boyfriend of a girlfriend, in order to raise money for shop number two.

In 1984, when The Body Shop was floated on the Stock Exchange, it had grown to a value of £4.75 million. Today the Figure is several

The fight against animal testing has always been a key issue for The Body Shop.

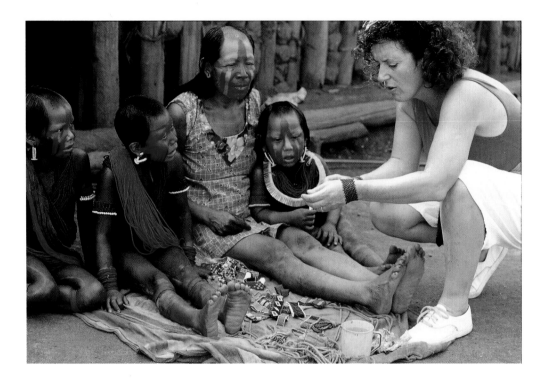

Anita Roddick spends much of her time travelling to see the people with whom The Body Shop is involved.

hundred million pounds. For me, there's only one explanation for The Body Shop's phenomenal rise. It's because Anita Roddick and her husband, who today is chairman of the board, have been able to apply the central ideas of this book to the core of their business.

Roddick's entry into the cosmetics business was spurred by irritation at the industry's business methods. Its unrealistic product promises, its use of idealised images (and advertising generally) – and its fixation with expensive packaging. The former teacher, whose commercial experience was limited to the restaurant and hotel business with Gordon, therefore decided to open a shop that offered cosmetics based only on natural ingredients, packed into the cheapest possible refillable plastic containers and sold without any promises of beauty or eternal youth. A totally environmentally conscious and completely unconventional way of selling cosmetics – which has simultaneously developed into a Corporate Religion and a Brand Religion.

The Body Shop spends little on advertising in the traditional sense – an essential reason for the incredible expansion is the free publicity the corporation receives.

The Body Shop and Anita Roddick preach their religion everywhere, and it has generated endless positive press. What started as an individual's campaign against animal testing has over the years turned Anita Roddick's personal involvement into a religion.

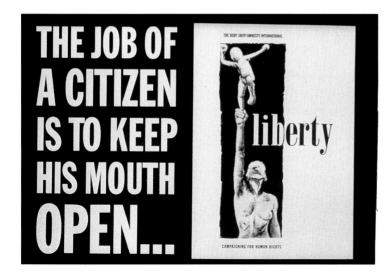

The Body Shop communicates attitudes.

The Body Shop's revulsion at the testing of cosmetics on animals became a springboard for actions which would – and will – make the world a better place to live in. In 1985 the corporation began to support Greenpeace, and it wasn't long before The Body Shop's premises were recreated with a combined platform of alternative cosmetics and grass roots. After Greenpeace, it was Friends of the Earth who combined forces with The Body Shop in a campaign on the acid rain issue. While helping these and other organisations, The Body Shop received a lot of public attention and sharpened its profile as 'the caring company'. The corporation was the doyen of the green wave and an icon for the socially and politically conscious consumer long before the owners of Brent Spar first saw the red warning lights.

Practise what you preach

When you set yourself up as a spokesperson on matters of principle, it is crucial that you apply them to yourself – right down to the smallest detail – to guarantee reliability in the eyes of the consumer. "We were scrupulous in ensuring that our own business practices accorded with our principles", writes Anita Roddick in her combined autobiography and management book Body And Soul. She remains scrupulous in seeing to it that the corporate values on which The Body Shop was founded are practised in ever more efficient ways.

In 1996 The Body Shop published its first 'Values Report'. The report is about ethics, particularly in connection with animal testing, the environment and social conditions. The points are summarised in a document entitled "Our Agenda" which not only sets out what the corporation has achieved in different areas, but also contains concrete

When action needs to be taken, Anita Roddick is right in the forefront – where the press photographers can see her.

Amnesty International is a long-standing partner.

mission statements on what The Body Shop is going to do in both business and ethical arenas. The fight against animal testing, which still is the core of the corporation's campaign identity, is systematised and helped on its way by a 'Supplier Purchasing Rule'.

This means that the corporation is committed to not using raw materials which after 31 December 1990 have been tested on animals for cosmetics purposes. To ensure compliance with the rule, all suppliers must sign declarations accordingly, and control checks are also made. The system is so effective that it has become ISO 9002 certificated (ISO is an International Standards Organisation for quality control). Full scale inspections of other areas are also carried out to see that suppliers are living up to the high ethical standards preached in the campaigns. The Body Shop has a number of employees whose sole job it is to ensure that company principle becomes physical reality. For example, the corporation has a Fair Trade Department which sees to it that missions concerning co-operation with distressed areas of the third world are carried through as defined in The Body Shop's Community Trade Policy – previously known as Trade Not Aid Policy. The company's current policy is simple and direct.

Helping the developing world through fair trading has proved a winning strategy. Together, The Body Shop's Ethical Audit Department and Fair

Trade Departments form the company's 'Values & Vision Centre' which is run by Anita Roddick. The Public Affairs Department co-ordinates the campaigns and monitors the corporation's products and working procedures to ensure they are environmentally sound and do not consume disproportionate amounts of energy. The Body Shop checks that materials from threatened environments are not used and that countries in the developing world are not adversely affected. This total consistency between word and deed is no accident. Anita Roddick's natural involvement permeates the organisation and her commitment has been crucial to its success. Those who have tried to accuse The Body Shop of "social swindling" have not seriously dented its corporate image. Internally, it has always been a strength that the boss herself is a model for the employees.

Trade and care as a Corporate Religion

In my view, it is of essential significance that Roddick's strong Corporate Religion has succeeded in involving the employees, not simply as shop assistants but as grass-roots activists. At the same time they have also learned to cultivate equally healthy business values, without which progress would not have been possible.

The Body Shop's approach to education is a good example of how trading and caring can walk hand in hand. Over the years, employees have been educated in a range of subjects including AIDS, alcohol and drug abuse, unemployment and of course, environmental issues. That education is combined with clear, professional information about product ingredients, and about customer care. To ensure that every Body Shop employee receives the message, individual countries send personnel to England to be trained as trainers, who then return to teach the employees back home. Employees embrace The Body Shop ethos and, hopefully, carry that spirit forward.

Not that The Body Shop should worry. It's second nature for everyone to use both sides of the recycled paper that is omnipresent in the organisation. Packaging is also re-used as much as possible, and many franchisees and employees personally contribute money to the causes which The Body Shop encourages its customers to support. The clear external profile attracts applicants who genuinely want to work for Anita Roddick, and cultivate the Body Shop religion. If people aren't interested in the message, they should leave the company.

Anita Roddick still travels around and meets employees in different countries. By so doing, she is also making sure that the strong Brand and Corporate Religion which The Body Shop has gained by connecting social and political issues with its products, will also control The Body Shop tomorrow.

Fig 4.13 The parent company is threatened

International markets will dominate the parent company because they are much bigger than the home market.

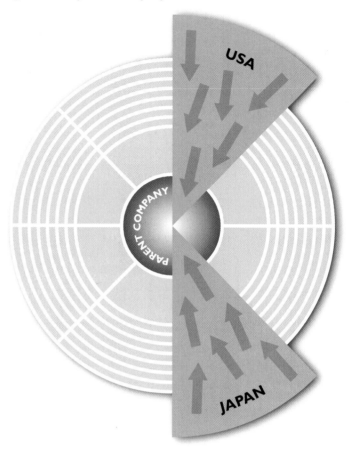

CASE-POINT

The Body Shop
The Body Shop is one of the best examples of how a Corporate Religion can walk hand in hand with a Brand Religion. Founder Anita Roddick's personal values of 'trading and caring' permeate everything that the organisation does. Staff are employed who share these attitudes and values, creating a reliability which rubs off on consumers. In this way, the synergy between the internal and the external is constantly strengthened.

The threat from large subsidiaries

The Body Shop is a relatively isolated example of an international European company which has had the luck to spread its Corporate Religion round the whole world. The vast majority of large European corporations seem to swear by non-homogeneous marketing in the different markets, where the subsidiaries market the company's brand(s). In the future, companies which take their brand building seriously will have to face up to the task of presenting a homogeneous expression to the world. As shown in Figure 4.13, international markets will dominate the parent company because they are much bigger than the home market. As already explained in Chapters 2 and 3, international European corporations have to turn the market adjustment theory upside down – even if the subsidiaries in five markets outside Europe have double the turnover that the parent company has in the home market. It is the only way in which the company can keep itself centrally focused and have time to react quickly to changes in the markets.

Unfortunately, international companies in Europe have failed to realise what the Americans have known all along: management's most important job is to take care of commitment and action in the whole organisation. American company managements are experts at running big systems. They have all grown up with an enormous home market and have no tradition for leaving the initiative to subsidiaries. There will be a lot more on this subject in the following chapter. But I'd like to finish here with one of the best examples of a Corporate Religion there is – and one for which all the different cultures around the world have proved no obstacle.

Hollywood influences the world via the cultural values and norms that are communicated through film and TV.

Consistent values consummate success

The (Walt Disney Company

Both in its products and its organisation, Disney sticks firmly to a set of universal values. Such devoted consistency may have its problems, but first and foremost we should regard it as the source of eternal success.

The Disney group doesn't only sell products. Disney sells an outlook on life. Disney sells values. Disney sells a culture. These values are as unchangeable as Disney's popularity is enduring – and they can seem outmoded, especially to Europeans. The Disney universe is built around a fantasy where all negative or controversial subjects – politics, religion, sex and drugs – are banned. When Disney characters take up arms there is no doubt that it is in the service of positive fantasy. They are depicted in a way which clearly separates them from the real world's instruments of violence.

"Mickey Mouse chokes individualism and changes children into consumers", blazed Le Figaro when Euro-Disney opened outside Paris. At least the first part of the statement could be questioned.

Walt Disney's values still control the company.

Disney promotes capitalism, individualism, the American dream and family values, especially, via its comics.

This ethos has been maintained despite the fact that such conservative ways of handling things have at times been exceedingly unpopular. The essential point to grasp is that the group has not been jumping around after unanticipated market trends. Disney is Disney and that's that. The consumer must come to the product, not the other way around.

Walt's way

In 1932 the Mickey Mouse Clubs had around 1 million members between them. To become a member you had to take Mickey's oath: "I will do good deeds at home, in school, on the playing field, no matter where I am... in short I will be a good American". A good American – Disney in a nutshell. Hardly surprising then that Mickey Mouse has become an immortal symbol for the core values of American society.

The Disney ideology – or religion – is not only built into the products. Certain values also permeate the entire organisation. It was Walt Disney who introduced and preached the values which have controlled the organisation's business ever since. It was regarded as an honour to be considered part of the Disney family – and as with all families there was a certain moral code which family members were expected to follow. Every employee had the right to make mistakes, but ethical mistakes which affect the company's image are not tolerated.

Disney theme parks are the best example of the ideology. James C. Collins & Jerry I. Porras describe in the excellent book "Built To Last – Successful Habits & Visionary Companies" how the newly employed at Disneyland go through a training programme several days long, which pretty well brainwashes them with Disney religion. Employees are regarded as participants in a show which makes the audience happy. The whole organisation's efforts are concentrated on that object. Nothing is accidental, the system covers every action – even at a distance. When a Danish company which produces electric light switches asked for permission to use Disney Figures on them, the answer was immediate. No. Disney's reason? They did not want any possible connection with fires in children's rooms. Even though the Danish Disney organisation is far away from headquarters, it has clear guidelines to follow. That shows you how much importance a strong religion has for a brand. No matter where you meet it, the organisation and brand have the same values. Collins & Porras write:

> "The Visionary companies realise their ideologies through tangible mechanisms, which are arranged consecutively in such a way that they send a series of successively strengthening signals."

©Walt Disney Company

© Walt Disney Company

© Walt Disney Company

© Walt Disney Company

1992

1995

Counter-pressure against EuroDisney was intense, but now they have gained a foothold.

The French culture fight

Very few things have gone wrong for Disney. But one of them is EuroDisney, or Disneyland Paris as it is now called. EuroDisney opened on 12 April 1992.

A deficit of 5.3 thousand million French francs in 1993 and 1.8 thousand million in 1994 shows the scale of the problem facing the tourist attraction, 39% of which is owned by the Walt Disney Co. The meeting between the Disney universe and French nationalism resulted in a culture battle. Disney had in broad outline maintained its culture and only modified EuroDisney a little in relation to American versions. Rightly so. Watering down Disney culture would ultimately do more harm than any short term benefits could justify. The cultural fracas that ensued was best illustrated by the fact that Frenchmen could not be served wine (or spirits) with their food at EuroDisney, which – in those parts – is tantamount to a contravention of human rights.

France is perhaps the most difficult place in Europe to implement a foreign culture, but Disneyland Paris gradually got a foothold. In 1995 the picture improved, with a record number of visitors (10.7 million) and a bottom line back in black to the tune of 114 million French francs. Progress has continued in the same vein. The following year 11.7 million people visited the park, generating a surplus of 202 million French francs. Voilà.

Michael Eisner almost out-Disneys Disney.

Not a religious movement

By the 1960s Disney University was well established. All employees must attend an information seminar about Disney's traditions and values. Disney has, in the same way as McDonald's, an internal bible which dictates how employees shall conduct themselves. The bible was written following Walt Disney's death, and they chose to go back to the old values which had always been synonymous with success. Each one of the 70,000 employees was also presented with a vision statement card. It summarises the internal bible in slogan form, and employees are expected to keep it with them at all times.

> *"When you investigate Disney, you can easily forget that it is a company and not a social or religious movement"*, noted Collins & Porras in their book.

The Walt Disney Company ran into problems after the death of Disney himself. They suddenly missed the man who had dedicated his life to the company. It is crucial that any top leader's religion is compatible with the company's – so that it can continue to operate solely from core values. Disney's problem was solved in 1984, when true believer Michael Eisner came to them. Eisner preached Disney's words almost better than Walt himself. The result is well-known – Growth with a capital G based on Values with a capital V.

CASE-POINT

The Walt Disney Company
The Walt Disney Company's stubborn adherence to conservative 'family values' has ensured the company's unassailable position as a religion in universal family entertainment. Walt Disney's values are so deeply rooted in the company that nothing can undermine them, no matter how unfashionable they may be at certain times. Their religion does not adjust to its market – the market must adjust to them.

CHAPTER 5

Commitment
and action

*A people who feel the calling
are the strongest force on earth
(Bjørnstjerne Bjørnson)*

To demonstrate a Corporate Religion mentality, management must create commitment in the organisation and turn words into action.

Corporate Religions don't appear out of the blue. Nobody wakes up in the morning with a complete vision ready for immediate implementation. It's hard work – the product of your labours should be hammered out of steel – and before a Corporate Religion can be developed, the company must first have a consistent and focused brand. With these in place, the next step is to get the whole international organisation to focus on the same brand values. The company's new homogeneous structure must be visible no matter where you meet its brands. The company must attract customers with the same value norms in every market. This way you ensure homogeneous market positions and brand values, which will also benefit future product introductions for the simple reason that it's easier to follow up on one defined target group than several.

What marks out the really successful companies is that they take care that the whole organisation does the things that management expects. The Coca-Cola Company is probably the best example of how strong commitment has been able to create what most would agree is the world's most valuable brand – worshipped as a religion around the globe. The fact that a whole corporation unambiguously follows a chosen mission is well illustrated by their brochure.

As the poster opposite shows, The Coca-Cola Company is one of the few international companies that works on

In February 1994 The Coca-Cola Company clearly expressed these connections in an internal brochure. Top manager Roberto C. Goizueta formulated the corporation's mission in the following way: "We exist to create value for our shareholders on a long-term basis by building a business that enhances The Coca-Cola Company's trademarks".

gaining the employees' commitment. The results prove that they have succeeded to a very considerable extent. Too many companies have big visions and big plans, but don't do enough to monitor if and how they are being carried out. That must be a discipline in itself – expensive, yes, but worth every dollar.

Commitment

You can create commitment in many ways. For example, it is created via:

1. Big visions
2. Enthusiasm
3. Product development
4. Education
5. Fashion trends
6. Marketing
7. Belief
8. Management building systems
9. PR.

Top management must lead the way and show everyone that they really mean it.

To this list you can add a tenth example – top management must lead the way and show everyone that they really mean it. The various cases in this book demonstrate that there is no fixed template in creating commitment to the vision of a company run by a Corporate Religion. With the aid of big world sports events Nike, for example, leads the organisation into the sports shops by remote control – and that creates commitment around their brands. McDonald's on the other hand runs its religion with permanent sets of rules for everything, with big training programmes designed to create the desired commitment to the mission, the culture and its extension. McDonald's route is both longer and tougher than Nike's, and both have their strengths and weaknesses. Nike's way of doing things obviously works, but it is dependent on the fact that they must unfailingly sponsor the champions of sport.

There must be a certain element of faith involved in being part of a company, because faith breeds motivation.

Think about the Catholic Church for a moment. It has built up a worldwide organisation on a faith which has created an enormous commitment from its global congregation. There are parallels to be drawn here about how you create commitment around a Corporate Religion in a company. There must be a certain element of faith involved in being part of a company, because faith breeds motivation. The management's task is first to ensure that the employees believe in the company – and then to take care that customers are motivated to believe in it.

A fashion trend is the most dangerous route to commitment, because it's a highly risky business building an international company on what are essentially changing whims – unless of course you create the fashion trend yourself, and that means you have to be very good indeed at understanding the mechanisms that actually make trends.

The obvious examples here are the international fashion houses. Setting the agenda for fashion is the motivating power of the whole organisation. The sales personnel in the shops follow fashion with intense interest – as soon as the new collection comes in through the door they already know it will sell. They have first-class commitment and a high sense of self-worth, because their brand and their shop has a tangible part in deciding what everyone else thinks is fashion. That kind of commitment can readily be seen if you walk into say, an Armani clothes shop. If Giorgio Armani constantly succeeds in setting the fashion agenda, he can also continuously renew the commitment of his employees by virtue of the fact that they are not just selling clothes but the right clothes, the real clothes.

The fashion industry has also been good at creating a platform to communicate from, and exert control from. The fashion show is a temple, whose exotic rituals, TV, the daily press and fashion magazines transmit to the whole world. By focusing on supermodels, the fashion religion has equipped itself with the ultimate divine messengers for consumers. It's important to get something out of the religion driven brands, so that you continually generate enough resources for developing brands that maintain and strengthen the company's leading edge. Armani has been good at that. He has not only stayed with extremely expensive clothes but has also managed to reach down price-wise to a wider group of customers without destroying the snob effect. Furthermore, he has conquered a lot of markets, so that he gets the values broadcast wide – and thus can constantly be ahead through marketing and product development. In this way Armani keeps the whole big machinery that a Brand Religion requires turning smoothly.

Armani has understood that it is about having a consistent brand – and having control over it. By having his own shops in the most important markets, no one gets the chance to destroy the non-material universe around the clothes.

Education as a commitment creator in business-to-business companies

Lack of knowledge is one of the main reasons for lack of commitment in big international companies. It manifests itself in a number of ways: What does the management want? What solution do the customers prefer to have? How do we give them the best solution?

If employees in the front-line are left to themselves to find the best way of doing things, the results will be highly variable.

If employees in the front-line are left to themselves to find the best way of doing things, the results will be highly variable. Some do fantastically well, others less well. It's not so surprising – a brand's values contain many possibilities, like so many different facets around the brand itself. But for a brand to become a success, its values must be communicated identically.

If a company leader feels that a certain salesperson is irreplaceable, then it's a sure sign that the brand's values are not homogeneous. It must never be the salesperson – however good – that the customers buy. It must be the company's opinions, values and products. Of course there is space for the human factor in every successful, religion driven, committed company. But it should add to success and not determine it. You can't build a brand's market position on personal charisma.

The most successful corporations are those that have understood how to harmonise the company's product on all parameters. Education is the best method. Generally speaking, people like to be taught how to do things better. If education is a problem in a company, then management has a problem. They have failed to concentrate on an obvious control mechanism.

Strong commitment to the company's mission can be created with the aid of a targeted description of everything around the product, the customer's interface with the company, and the education of the employees.

Most companies train the sales organisation in product knowledge, but it is just as important to have training in a systematised sales method that the company can become expert in.

Strong commitment to the company's mission can be created with the aid of a targeted description of everything around the product, the customer's interface with the company, and the education of the employees. The coffee chain Starbucks has developed a powerful strategy along precisely these lines.

Coffee Religion: Making 25,000 partners pour their hearts into it!

"The original Starbucks store was a modest place, but full of character. The minute the door opened, a heady aroma of coffee reached out and drew me in. I stepped inside and saw what looked like a temple for the worship of coffee. By the third sip I was hooked, I felt as though I had discovered a whole new continent."

The words are those of Howard Schultz, Starbucks chairman and CEO, recalling his first visit to a Starbucks store in 1982. In those days Starbucks was just a coffee bean roasting plant and five stores. 17 years on Starbucks has grown into a chain of more than 2,100 coffee shops. Starbucks is a "Third Place"; a comfortable, sociable gathering spot away from home and work – in its own way, an extension of the front porch. In 1997 Starbucks served 5 million customers a week, and the average customer came back for another cup 18 times a month. So how can coffee grow into such a huge business all by itself? It's a good question, and perhaps the answer can be found in the last cup of lousy coffee you drank!

Starbucks Coffee opened its first retail locations in Seattle in 1971. Today, the chain has more than 2,100 in USA, Canada, East Asia, UK, New Zealand and most recently in the Middle East.

This case is about recognising how essential supreme brand delivery is – each and every single time the customer experiences it. Whether it's the product in itself, the ambience and atmosphere of the outlet or the knowledge and passion of employees going out of their way to please customers and cultivate interest in the finer nuances of world-class coffee. It is about how a meticulously orchestrated approach to both training and inspiring employees can give them the commitment to live, breathe and thus grow the brand. At Starbucks – as in all other service companies with a break-through brand performance – the brand lies solidly in the hands of its partner. Before tracing out the training cornerstones at Starbucks, let's take a closer look at the uniqueness of the Starbucks value proposition.

Pouring romance into the cup

The starting point is an astute observation. Starbucks don't see themselves as being in the coffee business serving people. They are in the people business serving coffee. Semantics? Not in the least. Romancing the bean, romancing the customer and romancing all the senses through the in-store experience – these are the things that drive customer satisfaction at Starbucks. Put quite simply, they are fanatical about product quality. Whether it's about the raw bean, its transportation or its roasting, its preparation, blending, filtering the water, or the ultimate moment of serving – everything must conform to the most stringent and exacting standards. Beyond the naked product itself, the "Starbucks Experience" embraces the inviting, enriching environment in the stores, comfortable and accessible, yet also stylish and elegant. People come to Starbucks for refreshing relaxation, a break from the busy day, or perhaps a personal treat. Each visit has to be rewarding. Therefore, whether it's the living room style furniture, or the carefully selected decor and lighting – it all adds up. The hiss of the espresso machine, the clunk-clunk as coffee grounds are knocked out of the filter, the bubbling of the milk steaming, or the swish of the metal scoop shovelling out beans; these are all familiar, comforting sounds to the customer.

Aligning everyone behind the brand delivery

Management literature is rich on the concept of delegation. Tons of books pertinently point to the need for improving delegation. Many of them carry elaborate route maps showing you how to make it happen. There is one caveat though: most of them gloss over the point that out of all managerial delegations, delegating the brand is probably the most sensitive of them all. So let's take a look at how they do it at Starbucks, demonstrated through the Learning Journey, the five four-hour courses all new partners (Starbucks term for employee) must attend within their first 80 hours of employment.

Right from Day 1, new partners are immersed in the value system and the fundamental beliefs of Starbucks.
Starbucks training includes:

All new partners undergo introduction courses and training before they are even allowed to serve coffee.

- basic and finer coffee knowledge;
- how to passionately share coffee knowledge with others;
- general housekeeping, fundamentals and superior customer service;
- why Starbucks is simply the best;
- details about coffee beans, types, blends, growing areas, regions, roasting, distribution, packaging etc;

- how to smell and slurp coffee the right way, as well as identifying where it hits the tongue;
- describing coffee taste – awakening senses and getting into a whole new vocabulary. Familiarising with coffee aroma, acidity, body and flavour;
- answering frequently asked questions and talking coffee.

Starbucks puts a lot of effort into the job training. Before new locations open, friends and families of the new partners attend special pre-opening parties in the week leading up to the opening. The purpose is simply to train and make the team intimately familiar with "the real thing" before the doors actually open to the public. Proceeds from these nights are given to a local charity in the community of the new location. Throughout the day partners are encouraged to brew coffee for sampling and discussion with other partners and customers. This helps partners and customers alike to learn more about the different coffees that Starbucks offers.

The Bean Stock options

In 1991, Starbucks introduced "Bean Stock", a widespread and ambitious stock option plan. The idea is to link everyone into the overall performance of the company, bringing the same attitude to work as the CEO or any other shareholder. To be eligible to receive a Bean Stock grant, partners must be employed from 1 April to the end of the fiscal year, work at least 500 hours from 1 April to the end of the fiscal year, which is an average of 20 hours per week, and be employed by Starbucks the following January when the grants are distributed. To illustrate the value involved, partners earning $20,000 a year in 1991 were able to cash in their 1991 options alone for more than $50,000 just five years later! Because the pact between the partners in Starbucks is such a central theme, not surprisingly Schultz ascribes much of the company's success to the uniqueness of the partnership:

> "If there's one accomplishment I'm proudest of at Starbucks it's the relationship of trust and confidence we've built with the people who work at the company".

Starbucks sells several different types of arabica beans and merchandise in their retail locations, through a mail-order catalogue and via the internet.

> **CASE-POINT**
>
> **Starbucks**
> The most powerful and enduring brands are built from the heart: they are real and sustainable. Their foundations are stronger because they are built with the strength of the human spirit, not an ad campaign. Starbucks never set out to build a brand in the traditional sense. Their goal was to build a great company, one that stood for something, one that valued the authenticity of its products and the passion of its people. In the early days they were so busy selling coffee, one cup at a time, opening stores and educating people about dark-roasted coffee that they never thought much about brand strategy. Says Schultz: "We build the Starbucks brand with our people, not with our customers". This explains why advertising does not seem to have been the engine driving Starbucks. Between 1987 and 1997 less than $10 million was spent on advertising. In some years, more money was spent on training than on advertising.
>
> The Starbucks Third Place concept epitomises successful retail duplication without being perceived as a McDonald's operation in the coffee category. There's a deeper meaning to Starbucks. It is about values – in our terms Starbucks is a religion. Taking the Starbucks brand to its full potential is intimately connected to leveraging and extending the values that people attach to Starbucks.
>
> Entrusting people with the brand is risky business – far more risky than running massive advertising campaigns, where the message – however well executed – is within your span of control. Carefully ensuring that people are committed, and understand and accept both the why's and the how's of brand delivery however, can turn a risk into a powerful asset.

Everyone can be educated

The Starbucks story is interesting because it shows how you can add more value to the product through education. In the case of McDonald's, the employees usually come from the lower bands of the educational spectrum. You can argue that the less education people have to start with, the easier it is to educate them to your way of thinking. The converse often applies when big international companies are faced with the challenge of creating a homogeneous organisation at leader and middle manager level. Often it is these most highly educated that possess the greatest ambition; and an

It is paradoxical that successful companies attract capable, ambitious employees – the very sort who can pose the biggest threat to the company's existence.

ego to match. It is paradoxical that successful companies attract capable, ambitious employees – the very sort who can pose the biggest threat to the company's existence. Teaching them company culture is paramount and the goals have to be big enough for everyone to identify with – because only then can full commitment be created.

IBM is a good example of a company that has always recruited highly educated people – and at the same time has provided a lot of "further education" in the IBM religion. By deploying substantial resources on internal training, IBM has focused the "good brains" on their work. It is typical for successful companies in the business-to-business market to concentrate on the whole process of customer problem solving. Through knowledge and education you can run a strong Corporate Religion.

Education creates commitment

The companies which make demands on their employees and train them hard are also those whose organisations win greatest respect for their brand.

International companies that market to the private consumer usually have simple messages, and selling the products rarely requires a large amount of knowledge. That does not necessarily make education and training any less important to the organisation. On the contrary. Whereas the "professionals" tend to be naturally inclined towards training, the same attitudes do not carry over to products with a small knowledge requirement. However, if education is neglected here the result will often be that the company lacks commitment. No religion can survive just by being there.

The companies which make demands on their employees and train them hard are also those whose organisations win greatest respect for their brand. Nothing builds up around a brand by coincidence; and when the company make demands on the employees, the employees can also makes demands on the company. McDonald's know this very well – and so they have made education a central element.

Educating Ole

**No one can become a McDonald's franchisee
without first being educated in the burger religion.
This is the tale of Ole Madsen's journey into the
system.**

Ole Madsen holds the McDonald's franchise at the main railway
station in Copenhagen, Denmark. The route to his own restaurant
went via education, education and yet more education before he
could finally buy the licence and sign the contract. After that, there was
more education – or training, as the corporation prefers to call it. Ole
Madsen's case typifies the way in which the McDonald's religion
spreads through its restaurants. If you can't think the "McDonald's"
way, you have no business being in the organisation – let alone being
responsible for one of its restaurants.

The application process

In 1993, Ole Madsen sent an application to McDonald's Denmark in
which he presented himself and explained his wish to become a
franchisee. He was 40 years old at the time, a fairly typical age for
franchisees. Most new franchisees are between 30 and 40 years old,
which essentially has to do with the fact that a contract with
McDonald's runs for 20 years.

The application resulted in a conversation with a McDonald's
consultant. There are no formal requirements in terms of academic
qualifications, but the price of the licence is in itself a sorting
instrument. The £45,000 or £115,000 investment (lease and purchase
respectively) must be your own money – no bank borrowing is
permitted. That barrier to "wannabees" is the principal reason why the
majority of franchisees are previously self-employed individuals who
have well and truly mastered the saving habit.

Ole Madsen's conversation with the consultant went so well that he
was invited to take the next step – a five day training period in an
existing restaurant, where he worked on equal conditions with the
other employees, cooking burgers, standing behind the cash desk,
cleaning the floor and so on. These five days are critical in determining
the eventual outcome of the selection process. On one hand, the

applicant finds out if this is something for him or her – and on the other, McDonald's are able to see if the applicant has the right abilities to get on with the mainly young personnel. If the impression is still positive – as it was in Ole Madsen's case – one goes on to the next step of further education. It should be noted that during this period, lasting between a year and eighteen months, the applicant is not paid any salary. Working on the principle that all future franchisees must learn about the company and its routines from the bottom up, the applicant must first work as a rank-and-file employee in an existing restaurant. This is typically for a period of between one and one and a half years depending on when the possibility arises for opening a new restaurant. The applicant also participates in three courses, each of a week's duration. The subjects range from basic service to business economy and management. It is mandatory that a final test is passed. If everything goes well, the applicant will be offered a restaurant. Ole Madsen passed the test and had a bit of luck at the same time. He had only worked for six months on the shop floor when the possibility of a licence materialised.

Ole Madsen in front of his franchised McDonald's restaurant.

Just before the opening of the restaurant, Ole Madsen was, like all the other future franchisees, sent on a two week "Advanced Operating Course" at Hamburger University (sic) in Chicago. The teaching is a continuation of the courses that have already occurred in the home country. It involves team building, management practice and more besides. The student pays for transport, accommodation and food –

only the course fee itself is paid by the parent organisation. As usual, the course ends with an examination that must be passed.

In the restaurant

Well before the restaurant opens, the employees are recruited and begin work. Full-time employees start a month before the opening and part-timers 14 days before. The time is spent on – you guessed it – training, which takes place in already established restaurants.

Before they start, new employees receive a handbook in which the rules of cleanliness and hygiene are spelled out. Nails and hands must be spotlessly clean, shoes worn with the uniform must be well polished and have rubber composition soles – jogging shoes or sandals are strictly forbidden. Men must have short hair (less than collar length) and be clean shaven, while girls with long hair must wear it put up.

The thing that controls the everyday running of the restaurants is the famous McDonald's bible (otherwise known as McDonald's Operations and Training) which sets forth how the business must be run. The exact contents of this meaty manual are officially a business secret. However, it is well known that it's based upon what McDonald's calls Q.S.C. (Quality, Service and Cleanliness).

A large part of the manual is dedicated to providing detailed guidance on the preparation of McDonald's products. How many shots of mustard here, how many cucumber slices there, how to avoid touching the french fries etc. And everywhere you look, there are constant reminders of the paramount need for cleanliness.

Like everything else, attending and serving customers is systematised down to the last detail. Burgers must be served within 10 minutes of cooking (seven minutes for french fries) otherwise they are discarded. McDonald's has an ingenious system whereby newly cooked burgers are put into a waiting line together with a number that corresponds to a number shown on a special McDonald's clock. This makes it easy for employees to see when products must be trashed. In the kitchen, stopwatches beep every time the limit for required freshness of certain ingredients (salad, dressing etc.) is exceeded.

A special McDonald's clock makes it easy for the employees to see when a burger has stood for too long, and must be discarded.

The individual franchisee is continuously checked on by HQ, and once a year he or she must go to a business review. This is in fact a conversation with people from the organisation, typically one from the service department and another from the accounts department. To ensure that the knowledge the franchisee acquires at the beginning is not lost over the course of time, it is compulsory for franchisees to attend an "Advanced Operating Course" every five years.

With all this continuous employee training, the possibilities for carving out a career are relatively good. The career track never varies and runs through a series of stations en route. From an ordinary employee you can become an area manager with responsibility for either the kitchen or the cash desks. Next stop is shift manager, where you are given the responsibility for the day or evening shift — within this there are other areas of responsibility. At the end of the line, you can ultimately get to be restaurant chief — provided of course that you have had the necessary training at Hamburger University. The higher you rise in the hierarchy the more training you require. It's the only way to ensure consistent worship of the religion which successful corporations beam around the world.

All cooked burgers have a number on them. When the McDonald's clock indicates time-out, the burger can no longer be sold and goes in the garbage.

CASE-POINT

McDonald's

Education and systematisation down to the last onion ring can create awesome commitment and action in an organisation. The famous Hamburger University is only a small part of the educational activities which McDonald's puts its employees through. Nor are the franchisees treated any differently. On the contrary, they have to go through endless tests to reach this position. Only those with the "right" values can stay the course with McDonald's. The end result is a consistent cultivation of the company's most valuable asset — its brand.

The interaction between commitment and Corporate Religion

If education is an important motivating power in Corporate Religions, vision is just as important. Religion can't exist without it. Vision is what employees latch onto and feel something for. Every employee at McDonald's knows that he or she is a part of the world's biggest burger chain that opens new shops every single day. The same goes for Microsoft, again controlled by a vision that dominates its area of business. Customers sense that Bill Gates is the best at foreseeing what will happen in the future, because up to now he has played a key role in determining the path that information technology has taken. Today Gates has the same position that IBM occupied 10 to 15 years ago. And he can control his company via national newspapers and the trade press, where his employees can read about the company's mission, and feel proud. Since Bill Gates can talk personally with all of them, media pressure becomes part of the Corporate Religion. The media play an active role in ensuring employee commitment.

There can be many factors involved in running a company's Corporate Religion, but in most cases you can easily identify what it is that creates commitment in the organisation. In the case of Nike, it is sponsorship. At CNN, The World's News Leader, employees can share the station's enthusiastic ambition and vision with their friends and acquaintances who also watch CNN. The company has made a trademark out of always being on the spot when something happens somewhere in the world, and getting the best pictures home.

1. The company has a vision.
2. The company has a system that can create commitment.
3. The organisation is educated and trained in everything relating to the customer's interface with the company.
4. Top management sends the company's corporate religion all the way through the system, so no one is in any doubt as to which way to go.

So which comes first – Corporate Religion or commitment? Some may argue that when you have a Corporate Religion, commitment comes along by itself. Well, maybe that applies to companies like Nike, where the world's TV-screens also form the whole organisation's collective retina. But for the majority of companies, even though they have created a Corporate Religion in the international organisation, their success still depends on how good they are at generating commitment in every part of the organisation in every market.

The first Christians realised early on that if they were going to win converts and spread the word, they had to put things into a system. They created commitment with the aid of a Bible and a strong belief in certain events. With those tools in their hands, they found they could go just about as far as they liked.

Action

We have seen the role that commitment plays in companies which are run with the aid of a Corporate Religion. But how can management ensure that actions follow the words?

Action is ensured by:

1. Hitting the target group defined in your mission.
2. Carrying the company's corporate concept through to the market.
3. Marketing the brand in the right way.
4. Making the right sales effort.
5. Delivering the right service.
6. Educating the organisation in the right way.
7. "Educating" the market in the right way.
8. Checking to see that the target group is satisfied with the brand's performance.

Until companies set up a real international organisation with clear roles and a proper distribution of power, they will effectively remain at a standstill.

To make sure that action really happens in all the individual markets requires a lot of the international company's organisation. In the next chapter, I will be going into the details of how you can support the market with education, marketing and systems of analysis to follow the target group, monitor the results and gather the necessary information for product development. It is abundantly clear to me that international companies with a traditional organisation are simply not geared to this crucial task, and that's the main reason why most of them do not get as far as they would wish. Until companies set up a real international organisation with clear roles and a proper distribution of power, they will effectively remain at a standstill.

McDonald's has already been mentioned several times in this book, and with good reason. The hamburger chain is a shining example of a homogeneous company that has geared itself in a way that guarantees action for its corporate concept and its mission.

Even so, McDonald's is still not quite up to Coca-Cola as a religion for their customers. In its mode of expression the hamburger empire has made more adjustment to individual markets, whereas The Coca-Cola Company never hands over action in the marketplace to others. The main communication of the brand has always been controlled from its headquarters in Atlanta and the strategies for the implementation of campaigns have been the same. What impresses me about The Coca-Cola Company is that they have centrally controlled everything around their corporate concept – they have poured phenomenal resources into achieving that, instead of using the capital for establishing endless new factories and distribution networks.

The Coca-Cola Company has only 33,000 employees because the corporation has chosen to focus only on the building of strong soft drinks brands. With Roberto C. Goizueta in charge and Doug Ivester as a strong number two, the Atlanta-based corporation has increased its lead in recent years. Internationally, Coca-Cola presently has 46% and Pepsi 21% of the cola market. On the home market, which has traditionally been closely contested between the two giants, it currently stands 42:31 in Coke's favour.

When Fortune reviewed the cola war (28 October 1996), it was in no doubt what the company's magic ingredient was:

The Coca-Cola Company has chosen to focus solely on building strong soft drinks brands.

"This is the real secret formula of Coca-Cola: senior management's intimate engagement in the core business (...) Ivester and Goizueta have distilled their own jobs to the essence: brand builder, deal broker, stock broker, concentrate seller."

The corporation still uses national bottlers and distributors, and has not bound up the money in bricks and mortar and motor cars. On the contrary, they have used all their available resources for investing in the brand's propagation and strength. It has been done on a franchisee basis so that distribution happens in the same way all over the world. By investing in this way they have created commitment and taken care of getting the real thing when it comes to action. In every country Coca-Cola has its own co-ordination office with just a handful of employees who spread the religion and take the necessary actions (see Figure 5.1). Coca-Cola actually has a very clear market organisation which carries the responsibility for the religion. They have used marketing and total distribution as a means for building their cola religion and becoming market leader.

Fig. 5.1   Coca-Cola's mission propagation

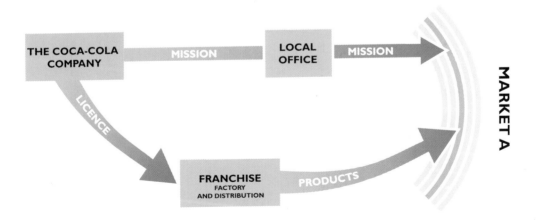

The Coca-Cola Company invests in its mission instead of factories and distribution systems. The production happens at local bottlers, but mission propagation is not handed over to others. Local offices implement the centrally formed strategy.

The mission is so strong and everyone so convinced about the goal, that no time is wasted in pointless discussion. Roles are clearly defined, power is properly distributed, and their time is spent on the culture fight.

Today, major world sporting events maintain the religious fervour. Coca-Cola probably uses at least as much money on sponsorship as it does on direct marketing. It gives the soft drink a reliable profile to be such a hugely visible part of big arena events. If the megastars quench their Olympic thirst with Coke, what better recommendation is there?

Another company that has gone as far as Coca-Cola to ensure that customers get the optimal product in the shape of attendance and service is Toyota. Mazda, Honda, Nissan, Mitsubishi and Toyota have since 1991 carried out an analysis of customers' satisfaction with car brands in all markets. In each market, this involves not only the corporations' own customers but those of the biggest competitors' as well. They all share the financing of this investigation, which is conducted by an impartial market research institute. The result of the investigation has been that, over time, all the Japanese corporations have markedly improved on the measured criteria – exactly because they have implemented continuous measuring. Other competitors are apparently happy to go their own way in blissful ignorance.

The Japanese boomerang

The five major Japanese car manufacturers investigate their own and their competitors' level of customer satisfaction once a year. Toyota has gone a step further with this by entering into direct dialogue with the corporation's customers. They are monitored through a "customer satisfaction" programme, which has a boomerang as its symbol. Why a boomerang? Because it comes back if it is sent off in the right manner – just like a satisfied customer.

"Customer satisfaction" in Danish

Toyota has gone a stage further, because the corporation is not content with these measurements alone. Over the last ten years especially, the corporation has worked in a goal-oriented manner to increase the quality level in the organisation and so gain the highest customer satisfaction in their area of business.

The fact that they put customer satisfaction measurements into their system can be seen as a natural development.

No car is better than the service behind it. That is the philosophy behind Toyota's "customer satisfaction" programme. They take the attitude that the car is the core product, which is expected to work. The experience of quality comes from the surrounding services provided by the dealer.

The corporation itself asks all its customers about how satisfied they are with their purchase. This dialogue is incorporated into a customer satisfaction system (affectionately known as CS), the results of which are actively used to assist the company in improving their efforts. These continuous CS measurements are operated in all markets. The basic principle in each case is the same, but the degree of sophistication varies. One of the countries furthest ahead in this respect is Denmark, which in 1963 became the first European country to import Toyota cars.

The Danish organisation has 2,500 employees working either among the 100 dealers or at the main importing office. The corporation has two main objectives: to be Number 1 in both sales and customer satisfaction.

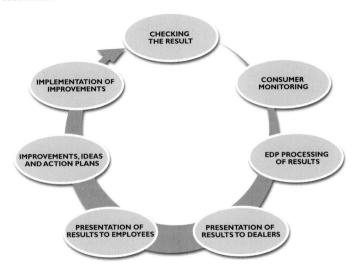

CS Circulation

CS measurements are not a stand-alone activity. They are vigorously followed up and represent just a small, albeit crucial, part of what Toyota calls the CS Circulation.

In terms of Danish sales, Toyota was the top car brand 11 years in a row, from 1985 to 1995. In 1996 they were ousted from the top slot by Volkswagen. Regarding customer satisfaction in Denmark, however, Toyota is still in pole position as they have been since measurements were first made in 1991.

How seriously the customer satisfaction programme is taken in the organisation is illustrated by the fact that the person responsible for CS measurements – the education director – has the same level of seniority as the sales and marketing director. They both report directly to the top.

When CS measurements began, it was made clear to everyone that this was no short term stunt – it was going to continue. Initially, there was quite a strong tide of resentment among the dealers and employees – who were now to be assessed directly by the consumers. This reaction was hardly surprising – nobody likes being watched over.

Nonetheless, the implementation of the programme has proved a considerable success, which says a lot for the management who put a great deal of effort into explaining the idea properly to all involved. For example, meetings were held with every single dealer to explain the whole process and the thinking behind it. Resistance was overcome when it became apparent that the measurements were not some kind of passive supervision, but would be actively used to make improvements which would ultimately be to the benefit of the entire organisation. Besides the CS analysis, the educational director is also responsible for non-technical education which is primarily designed to cultivate attitudes. This education is to a large extent planned according to the results obtained from the CS analysis.

Monitoring the motorist

Everyone who buys a new Toyota receives a questionnaire from the Danish head office 21 days after the date of purchase. It contains 25 questions on subjects ranging from the sales process, the dealer's facilities, delivery of the car and the car itself. A typical question runs: "How did you feel you were treated by the salesperson?" The respondent is asked to put a mark against one of five categorised answers, or if they can't remember how they felt three weeks ago they can respond "don't know". The same categories apply to all the questions.

Those consumers who have taken their Toyota into the garage for spare parts, service or repair during the course of a year receive yet another questionnaire. In practice, this means just about everyone. The new questionnaire is designed to elicit consumer impressions of after-sales service. It is constructed on exactly the same lines as its predecessor and also comes direct from the head office. In 1996, the response rate was 57% for the first questionnaire and 38% for the second. Practical delays in sending out the latter may be the reason for the diminished response and the company is working to improve on it.

What the measurements are used for

All responses are handled in a central EDP department. The results are presented as radar diagrams, which are updated on every dealer every third month.

This method of presentation enables the dealer and the employees to quickly see how they are performing against the various criteria.

The score is compared on the radar diagram with both the country average and the best dealer in the region (Denmark for example is divided into 7 geographic regions). A concrete action plan is written against each segment of the diagram, with follow-up to ensure improvement on weak points.

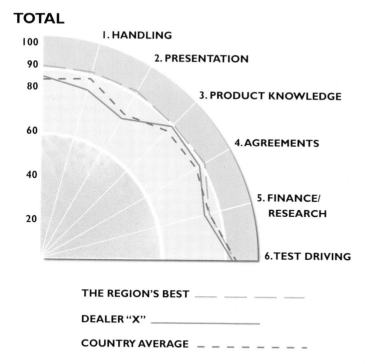

TOTAL

*A section of a radar map
for a Danish dealer.*

100
90
80
60
40
20

1. HANDLING
2. PRESENTATION
3. PRODUCT KNOWLEDGE
4. AGREEMENTS
5. FINANCE/
   RESEARCH
6. TEST DRIVING

THE REGION'S BEST ____ ____ ____ ____

DEALER "X" _____

COUNTRY AVERAGE _ _ _ _ _ _ _ _

The sales staff

The dealers receive employee assessment scores not only as a total,
but also broken down by individual. Every sales person is scored on
how their efforts are assessed by the customers. As is commonly the
case, Toyota Denmark continually runs sales competitions. The CS
assessments form part of these competitions, in the shape of plus or
minus points. Bad ratings thus carry penalties for the individual. Some
dealers also have individual salary arrangements which incorporate
ratings. But it is more common to have collective bonus arrangements
calculated in relation to CS measurements.

Elections

Toyota consciously works to make the results visible in the company.
Results boards display the latest measurements for dealers, employees
and customers to see. Visibility is an important condition for
motivating the dealers to be a part of the improvement process.
Toyota uses the boomerang as a symbol of the CS programme
because a boomerang comes back if it is sent off in the right manner
– just like a satisfied customer. And in order to manifest the dealers'
proud successes in something tangible, gold, silver and bronze
boomerang awards are presented.

Answers given in the consumer questionnaires are scored according to a fixed point system: excellent (100), very good (80), good (50), less good (0) and bad (-50). Twice a year the results are totted up, and boomerangs are awarded as follows:

The Sales Department
Gold: 88-100
Silver: 84-87
Bronze: 81-83

Garage
Gold: 83-100
Silver: 79-82
Bronze: 76-78

The first time a dealer gets a "gold", all relevant employees receive a personal gift, for example a watch or a Cross pen set.

International exploitation

The person responsible for the CS measurements in each country is also responsible for communicating the results further through the international system. The European importers report their results to the European head office in Brussels every three months. The most important results are made available to all importers, who can then compare themselves with others. This exchange of results is followed up once a year, when those in charge of CS for each market meet for 2 or 3 days to exchange experiences. Finally, the results go to Japan, where the information from consumers has an influence on product development.

CASE-POINT

Toyota
Toyota has efficiently systematised the measurement of customer satisfaction (CS), or the lack of it. Combined with analysis of competitors' customer satisfaction, the Japanese car manufacturer obtains a clear, unfiltered picture of the general state of things. Measurements are not just a form of passive supervision, but are used to create action in the organisation. Whatever is not scoring highly enough is improved. CS measurements are given high priority – the department which controls the CS programme is acknowledged as the most important department in the whole Toyota organisation.

Control of campaign and sales activities

One of the best ways to ensure action is to measure the effect of the sales and marketing effort on the markets. When you measure effort, you find out how strong a position you have with the target group in terms of knowledge and preference – and also how much the consumers are involved in your brand. It's important to know this in order to achieve the market position you want to attain; and when you think about new product development, it makes sense that the responses you get from the market come from the people you want to trade with in the future.

One of the best ways to ensure action is to measure the effect of the sales and marketing effort on the markets.

Far too few companies carry through the activities they have planned. If the parent company thinks that planned activities have been actioned – when they have not – the gap between the centre and the subsidiary just gets bigger and bigger. Analyses of international companies which still retain the traditional structure of parent company and sales corporations as two independent units, show that it is not unusual for only 20-30% of the activities that originate from headquarters to be carried out as planned. That adds up to a lot of wasted money and resources, compounded by the fact that the parent company thinks the market information it receives is one thing, while what it is actually getting can be entirely another.

Far too few companies carry through the activities they have planned.

Action requires good planning

In traditional international companies, the product is usually completed before the marketing starts. This can have a number of serious consequences.

The main problem is that product development is often unpredictable and usually is kept firmly under wraps, away from the prying eyes of competitors – either real or imagined. As a result, there are insufficient lead times for either marketing or sales preparation because new products are revealed at the last moment. The effect of planning as a discipline is therefore minimalised and the initial success of a new product becomes dependent on whether the market thinks it is a good idea. Under these circumstances you might as well forget about having a marketing plan of any description. Is this the worst possible scenario? It is, and it happens to most international companies most of the time.

If you want controlled action in the marketplace you must have long-term planning, so that the markets are prepared and you get your training and education programmes in place.

If you want controlled action in the marketplace you must have long-term planning so that the markets are prepared and you get your training and education in place. Until you do that, you cannot expect any campaigns to be properly carried out. If you don't get this right you are finished – no amount of subsequent adjustment will bring you back on track. Watch out also for those who don't want to participate in the new campaign because they are happy running the old one, thank you. The only thing that matters is what the customers and the users think. Anyone else's opinion is irrelevant.

The most difficult thing is to get the control machinery to deliver input for product development and marketing, so that new campaigns and concepts can be developed which the planning department can action through the subsidiaries along with new education programmes.

It takes a lot to stay at the forefront of development and control an international company optimally. Even though it looks easy being Nike, Microsoft or The Body Shop, they work hard at constantly staying at the cutting edge and optimising their market position.

If you have the mind for it, you can control your company via a Corporate Religion and get it to grow with explosive power. The difficult thing is to get the religion established in people's minds within the whole organisation – so that it is not connected with just one person as with SAS, Microsoft and The Body Shop. The religion must be made in such a way that it can continue long after the first visionary leaders have retired.

The Coca-Cola Company continues to be the best example. The company has existed since 1886 with the same religion and the same attitude of total commitment, total control and the demand for action. Successful international companies have often had the same leader for a long time. But there are also examples of new leaders who succeed in continuing the religion of the company. The task for the "newcomers" at Microsoft, The Body Shop and Nike, which in record time have created international super-brands, will be to transfer the Corporate Religion being run by first generation top management into a permanent culture within the company. That means developing a system to ensure that the company's Corporate Religion constantly renews and strengthens itself. It will be very difficult, very demanding, but very rewarding.

CHAPTER 6

Consequences for the organisation

*When a country's religion starts
to totter, so does everything else
(Friedrich von Schiller)*

The introduction of the Corporate Religion concept has a number of consequences for the company's organisation and implications for the future. This chapter explores them, and suggests what organisational structures could look like in the future.

The organisation is the means, but without change it will take on the mantle of a goal.

When companies go through the development process from national to international company, the majority do not change their organisation at the same time. They continue as before and build small copies of themselves in the form of subsidiaries. The basic problem is that companies continuously fail to realise that the organisation needs to be changed in line with the international tasks that have to be solved. It's a question of controlling your own destiny and not letting the past lead the company into the future. The organisation is the means, but without change it will take on the mantle of a goal.

Over the long term, the company has lost if it does not tighten up and make itself consistent – a place where nobody is in any doubt about where the power centre lies.

Most international companies are taken apart from within by their own organisation. It becomes a goal in itself to create independent power centres in the parent company and the individual subsidiaries. That results in a non-homogeneous company pursuing an erratic course. The cause is simply bad management – leaders who neglect to adjust the international organisation to the international structure. The company becomes heavy, slow to react and less profitable. It survives only because the competitors are no different. But over the long term, the company has lost if it does not tighten up and make itself consistent – a place where nobody is in any doubt about where the power centre lies.

In a chaotic world, brands must be consistent. And the international company must adapt its organisation accordingly. Every consumer is actually looking for something that lasts – and consistent brands contain the security that consumers are seeking. The necessary condition for creating a consistent product is that the organisation itself is consistent.

Reuniting the power centre and the consumer

As we saw earlier, the company must create a system so that it can constantly monitor target group consumers, because that ensures that the information flows directly into the company's nerve centre. If information is reliable, it can be used for product development, estimating the effect of the marketing effort, saying something about the brand's position in the market and for planning new marketing activities. But it can only happen if the company's organisation is prepared to get it – information does not arrive by itself.

Knowledge exchange in the company builds on an inward focus. A lot of the information about how the market is behaving and how the target group understands the company's products comes from the subsidiaries. How useful the information is depends on how good the subsidiary is at gathering it and passing it up the line without subjective filters. Therefore there must be fixed guidelines for how data is gathered and processed – otherwise it could end in disaster.

There is a tendency for companies in the professional area to place their destiny in the hands of their sales-people. It's a mistake – because the salesperson only comes into contact with the purchaser – not the decision maker behind the purchase.

Successful international companies always have some kind of direct and outwardly directed continuous monitoring system. Lesser companies might conduct market research, but it is usually very sporadic.

Fig 6.1   Direct information flow

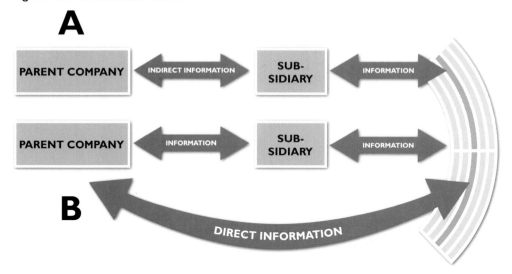

A: *The normal situation: information from the end user goes through the subsidiary's filters. Much of it gets no further.*

B: *The correct situation: unfiltered information from the end user goes directly to the parent company. This is direct information flow.*

You don't have to delve very far into most company information-gathering systems before it becomes clear that most of what they get is based on the salesperson's observations. It spells catastrophe.

As Figure 6.1 shows, the information has to go through too many subjective filters, each with their own interests that they feel duty bound to add – and why? Because the subsidiary is sales controlled – it is with those eyes that they see everything. Compound that with the power a big subsidiary can wield in an international organisation, and you have the perfect recipe for conflict with the parent company. Worse is in store, because the parent company must also use the information coming from the other subsidiaries. The problem grows in direct proportion to the number and size of the subsidiaries. Many of them function as middle-sized companies with full manpower and a strong need to assert themselves. From the MD right down to the youngest salesperson – they all do exactly what they think is right for the company. Their efforts are often not in line with the overall "brand policy".

Theories of market adjustment and motivation argue that the subsidiaries must have the greatest possible latitude.

If there is total central control over what everyone does – and how they do it – then you have a perfect situation.

But it is rarely like that. Theories of market adjustment and motivation argue that the subsidiaries must have the greatest possible latitude. International companies which believe this will lose the global battle.

As I mentioned earlier, it is the brand's non-material and emotional values that grow ever bigger while the product itself becomes progressively smaller. That is why there is the need for total control of everything – right out to the furthest link in the chain. Otherwise it is the very life of the brand that the subsidiary puts at risk.

It is for the same reason that the international company must change its organisation from an inwardly to an outwardly directed focus. That can only be done by changing the organisation and power structure in the company.

The subsidiary must be integrated within the total organisation so that market adjustment does not give the subsidiary carte blanche to change everything in the local country. On the contrary, the local country must be converted to the company's culture. The company, both parent and subsidiary, must concentrate all their efforts on it.

As Figure 6.1 shows, there must be a direct connection between the customer/user information gathering point and the power centre. And that same power centre must also ensure that its strategies and marketing get all the way out to the customer/user with equal directness. It sounds simple, but it isn't. Subsidiary power barriers and their own priorities about what they do and how they do it present formidable obstacles.

Making the non-homogeneous international company homogeneous

Multiple power centres can only be divisive; they must be reduced to one power centre. When you have two or three heavyweight subsidiaries, the task becomes doubly important. Nobody is immune to this danger – even though both America and Japan have the apparent advantage of a very large home market for example, you saw how a mighty corporation like IBM was split up between several regional centres.

Homogeneity is the big challenge.

Homogeneity is the big challenge. If the company is only operating on the home market, the distance from the top to the bottom of the organisation and out to the consumer is usually short enough for signals to get through unscrambled. Having said that though, you do see plenty of examples of national companies which lose control of their market the instant they step over a national border. It's as if there's an invisible border control which won't allow marketing to cross.

Fig 6.2   Making the international company homogeneous

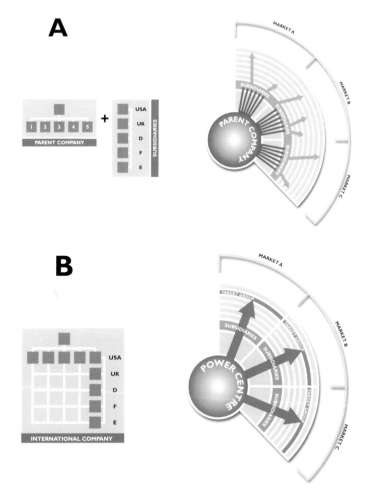

The international company must be reassembled so that it can operate effectively in the market. Figure A shows the non-homogeneous method of doing things, where the subsidiaries are too autonomous in relation to the parent company. Contrast this with figure B, where the control over the subsidiaries is back with the parent company. It's a safe bet in this scenario that the company and its brands will be homogeneous everywhere.

During the evolution of the business world, it has been seen as a healthy principle to let individual countries control themselves, because they probably know their local market best. But when target groups become global, total management control at the local level exerts a drag force on the dynamic international company.

There can be no doubt that market adjustment – in the traditional sense – has played out its role. At present, there is frustration building up in companies, where power struggles are raging.

Market adjustment – in the traditional sense – has played out its role.

Everyone can see the symptoms, but no one seems to know quite what to do – or is really interested in the solution: the subsidiaries must give up their total control and top management must start leading.

The solution is either better co-ordination or greater central control and management responsibility. Often, senior managers are worried about antagonising the subsidiaries, which can blame it all on the parent company if it goes wrong. But if they continue as they are now, it will go wrong anyway. The company can only strengthen its chances by finding a focus – and following it. The reason why top management react as they do, is because they accept the situation as it is now, where the subsidiary has all the market knowledge. In the new homogeneous international company, it is the parent which has all the information. This increases the chances of success, since the level of customer knowledge in traditional subsidiaries usually leaves a lot to be desired.

Fig. 6.3 Information flow in the international organisation of the future

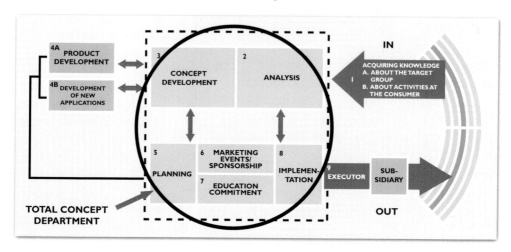

The organisational structure of the future will be far simpler than those we know today. The organisation consists primarily of a department for incoming information and one for outgoing information, united in a single total concept department.

1. Information is gathered from the markets – on both the target group itself and on follow-up of activities being carried out.

2. The gathered information is analysed and processed to build knowledge for further work.

3. Concept development is the heart of the organisation. Based on analysis, it is the development of concepts – not products – that will ensure the future of the company.

4. (A) Product development occurs through continuous interplay with concept development.

   (B) At the same time, the department must find new applications for the products.

5. The starting point for outgoing work is the planning department.

6. The marketing department must be supplemented with a department that specifically handles events and sponsorship, which is no less important than traditional forms of communication.

7. The education department is responsible for ensuring the constant commitment of the organisation.

8. The last link is the implementation department, which in co-operation with the subsidiaries has the responsibility for ensuring that action happens.

9. The subsidiaries put the mission into practice.

The first thing to do is to break down the existing organisation.

Corporate Religion requires a complete new organisation

The first thing to do is to break down the existing organisation. The subsidiaries must be stripped of their autonomy and reduced to co-ordinating units. That is no easy task – it requires that top management participates much more actively in establishing the global market position rather than seeking to control on the basis of economic results and forecasts.

In setting up the new organisation, it is essential to concentrate on what the organisation does, and not on what it looks like. We start by setting up the "healthy cycle" for the international organisation.

The healthy cycle shown in Figure 6.3 is a very simple model, but only a tiny percentage of international companies actually follow it. There are important benefits to gain by doing so, because then the company can start instilling competence back to the main centre and create the right set-up for the single company. The goal is to create a global company – the organisation is then arranged accordingly.

1. Acquiring knowledge

The whole process starts with obtaining the fullest information about the customers/users in the most important markets, plus smaller markets with big potential – to provide the best decision-making material in the power centre. Besides gathering data about consumers and the brand position in the market, it is important that the company has a control system that monitors the implementation of marketing activities and education programmes.

The company must control action at a distance. Therefore, it is important that every employee is fully aware of this, and is fully committed to making it happen.

2. Analysis

A central analysis and control department must be established. Its function is crucial in the effort to get the right information about the target group in the different markets and the brand's market position, opportunities, threats, strengths, weaknesses, competitors etc. It is also equally important that the effect of marketing activities, PR and events are carefully analysed to see what works, what doesn't work, and how well the activities were carried through.

The most difficult task is to compare analyses and results from the different markets to make a joint basis for decisions. The department must find the 'global road' for the brand and – together with the development department – test new product types and new product opportunities within the brand band.

Using the same resources which were previously tied up in the subsidiaries, management now gets real information "on line", without two or three years of delay and subjective distortions. Now they have the real market picture.

3. Concept development

In the traditional organisation there is usually a product development department. Since the brand's value today largely consists of everything but the physical product, new criteria must be established for development.

Fig 6.4   The tasks of the development department are extended

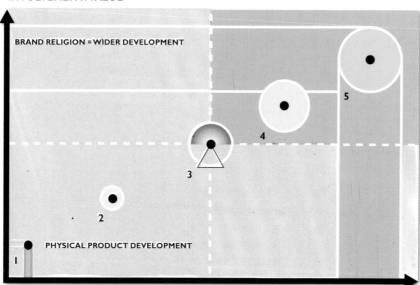

In the new international company, this is the central department. It is here that decisions are made and the future is planned. The time where it was sufficient to have a product development department has passed. As the figure shows, the product itself is only a small part of the development work. The extent of this work depends on the arena in which the brand competes.

1. *Traditional (physical) product development.*
2. *Concept development is linked with product development.*
3. *A holistic development of the whole company becomes necessary.*
4. *Further efforts are put into developing activities which consolidate the brand's status as a brand culture.*
5. *The ultimate brand – a Brand Religion – requires an enormous amount of continuous development effort, where the product itself occupies only a small part.*

In close co-operation with the analysis department, this department's most important function is to gather all the relevant information about all the brand's values. It is this information the company uses for developing new products, product improvements, product positioning or a new and more efficient advertising campaign.

It is also necessary to continually measure how strong the brand is and how much the brand band is being stretched. Can we introduce new products to make the brand band stronger?

This function is distinctly different to traditional development departments in that its starting point is the brand band and the brand values associated with it, rather than the physical product.

This is the company's nerve centre where the Corporate Religion is created and continuously modulated – the true power centre in the company. The department should be very close to the senior management, who must constantly participate in the department's work.

Every year the department's recommendations for adjustment to the Corporate Religion must be considered and decided on. When the decision has been made, everyone must follow it. It is passed to the operative departments, i.e. product development, product applications and marketing. They adjust the existing concept and develop new campaigns and product launches to strengthen the brand band.

4. Product development and development of new applications

In the new model, the product development department does not have free rein as is the case with many technologically driven international companies. It must co-operate closely with the development department to get something that fits the brand positioning they have in the market. A product invention may be a work of genius, but if it lies too far from the company's brand position for the brand band to cover, then most companies will have difficulty in getting it introduced successfully on the global market. What it really calls for is a new brand.

It makes sense to control the physical product development work so that new products stay within the frames which the concept development department has set for the brand band. But this is where it goes wrong for so many international companies – product development happens outside the primary market. That's why product development work must be controlled by the agreed concept, which in turn has its starting point in consumer trends. Not that you should be following in the consumer's footsteps. You should be ahead of the game and shaping the trends. IBM discovered the consequences of ignoring this point to their enormous cost when they failed to take the consumer PC trend seriously and carried on developing mainframes.

Product development work must be controlled by the agreed concept, which in turn has its starting point in consumer trends.

When other manufacturers jumped in and responded to the consumers' call, IBM was taken completely by surprise. Because they hadn't kept their ear to the ground, IBM had difficulty adapting themselves to the new situation.

It can be a great advantage if international companies establish a real development department for the use of the product, since there are usually many new possibilities to be discovered. If you can develop new applications for existing products, you optimise both your resources and the market potential.

5. Planning

Most traditionally-structured international companies have a marketing department, which in many cases is little more than a side-show to the sales organisation since it is the latter which holds the power. The marketing department is hemmed in between sales on one side and product development on the other. The information they get from the subsidiaries is neither accurate nor representative of the market's movements. Often the sales managers press product development for obvious, short term sales solutions: "If we can offer the new feature that our competitors have just introduced, we can sell a lot more", goes the argument. At the same time, traditional product managers can't contribute much of substance, because they have too little insight into the market – and that virtually guarantees that all new thinking will be narrow-minded.

The traditional marketing department must become the operational arm of the development and planning departments. It is the latter who decide what the company shall market. The planning department's most important role is to have a complete overview of what is happening in the subsidiaries and what has to be carried through to keep the market position – or to win further market share. Most international companies first develop marketing campaigns and then start worrying about how to implement them. When you are working on the big scale, it's got to be done the other way round.

The question must be: What do they need out there in the market and what can our organisation deliver? When you've found the answer, then you can develop the appropriate marketing campaigns and education package.

The concept development and planning department are together the most important departments in the international company. Therefore, they ought to have one boss – the highest in the company – who unites them. If those functions slip one centimetre further down in the organisational diagram, the organisation will be dragged into endless power struggles between head office and the subsidiaries.

The planning department works simultaneously with both the long and short term view. At any given time, you need to run short term marketing activities with associated education. But these activities must also fit into a larger context, so that the long haul of the brand is ensured. There is a great advantage in uniting everything in a central department, because different markets will be at different points on their learning curves, and their knowledge will vary accordingly. Gathering a company's knowledge centrally provides a much better basis for decisions – indispensable if you are going to run an international brand with the same values in every market.

The planning department also ensures that resources are not wasted on any development, marketing or education activities that the organisation cannot carry through. In co-operation with the development department, which contributes information on what is needed for running the brand in the market, the planning department provides input to the subsidiaries in good time, so that they can actually carry out the plans in the intended way.

On the basis of input from the analysis and development departments, a proposal is made for the coming year – plus a rolling three year plan. The proposal must be presented in a common forum with the most important departments and the subsidiaries present so that all points of view can be heard.

Everyone is given time to study the plan's requirements in detail and come to a considered opinion about it. The same forum then reconvenes and adjustments are made, but agreement must be reached.

When the plan is decided by those charged with the task, it is decided for the whole company – because the international company's spiritual leader is in charge of both the incoming and the outgoing information departments. It may seem obvious, but very few senior managements actually participate in this work, even though the company's future is being decided here. Most of them go for financial results, but results can only be history. And if a forecast isn't based on real knowledge, it is valueless. These practices tell them next to nothing about where they actually are in the major markets, yet so many international company bosses persist. Figure 6.5 shows how high in the organisation the incoming and the outgoing information departments must be positioned to make corporate sense. By using plenty of time in the planning phase, international companies save a lot on resources during the rest of the process. Marketing and education are now fixed tasks that must be implemented at certain times in specific markets.

6.a Marketing

In the new international organisation, the marketing department gets a defined task from the development and planning departments. But the task is still a major one.

Marketing concepts and campaigns must be global, with

their roots in the most important markets – plus some smaller ones. To attain the optimal result, it requires an interactive process between the end users in the markets and the marketing department. It also means that concept development should run in parallel with technical product development, rather than waiting until the product is virtually finished. The development department are responsible for watching over this, and when development projects are on the large scale there must be very close co-operation between these two departments.

The marketing department is now global. Projects become bigger and so development takes longer if differences between markets are taken into account. But under all circumstances the brand's common denominator across all countries must be recognised and defined. Introducing the split between development and marketing enables the marketing department to focus more strongly on the actual implementation of the campaigns. In the case of consumer durables, marketing pressure – aided by the optimal media mix – is essential for running brands successfully. With business to business, it is important to build up effective marketing systems and find methods of putting pressure on the end user. This can be achieved in a variety of ways. In both cases however, companies must be able to both attract and keep customers. Knowledge acquired from all markets needs to be transformed into efficient methods that can either be tested first in certain markets or implemented fully from the start. No matter what method is used, it is always a continuous learning process – a fact which many companies tend to forget.

Introducing the split between development and marketing enables the marketing department to focus more strongly on the actual implementation of the campaigns.

The marketing department must focus on how best to reach the customer. If databases are to be used that the subsidiaries are unfamiliar with, the company must ensure that they are taught in order to ensure commitment and action in every market. Good ideas are not enough by themselves. They must be carried through in a planned fashion in every single market you enter.

6.b Events/sponsorship/knowledge

Many large international companies control their brands and their business with the aid of sponsorship and events

– or a mixture of the two. These areas should command high priority – and have a central place in the organisation. This is not just something that the marketing department does as part of its daily duties. At Nike and Armani, sponsorship controls their whole business. It is also worth noting that companies which involve themselves heavily in sponsorship often need to use equally large resources on traditional marketing and advertising functions. For international companies operating in the professional product market, communicating knowledge to their customers is of vital importance. It makes sense for them to have a knowledge department in close connection with the development department, in order to ensure that this externally oriented function is part of the marketing mix. Many companies have a hidden store of knowledge that customers would love to have access to, and which would strengthen the company's market position, but most neither realise this fact nor are capable of transmitting it. Others simply do not understand the mechanisms and just continue along the "product feature track". The mechanisms are actually the same regardless of whether it is an exchange of knowledge across borders or between doctors, and it applies equally to pharmaceutical research as to sports events. If you want a strong standing in the professional market, it is important to have good contacts with the leading authorities in that area. The organisation must act on that fact – and become a part of it.

The pharmaceutical industry is a global industry where the exchange of knowledge goes across borders. The most successful companies are those that understand how to connect knowledge development to the doctors and at the same time use this knowledge in developing products.

7. Education

Education is the new imperative in companies of all kinds. Most new products contain more and more knowledge – and that requires strict control of the tiniest details if the product is to be experienced identically by all consumers.

By deciding on a fixed plan in good time, and considering all the interfaces that the subsidiaries have with the customers, the education department can work in a goal-oriented manner. Many successful companies exert influence through education, like Disney and McDonald's – which with its Hamburger University trains the employees down to the last sesame seed. That makes education a management tool and a part of ensuring the implementation of the company's plans.

8. Implementation

You cannot run an international company through a Corporate Religion without focusing on commitment and action; especially if the company makes products which have a short life. The company must put in place a priority function whose sole task is to ensure implementation. Under normal circumstances, this is done by the education department and the marketing department. By maintaining tight discipline around implementation, the respect of the subsidiaries is earned because they know they can rely on things coming in time. What has been planned must be carried through – and if expert knowledge is required to carry campaigns through, the control function must make sure that it has it.

9. The subsidiary

The subsidiary must be re-established as a co-ordinating unit connected to the company's nerve centre. The subsidiary must never become an independent unit covering all functions. Not only is it too expensive, but it also generates all too many part solutions. As we have seen, the company plan is defined and agreed through consensus. After that, it's a matter of carrying it out. The subsidiaries must be peopled by those who implement and not those who want to develop their own products and ideas – which only serves to put a spoke in the wheel of progress.

It is essential to divide the task so that the power centre develops and the subsidiaries implement.

When running a company via a Corporate Religion, the most important functions are those which ensure the timely arrival of information where it is needed – co-ordination, analysis and control. It is the only way in which top management can retain a constant overview of the global market position and the brand's market position. The implementation department must have a co-ordinating link with the education department and with the subsidiary to make sure that all planned activities are carried out.

As shown in Figure 6.5 it is essential to divide the task so that the power centre develops and the subsidiaries implement. That is your guiding principle when recruiting people to work in the subsidiary. A common objection to this is the assertion that you can't attract capable and motivated people this way. That's complete nonsense. If it were true, then Coca-Cola would be marketed in very different ways around the world and McDonald's would be selling everything from burgers to deep-fried caterpillars. Wherever your location, it is highly motivating to sell a brand with global values. The two companies just mentioned prove this every single day.

Fig 6.5 Division of tasks in the homogeneous international company

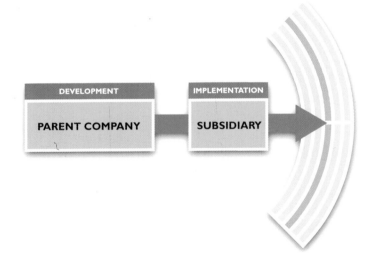

The right division of tasks is for subsidiaries to carry out what is developed centrally.

The difference between the global megabrands and the less developed brands that issue forth from international companies, lies entirely in top management. It has to be here that someone lives up to their responsibility and creates a homogeneous international company where everyone knows what the tasks are – and ensures that they are carried out as planned.

Different stages of development

Very few companies are so far advanced in their development that they can view the global market as a homogeneous market. The Corporate Religion idea is based on the principle that you run your company by binding all its departments together in one homogeneous entity. Most international companies will be on their way up the curve shown in Figure 6.6 – in some markets they may have developed strong positions, whereas in others they may be weaker. The picture can require some differentiation, but the Corporate Religion concept will still make it easier to carry through identical global implementation.

The transitional phase from an non-homogeneous to a homogeneous international company always has its difficulties. A Corporate Religion has its starting point in the major markets where the company is strong – the position in minor markets can be very different. To deal with such disparities, it is better to proceed as shown in Figure 6.6 and to divide the markets according to stage of development. In group C, the product is the driving force, in group B it is the product-concept and in group A, the religion. You have to be aware of this division from the start, otherwise it will not be possible to carry the activities through and the project will collapse.

At the same time you also ensure that the company's Corporate Religion, which is based on the most developed markets, is carried through in even the weakest markets – because you have adjusted it to the latter's less advanced stage of development.

By taking into account the fact that the Corporate Religion will be implemented in markets at different stages of development, you safeguard the company against relapsing into decentralised control. However, there must be a clearly defined plan for lifting the markets up as indicated in Figure 6.6. It's no use starting with some concept in the small markets, and then changing it later when they are more developed. Everyone must put all their efforts into attaining the big goal, the company's Corporate Religion. It is important to remember that

It is important to remember that when we talk about adjustment, it is adjustment of systems – not of the concept. The concept is fixed. That is what the company sells.

when we talk about adjustment, it is adjustment of systems – not of the concept. The concept is fixed. That is what the company sells. In relation to the international concept, most international companies usually choose a very broad common denominator in order to cover everything. But the religion driven company is a very different organism. It chooses one path and aims at one very specific position. It's a fact that many international companies shrink from building a strong positioning.

Fig 6.6 Effort is adjusted to the market's stage of development

STAGE OF DEVELOPMENT

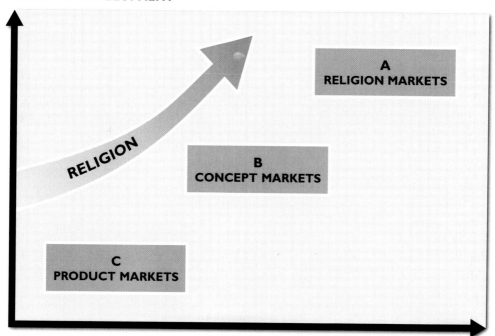

When the religion process starts, the various markets will usually be at different stages of development. This has to be taken into account in the implementation. The most developed markets which can carry through the optimal Corporate Religion idea are gathered together in a homogeneous group A. Those that have advanced far enough that they are run by the concept are collected in group B, while the less developed product based markets are gathered in group C.

The centrally developed implementation strategies must be adjusted to the 3 groups.

When you do that, you can pretty well guarantee a toothless organisation as a result. It's the uniqueness and the international homogeneity that sells and brings success.

It can sometimes be necessary for a company with a strong Corporate Religion to drop those markets where the religion is too difficult to carry through successfully. The global market is big enough – it's far better to aim at markets that fit the soul of the company and its Corporate Religion, than dilute the concept just to get everyone behind you.

The religious focus

Focus is crucial to Corporate Religion. When the effort is focused, it is no coincidence that the company grows. Forget about sudden market influences. Everything is analysed and interpreted in the finest detail. It isn't an application from a dealer or agent that decides where your brand is next going to be marketed.

New markets are seldom investigated thoroughly enough. Sales potential is assessed without looking at its relation to the company's concept and profile. But it is the concept that decides if there is real potential in a market. At first sight the market may appear to be large, when in reality it may be small or even unattainable. Another issue could be that the company has built a certain marketing system – and it becomes a condition for success that you can carry it through. A good example is Procter & Gamble. Most of the company's products are aimed at the housewife. The company's investigations have showed that everyday products are best sold using TV commercials.

The global market is big enough – it's far better to aim at markets that fit the soul of the company and its Corporate Religion, than water the concept down just to get everyone behind you.

So Procter & Gamble has built a lot of systems for determining what is required to get a certain market share. To this must be added knowledge about the total marketing mix, promotions, sampling activities, coupons, salesforce size and media pressure. Procter & Gamble never goes into a country where they cannot broadcast TV commercials. A religion driven company ought to scan the global market for markets that fit their religion, and aim at those.

New organisational thinking

When you take the step of introducing a total concept mentality, you actually divide the company into two parts: development production, and finance logistics, and the pure concept organisation (see Figure 6.7).

Creating these two units maximises available energy and generates a dual capacity to run these important areas. This avoids the risk of one half receiving more motive power than the other – it is virtually impossible for one person to fulfil both leadership roles. The key benefit of this division is that you can bring under one umbrella everything which gives the company its brand value. And you get the perfect opportunity to control the total flow of information. It is especially important that product management, segment management and portfolio management are united, and that areas such as product development and design – which are concerned with the external concept – are also included.

Many companies resist this way of thinking, because development is traditionally allied to production. That will not work in the future, when customers and the customer mission determine the direction the company takes. Concept development must be separated from technical development, the former joining the total concept department, while the latter becomes part of production. The most important result of this simplification is an integrated view of the market, which enables you to take a unified approach instead of isolated initiatives. This is essential for practising a total concept way of thinking. No matter how good the intentions in traditional organisations, empire building will always act to undermine unity of purpose.

The traditional sales and marketing functions will need to be completely redefined. The company is now the brand – the product managers will become concept segment managers, while the traditional sales and marketing manager will become the group manager and driving force of the company, forging the vital link between the company and its customers.

The concept manager will be the company's religion leader and will have different qualities and qualifications to the traditional role model of a senior manager today. The job will require development and communication skills, the ability to lead from the front, a contagious enthusiasm, courage and foresight.

The era of careers and career ladders has passed. It is knowledge, insight, enthusiasm and identification with the task that will count in the future.

Fig 6.7 Management tasks in the organisation of the future

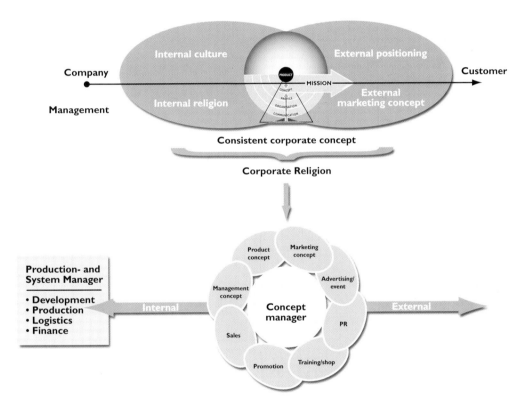

Everything concerning the concept must be united by one person, the concept manager, who simultaneously becomes the company's religion leader. He must be supported by a system- and production manager, who is responsible for development, production, logistics and finance.

CHAPTER 7

Consequences for top management

The leader is the wave
that pushes the ship forward
(Leo Tolstoy)

There can be no Corporate Religion without a re-evaluation of the top management's role. This chapter confronts the issue.

Too many international leaders leave the power struggles to others and hide behind the organisation instead of leading from the front. Developments have happened so fast that traditional international company management hierarchies with their financially-based attempts to control decentralised, self-governing units, are dead in the water. Companies need strong spiritual managements, who keep them on course with the focus on a strong brand position – otherwise they will be destroyed from within by internal battles. The international boss who wants to lead with the aid of spiritual values, must recognise that steering the company with a Corporate Religion is the most important task.

Spiritual focus

Financial control never created anything. It is a necessity for controlling growth, but let's not forget that it is growth that creates value; and it is value that has primary importance.

The new international leaders must release themselves from the weighty burden of administration.

International leaders bury themselves under piles of administration, while all the company development is left to others further down in the organisation.

The consequence is that the company loses the benefit of its good ideas, which cannot penetrate upwards to a top management with its attention focused elsewhere. The new international leaders must release themselves from the weighty burden of administration. At the same time, the focus must be directed towards the company's future establishment instead of towards the day-to-day control of the house economy.

Fig 7.1 Top management – the future focus

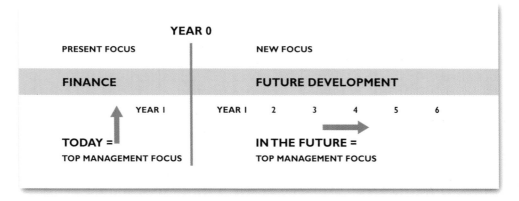

Today, top management primarily focuses on the financial past and the budget for the year ahead. In the future, the focus must be moved to vision and development.

Most companies go through an intense phase of development at the start, where their small size makes it easier to keep tight control. The bigger and more international the company becomes, the more difficult it is to control it. As generations of company management come and go, it gets progressively harder to maintain a homogeneous management and company culture. I should point out however, that it is not always the best course to keep the original culture. It must be seen in relation to the position of the brand – not in relation to the ego of the leader, which unfortunately is often the case. Making decisions behind closed doors won't fit the bill either.

There is a need for a real commander, visible in the organisation and willing to lead from the front.

There is a need for a real commander, visible in the organisation and willing to lead from the front.

The company which is managed by its founder doesn't usually suffer from management identity problems. But if the founder is deceased or has otherwise left the fold, problems can arise. The difficulty centres around getting the leader's message out through the organisation. So often, managements fail to focus on communication because they simply do not realise how important it is.

Little if any information comes from above. In large international companies especially, management turns to control by numbers when their organisation becomes too big or diffuse for them to oversee. What's really needed is progressive management which can tell the whole organisation where they are heading, why and by what means.

Spiritual management with the founder as leader

Behind almost every major international company stands a charismatic founder figure or perhaps a leader from a succeeding generation, who has driven the company from the start by the force of personality. Sometimes, it can be a team rather than one specific person, but in each case there exists the same homogeneous attitude to the business. With strength at the top, the company will adjust itself to this management and nobody will be in any doubt about the course being set. It creates an efficient company with short communication channels and a clear focus.

As long as the management keeps its focus on market developments, is capable of translating them into competitive products and understands the importance of building out and strengthening the brand's position, the company shouldn't get into difficulties.

Most entrepreneurs however are usually development oriented and often possess a technical background. They have the tendency to devote their attention to the physical aspects of the product, and rarely understand the importance of building a strong brand.

Company founders become increasingly distanced from the market as time passes and the company grows.

Another pitfall for company founders is that as time passes and the company prospers, their distance from the people at the sharp end increases in direct proportion to the power they acquire. Often the result is that they retard company development because their thinking becomes fossilised and things can quickly go from bad to worse if the founder withdraws into the ivory tower, fulfilled and satisfied by the good results, without a new spiritual leader ready and waiting in the wings.

A new administrative leader is no substitute, because vision disappears. You might dispute the truth of this by pointing to the development department, whose essential task is to be forward looking. But if focus vanishes from the top, it will very quickly copy itself throughout the entire organisation. It is an unfortunate fact in big companies that several years can elapse before the lack of development shows its effects on sales. This explains why, in the short term, a new administrative leader can often get some financially favourable results but vision is being more and more neglected, and then one day – when the brand can no longer hide the lack of product development – something will snap and the company gets the message the hard way.

It is an unfortunate fact in big companies that several years can elapse before the lack of development shows its effects on sales.

This is a particular problem for industry in America, largely because top managers get the kind of lucrative deals with share options that make it enormously advantageous for them to maximise the company's value in the short term. Then they can sit back and smile at their bank balances – but what about the company's long term position in the market?

Those who focus only on the past history of company results are already losing ground in the market, because the market is a dynamic quantity. Many are being saved by the fact that their competitors are hampered by exactly the same kind of myopic management, did they but realise it. Maybe that explains why most areas of business move forwards in sudden leaps – because someone suddenly arrives with an innovation that forces all the others to react.

Company founders are usually at the cutting edge of their markets, either because they have created the markets with product innovations, or because they have found a niche in the market for their products. They know their niches, and are good at reading both the market and the consumers. The problem for founders arises when the company grows so large and international that they lose their overview. To maintain their grip, they turn to control by money and slowly drown in a sea of statistics.

The problem for founders arises when the company grows so large and international that they lose their overview. To maintain their grip, they turn to control by money and slowly drown in a sea of statistics.

In this situation, it is far better for a founder to step aside and leave dynamic management to a new innovator or have others to take care of the financial control, so that he or she can continue to monitor the market and develop the company. As long as the founder is physically present in the company, nobody else sets the agenda. Usually there will be a very strong sense of spiritual management, as most founders involve themselves in everything. They send out signals to everyone, so that nobody in the company is in doubt about the direction they are going. Bill Gates is a good example in this connection. Microsoft also provides visible proof that if the ideas and the energy are there, the results will follow.

The tenacity of the traditional entrepreneur needs to return to international business. If you sit on your laurels it can be hard to get back up again.

Spiritual management in companies with second generation management

How do you transfer entrepreneurial flair and establish just as strong a management as the one that the founder practised?

Most international companies are in their second generation of management and it is here that the big challenge lies. How do you transfer entrepreneurial flair and establish just as strong a management as the one that the founder practised?

When you have a company culture, it does not necessarily mean that you have a strong and forward-looking management. The future will only arrive in an organisation that is being driven forward. It is all too easy to underestimate the importance for employees in a big organisation of having a visible management and clear goals. Financial targets and salaries are not enough by themselves. They must also have spiritual sustenance.

A company will get an optimal return on its efforts when it has visions, and goals for market positions, implementing activities and individual employee performance. This must be seen in relation to a far bigger goal defined by the bosses. They must present clear and visible goals and at the same time give it a spiritual base. It is essential for success that the goals do not alienate the employees. On the contrary, they must be motivated by them. And the more that the goals and the visions catch on in the market, the stronger and more goal-oriented the organisation becomes.

Most major international companies are in either the second or third management generation. It's worth reflecting that in every case there was once a person or a group of visionary and innovative people in charge of the company which at some point enabled it to make the upward leap. The goal was clear, and the company has had a strong spiritual management. It is crucial to promote that condition so that it becomes a permanent feature of the company. The success culture becomes the company's own culture, so that the dynamic and visionary management culture is passed on from one generation to the next.

It is the long haul that creates the solid international position. Though fast movers like The Body Shop, Microsoft and Nike are impressive, you have to admire a company like The Coca-Cola Company for being capable of transforming its dynamic and aggressive approach from generation to generation of management. That is one of the reasons for the company's tremendous international position. Innovators such as Bill Gates and Anita Roddick are textbook examples of strong spiritual leaders creating fast growth, but for both of them it will be decisive how they build a strong second generation management and culture that can keep the companies in front. Those companies which have managed this transformation with renewed growth are characterised by the fact that they have continued the dynamic and spiritual management. You can always get a leader, but to find one – or a group of them – who can continue the spiritual management is a far more difficult task.

Corporate Religion requires a very strong management

Top management has to prioritise its resources in the future if it wants to get back into the management role. It begins with changing the organisation. To be able to run the international organisation via a Corporate Religion, management must use a wealth of resources in monitoring the market, developing and sustaining the religion and shepherding commitment and action in the organisation. Top management must therefore release themselves from the traditional tasks which have been defined by the old

Top management has to prioritise its resources in the future if it wants to get back into the management role.

school, where the role is static and financial tasks take up most of the time. Time must be allowed to watch the global market, so that opportunities to take the lead are not missed.

Fig 7.2a Traditional top management focus

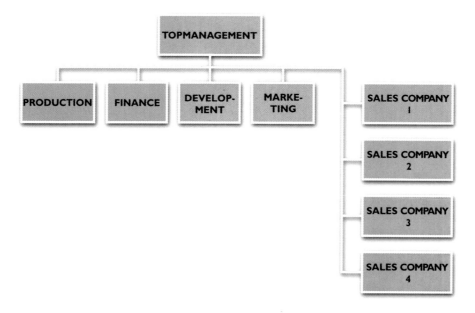

In most organisations, the top management's focus is far too diffuse, because too many individuals and subsidiaries are reporting directly to the top.

The company leader becomes spiritual leader, and the two people in charge of the inward and outward information departments respectively must report directly.

The way that international companies are organised today obstructs the path to more progressive management because the organisation steals the time which otherwise could be used for constructive management building. The new international organisation must be adjusted in accordance with the Corporate Religion idea, so that the organisation itself produces the dynamic and forward-looking effort. The company leader becomes spiritual leader, and the two people in charge of the inward and outward information departments respectively must report directly. In the new order, the subsidiaries do not have this direct line of reporting, as it would shift the focus away from the central Corporate Religion. A tough line needs to be taken here, otherwise the power struggles between subsidiary and parent company will grind on indefinitely. The difference between the two organisations is that in Figure 7.2a the organisation depletes the leader's resources, while in Figure 7.2b the leader can focus on running the company via a Corporate Religion because of the way the organisation is structured. The condition for getting strong management is that space must be created for the leader – by making drastic organisational changes if necessary – so that he or she can lead again, instead of being led by the organisation. Now the leader's resources can be devoted to ensuring a firm foundation for the company's future growth, while others take care of the company's current income. If the leader is constantly ahead of the game, runs the company via the Corporate Religion, makes sure that the company is at the cutting edge of the market and sees to it that the implementation is perfect, everything else will follow.

In this way the international company moves in a positive circle, where the leader and the management become stronger and increasingly visible, and the focus is firmly

Fig 7.2b   Future top management focus

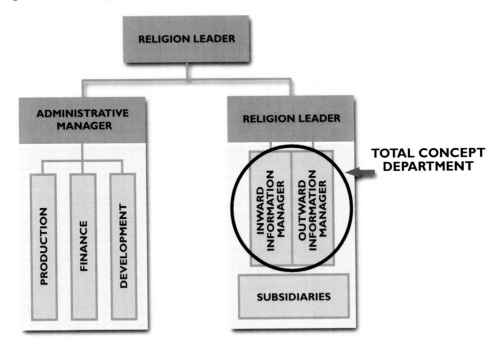

The religion leader must be directly involved in both inward and outward information. This can only be achieved in practice if all the practical tasks are left to an administrative manager.

fixed on the development and the implementation departments. That in itself creates stronger commitment and action. The company thereby strengthens its position in the market, bringing company and market closer to each other. We all know the truth of this. Our colleagues and customers can easily take up all our time if we let them. We have to get a grip if we want to break the bonds and reclaim our own decision space.

Corporate Religion requires a visible management

It is vital for the effective control of international companies that the management is highly visible. Not only must they formulate the mission, they must also practise what they preach. Large organisations are always blighted with cumbersome systems, and so the goal must be to make the channels in the organisation shorter from top to bottom.

The new communication media could well solve some of these information tasks. The technology is there, but so far there are not many managements making a conscious effort to use it. Companies often content themselves with an internal magazine, run by a benign staff who always seem to have difficulty finding good editorial content. The product is usually excruciatingly bland, with virtually no contributions from the top management.

In most international companies the top managers hide when they should be doing the exact opposite. The employees want to understand what makes them tick, and what they think. There are plenty of examples of leaders who make the most of visible management – the President of the United States for one. In election campaigns the President is at the epicentre of it, and the same goes for the management of the country. Of course we all know that the President isn't deciding things alone – there is a massive network of advisers and a party involved as well. But the President is the mouthpiece for decisions, and leads an entire nation through personal communication.

International companies can learn from this, and use visibility as a tool for more effective leadership. This approach also ensures that messages are received direct and undistorted in even the furthest outposts of the hierarchy.

Bill Gates knows this well. He is the President of both his company and the EDP business in general. It is hardly surprisingly then, that when Mr Gates travels abroad he is often accorded presidential status and received by government ministers.

Employees in large organisations want to know something about the big picture, since they are usually just a small detail of it. They need the full story. If new products are launched, or if the company changes its policy or course, it is nice to know why; and the messages penetrate further if it is the leader who tells them. A short time after Jan Leschly had been put in charge of the international pharmaceutical giant SmithKline Beecham, he went round the company's major plants and spoke to everyone. By meeting his employees personally, they all saw who he was and what he wanted. He delivered a personal message and gave an excellent example of a leader taking the time to become visible to his people. From that position it is much easier for any leader to get a Corporate Religion through.

Employees in large organisations want to know something about the big picture, since they are usually just a small detail of it. They need the full story.

Corporate Religion implies a new type of leader

Today's international company leaders must find out if they are the innovative type who can – and want – to function as the spiritual leaders of their organisations. If the answer is no, then find someone who can.

The international company must be led by an innovative leader who can take the company onto the international offensive. He or she may have an analytical or development oriented nature, but first and foremost the job involves communicating with a big organisation. Next comes active participation in the development, maintenance and dissemination of the company's Corporate Religion, the central management tool. I am aware that the type of leader being described here is not particularly fashionable, nor are there many around who

Today's international company leaders must find out if they are the innovative type who can – and want – to function as the spiritual leaders of their organisations. If the answer is no, then find someone who can.

possess both the profile and the necessary international experience.

The spiritual leader is the antithesis of the administrative, product-oriented type who are so easily dominated by the book-keepers. The prevalence of the latter may be connected with the fact that around the end of the '80s there was a tidal wave of company mergers where everyone was concerned with achieving world domination – and at the same time wanted to spread the risk. As a consequence of this, it was the money men and the administrators who emerged from the top of the companies.

The branded goods industry was also in panic at this time, because the chains and the consumers were no longer willing to pay such high prices for brands. That forced companies to focus their efforts on fewer, stronger brands, sparking off a mass of non-core business sell-offs and a new wave of core business company acquisitions in order to achieve greater economies of scale. International corporations either developed into massive holding companies stocked to the roof with business units, each of them specialised in a specific area with a specific brand – or they became single international companies where the company 'is' the brand.

In both cases it is important that the leader manages the company in an innovative and outgoing manner. To build strong brands in the markets the leader must be focused and powerful – in other words a commander, who gathers information via his intelligence services, from which the strategy and tactics will be made. The commander must lead from the front – and always be in the thick of the action. When the army goes into battle, it must be so well prepared and motivated, that success is not dependent on chance.

The fashionable manager's time has passed, and along with it an era where form, friends and network were valued the most.

The fashionable manager's time has passed, and along with it an era where form, friends and network were valued the most. Since most networks are country based, such power structures can only stand to fall when international leaders show international results on an international stage. You have to manage the global market – and as I have shown, there is only one way to do it. This is where the book-keepers drop out of the frame. The global market has become so huge that it is only the best and most dedicated who triumph. The ability to achieve victory and the will to win are the most important personal attributes – not a golf handicap.

One consequence of having a first class spiritual and innovative leader is that dedication to the development of the Corporate Religion happens at the expense of dedication to production, finance and logistics. Logistics in particular becomes a more important parameter, the more global the company becomes. To address this issue, we can therefore imagine different management structures as shown in Figure 7.3.

Fig 7.3   Management models

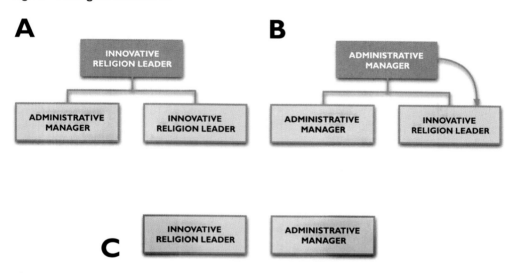

The crucial thing is to have an innovative religion leader in the expediting role. As the outline model shows, there are several possible solutions.

In A the innovative leader controls the "extrovert" part of the business, but at the same time has a strong administrative leader who controls production, finance and logistics. The model is a good one, because it gives the religion leader's word greater weight out in the organisation and also allows his or her efforts to be concentrated on managing the religion aspects of the company.

INNOVATIVE RELIGION LEADER   ADMINISTRATIVE MANAGER

In B you have a leader who does not have the innovative abilities, and perhaps cannot produce enough of the dynamism necessary to run the company with the aid of a Corporate Religion. Here it is important to realise one's limitations. The innovative role is indispensable for the company, so it has to happen in another way through another person selected for the job. It makes sense therefore, to make the innovative leader the spokesperson – or Corporate Religion manager – for the company as shown in Figure 7.3.

In C a dual management structure is involved, which demands a lot from the two top leaders. They must be able to work together, respect each other and be able to reach 100 per cent agreement, at least in public. If they succeed in that aim, it is an optimal solution because the company gets both an innovative, outgoing individual and one who can keep control of the company, the latter acting as a counterbalance to the former.

The leader of the future must stand at the front

The international companies which have the growth and the strong brands are generally those where the management involves itself.

International companies have become so big that it is almost impossible for individual employees to work out who it is that decides. This forces management to find ways of demonstrating to the employees that they participate in the daily business. The two founders of Mars Inc., whose main brand of course is Mars, travel round all the subsidiaries each year. This way, the employees can see for themselves that the top management concern themselves with the company's daily business – and that strengthens the company internally. The international companies which have the growth and the strong brands are generally those where the management involves itself and gets directly involved in the global development process. The management participates in analysing the single markets, it develops the religion – and adjusts it to new products, campaigns and media – all the way to the final implementation. The Corporate Religion leader has the responsibility for the global market, where the subsidiaries have now become co-ordinating units and the leaders of the subsidiaries have become regional sales managers.

So if the leader wants to develop and run the global company, he or she must be deeply involved in the operations. The trick is to find the limit of that involvement, without affecting other resources – for example the energy you have to put into the analysis and development of future products, the brand's future identity and the continuous cultivation of inward and outward information in the organisation.

Systems for supervising the global market

When the top leader is participating in developing the brand, systems must be put in place which can measure key parameters so that the leader can follow the world market from a distance. For most company managements, it will seem an expensive exercise until they realise how resource saving it actually is. What's more, the company gets usable knowledge and not the subjective interpretation of regional reality from different subsidiary managers.

The problem in setting up the system is that the external data that the company needs, also requires agencies which do the analyses in the same way in every market. In some instances, it might be wise to consider doing part of it yourself. At one time, Gillette focused on the whole question of price, and how much a brand can modulate it. They set up a tracking system where a basket of different everyday necessities was used to follow price development and to set the price at the right level in the American market.

In the March 1996 issue of Fortune, manager Alfred M. Zeien says:

> "A lot of people argue you should charge what you can get. Gillette believes consumers have a relative value consciousness. If the price of something gets out of whack, they feel as if they are getting ripped off."

The example illustrates how important Gillette feels it is to continuously know where the price of an article lies in relation to other articles. For them, it is important for the brand to maintain a certain price/value-relationship.

Therefore, they must measure it directly. Gillette does not have the time to wait for traditional sales reporting.

Another good example is Toyota which, as I mentioned earlier, has implemented a global measurement of customer satisfaction. Here the company gets a direct measurement of how the company's dealers function and how satisfied the dealers and customers are. After that, Toyota can compare levels for customer satisfaction across borders and set up norms for what they can reasonably demand. With the ultimate measurement system, Toyota knows the temperature of their brand. They can follow the target group and find out how well their Corporate Religion is being accepted in the markets. It is a system which requires many resources. On the other hand, the corporation has full control of the target group and the organisation at the same time.

CHAPTER 8

Implementing a
Corporate Religion

Are you one who watches?
Or intervenes?
Or who looks away, and steps aside …
(Friedrich Nietzsche)

Without realising that a company can get into a higher
gear, no one will introduce a Corporate Religion. There
must be a will to become better than the others. Dynamic
and well-functioning companies, on the other hand, can
easily choose to be run by a religion. The idea can only
make the company even more vibrant.

To transform an international company into a Corporate
Religion company in practice means that the company
must effectively start from the beginning again. The
difference is that the new religion-run company has to
accommodate the original company into its changed
structure. If the existing organisation is taken as the
starting point, corporate inertia may force the company to
continue along basically the same track.

Figure 8.1 shows a timetable for the implementation of a
Corporate Religion and we will now look at each stage in
turn.

1 Internal analysis of the company's product programme

The most important thing to be clear about is what you
market and sell. Is it the company, a brand, or a mix of the
two? Or are you selling lots of different products? If the
latter is the case, radical changes will be needed unless all
the products can be integrated into a single unified
concept which makes sense to the customers. You may
have to contemplate splitting the company into different
business units, each with their own brand and religion.

As shown in Figure 8.2 there are several different ways of doing it. A shows a company where different brand divisions have been established, which function as independent businesses. B is like Mars Inc. where the same organisation runs different brands. This model clearly gives the greatest economic advantages, though there are limitations on how many brands an organisation can handle without affecting efficiency.

You may have to contemplate splitting the company into different business units, each with their own brand and religion.

Fig 8.1 Implementation of Corporate Religion

TIME TABLE

1. Internal analysis of the company's product programme.

2. Analysis of brand values in selected markets.

3. Assessment of the brand's business opportunities on the basis of the analysis.

4. Development of a Corporate Concept.

5. A total description of the company.

6. Defining the Corporate Religion and the system set-up to ensure commitment and action.

7. Trials in selected test markets.

8. Adjustment of concept and religion.

9. The old international organisation is dismantled and a completely new one is built up from the base.

10. The organisation is changed globally all in one go.

11. The religion must be impressed on everybody from the beginning

12. The religion is established during the course of one year.

If the individual brands are very different, it is difficult to get a Corporate Religion idea to function. But if there is a main brand, as in the case of The Coca-Cola Company, which also has smaller brands such as Fanta and Sprite, it then becomes possible since it is the Coca-Cola religion that runs the company. It is ideal if you can unite the complete product programme or at least the main part of it under one main brand which commands the resources for real investment.

As Figure 8.3 shows, the goal must be to unite the complete product programme into one brand, where the brand values are relevant to every product. No product can be permitted to conflict with the brand. It can be a tough decision, but some products may have to be sacrificed in order to get a strong and consistent brand.

2 Analysis of brand values in selected markets

How wide can the brand band be, and still give the re-formulated brand a meaning? You must find out by testing it on the concept level among the target groups in selected markets. The analysis has to reveal whether the values that the company thinks lie in the brand are also the values which the consumers think are important in relation to choice. At the same time you must test which products can usefully be accommodated in the brand band and identify those which detract from it and silt up the message.

Fig 8.2 If the company can't unite all the brand identities, it must be divided into separate business units

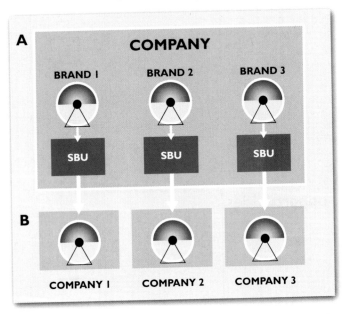

Dividing the company into separate business units may be necessary in order to communicate in a focused and effective way. The crucial thing is that the company should not appear divided, in the eyes of the consumer. Economies of scale achieved by drawing on the same production and logistic machinery, for example, can easily be exploited. Toyota/Lexus is a good example of this.

The analysis must present a clear picture of which concept the brand must be built on. It must uncover the differences which exist in the individual markets, and pinpoint those values which connect all the markets.

In practice, consumers in different markets tend to attach the same weight to the core brand values. It is only the peripheral brand attributes that separate the countries. If it proves impossible to find common denominators, you must try again and this time build in some wider values – or else consider dropping the idea of a global brand completely. That's a rare occurrence – usually it is possible to find a way into the global market.

Fig 8.3 Many products, few brands

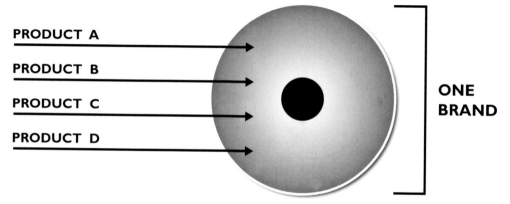

PRODUCT A

PRODUCT B

PRODUCT C

ONE
BRAND

PRODUCT D

To get your efforts efficiently focused, the different products must be united under one brand or just a few brands. The acid test is that the brand remains strong and consistent when more variants are added to it. If a product doesn't support and strengthen the brand values, drop it. Nothing must be allowed to make the brand weak and inconsistent.

3 Assessing the brand's business opportunities

The analysis may indicate that you have to divide your business up into two brands, or re-evaluate your product range. These are major decisions, as the traditional international company has developed without the necessary control. Without such action, consumers won't see the company's complete product portfolio the way you want them to. They have to understand and relate to the re-formulated brand and its values. The solution is either to sell off, or operate with two brands.

If the latter course is chosen, you must carefully consider whether there are sufficient resources available to get penetration in the global market with both brands. If a middle solution is chosen with a main brand and a smaller follow-my-leader brand, it is important that this priority is made clear within the organisation. Of course the smaller brand must be properly supported, but nobody should forget which brand is the revenue-generator.

Fig 8.4 Consumer perceptions of brand values

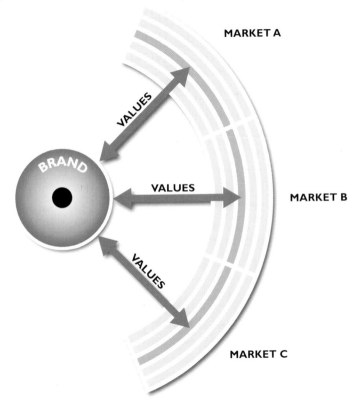

The consumer's view of the brand must be analysed in a series of key markets. The analysis must show if there is a connection between the values which consumers find important in relation to brand choice, the values they connect with the brand and the values which the company is trying to attach to it.

4 Developing the Corporate Concept

Can the company set up a mission for the brand which can form the core of a Corporate Concept?

After having worked out whether the company must be recognised as the brand – or whether there are going to be several brands – you can continue. Which brand values does the market prioritise? How wide can the brand band be? And which products can it contain? Can the company set up a mission for the brand which can form the core of a Corporate Concept?

First of all, you should set up a mission defining your company goals, and how you want to pursue success. Part of that involves making a decision about which Corporate Religion will take the company where it wants to go. After that you can start finding out which products and concepts fit the objective of achieving a certain market position. Don't take anything for granted. That will give you the best analysis and the best starting point for new thinking.

Most companies have a certain market position and certain products out of which they make a living, so in practice they work outwards from that. But think about what Jan Carlzon did. His re-positioning of SAS stands out as a shining example. In developing the concept, the whole idea is to get the concept pushed as high as possible up the involvement axis. The more you can involve the consumers in your brand, the greater the value, and the stronger the brand position becomes. As several cases have demonstrated, increased involvement can lead directly to bigger profits so you must constantly try to get brand involvement established as much as possible, both via rational and emotional values. In the development phase, forget the brand's present position and look at the possibilities the brand offers. Give yourself space – it's here that the innovative leader truly justifies his or her position in the company.

As I have already mentioned, the company has to shift direction from the product oriented to the mission driven. The mission is the company's guide, because it defines the wider brand values which will create increased involvement and increased brand value. Figure 8.5 shows the development model for a Corporate Concept. A shows that the mission must have its starting point in the international target group. On the basis of the mission statement and the product's opportunities, strengths and weaknesses, a concept for the brand is chosen. The concept is determined first, and then everything else is adjusted accordingly: profile, organisation and mass communication. Sponsorship or knowledge initiatives are also adjusted to fit the concept, so that everything is mutually supportive and forms a consistent stream. Companies need to recognise that if they

Fig 8.5 Developing a Corporate Concept

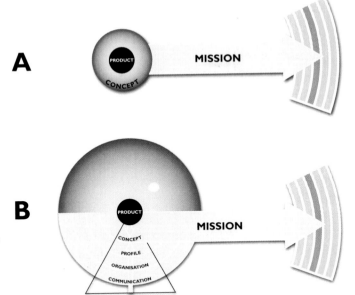

The development and communication of a Corporate Concept should happen in steps: When the brand concepts and the mission are determined (A), they have a direct influence on the profile, the organisation and the communication – Corporate Concept (B).

want to climb further up the involvement axis, a consistent concept is required. There must be a Corporate Concept where brand and company flow together – today's consumers have become much more aware and are not fooled by empty words. In Figure 8.5, B shows that the brand that the consumers meet is much wider than the brand which the individual product represents. When companies redefine themselves, as SAS did, it is crucial that the management does not content itself with intentions around a new objective or a new company concept. It must be carried through all the way; all the links in B must be included.

5 A total description of the company

When the Corporate Concept description is in place, the company has already come a long way, but the ultimate goal is to construct a total description of the company. A description which brings the internal and external company into perfect harmony. The external market position forms the starting point, relating the whole company to a set of values which can deliver the desired brand value.

This process concerns the company's personality and its development. What matters here is the company's soul and belief rather than products and packaging. Many companies make partial attempts in this direction but very few are capable of creating a coherent Corporate Religion which unifies the whole company in a value-related and spiritual dialogue with the market. In certain circumstances, it may be appropriate to have different cultures in the company, depending on whether it is the production department or the sales department of the company which has primary contact with the market. But it must be made clear who it is that understands the market, and is going to develop new products and new solutions for the future. It doesn't matter if the company is driven by an introspective production culture if what is really being sold is a solution or a concept which builds on something entirely different to what is considered as the product.

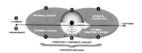

See Figure 4.7 for explanation

Imbalance can kill a company. It becomes more and more important to have a total understanding of the market position and how to keep the company continuously in the lead. The values delivered by separate parts of the company must be known. If there is an imbalance between the internal and external positioning, it must be there as a result of deliberate choice rather than as an oversight. It's a bit like a play. Everyone has different roles and they must know them inside out in order to achieve the best result. But first the play itself must be written, and written well. It needs a good plot, a good director, and a blend of audacity and commitment.

6 Defining the Corporate Religion and the system set-up to ensure commitment and action

In most cases the religion is automatically defined at the concept and mission stage. Sometimes however, there is not necessarily a connection between the brand's concept and the Corporate Religion by which the company wants to run itself. The most simple and efficient way is to define a mission statement for top management to manage accordingly. For the company to become as focused as

SAS succeeded in becoming, the religion has to be formalised so that everyone understands it. The top management must communicate the message. The religion must not be seen as some lofty and esoteric objective; it must result in concrete actions for every single employee.

The essence of the Corporate Religion idea is about bringing back the human factor into the dehumanised machines that characterise massive international organisations. Corporate Religion must be a complementary management principle to the financial, and should get each individual employee thinking each day: "What have I contributed to the spirit in my company?"

Corporate Religion must be a complementary management principle to the financial, and should get the individual employee thinking each day: "What have I contributed to the spirit in my company?"

Most senior managers crunch lots of numbers and read even more reports, but I've never seen one conclusion drawn from such statistics. If that were ever to happen, my guess is that it wouldn't travel far down the corporate corridors. There should be a notice pinned to the wall of every director's office – "Financial management is habit forming". Top managers who want to instil a Corporate Religion must really force themselves to put just as much

Fig 8.6 Value based growth management

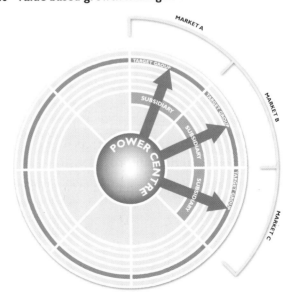

The same target group is influenced across all markets with a consistent concept with information flowing freely between consumers and the parent company which becomes a power centre.

effort into it as they did with their number analysis and financial reporting systems.

The intention of this book is to get spiritual management onto the agenda. If companies reach the problem recognition phase, then the whole movement will be under way, and will not stop until the religion is in place. The religion must be communicated by the top leader, and reach out to everyone. To create commitment it is vital that you have clear visions and a visible religious management, that operational management systems are set up for building the religion, and that its implementation is properly controlled. At the same time, the organisation must be managed in the right direction through education. This is where many companies hit difficulties, by thinking that everything will steam along nicely by itself. Commitment must be created in the organisation, so that activities are carried through according to the religion and individual countries do not revert to their former habits. Figure 8.5 shows that strong management is necessary from the top all the way out to the markets in order to ensure commitment and action. The concept religion will attain value when the belief is transferred from top management to the complete organisation – and when it creates commitment and action. Those who understand how to organise it create focused companies. A totally focused international organisation which has diligently pursued a Corporate Religion over several years is likely to succeed, because it becomes in itself a strong factor in the market. To ensure action out in the organisation it is essential that there is long-term planning, that implementation happens on time, and that campaigns and their effects on the target groups are controlled and monitored.

It is around control and timely implementation that the chain breaks in traditional international organisations, where too much time is consumed by bureaucracy and squabbling, and where the sales dominated company focuses on sales promotion instead of on the brand's position with the target group. It's the short sighted who go for the safe financial result rather than the company's future position.

7 Trials in selected test markets

Change nearly always meets resistance. The reorganisation of an international company is such a mammoth decision that the new concept and the new Corporate Religion must first pass its test in selected test markets. The difficulty with such a test lies in assessing whether the new concept will generate sufficient penetration with the target group during the test period. But difficulties are there to be overcome, and an accurate evaluation must be made which shows whether the religion idea is working or not.

Success depends on several things: the concept itself must be tested, along with the new brand values and possibilities for a wider brand band. The latter cannot of course be fully measured until the complete company is reorganised, which may take up to two years.

8 Adjusting the concept and the religion

When the test results of the new concept and the new Corporate Religion are fully reported, necessary adjustments to the concept and religion can be made.

When the test results of the new concept and the new Corporate Religion are fully reported, necessary adjustments to the concept and religion can be made. You must not press forward with extensive changes to the company until you have found the right solution for both the brand and the company. These are radical changes which must be carefully considered. It's better to get things right than implement a half-baked solution.

9 Dismantling the old international organisation

It would be a mistake to try to run the existing organisation via a Corporate Religion idea. If the right framework in a new and optimal organisation is not created, the only thing you will strengthen will be the company's problems. The subsidiaries will continue as before and the distance between the parent company and the market will simply widen.

The transformation to a religion-run company can only be successfully launched if the old company organisation is dismantled and a new one is built up from the bottom. The role of the subsidiaries in particular must be changed from self-governing provinces to co-ordinating units for the global brand which is controlled by the Corporate Religion.

Fig 8.7 Future top management focus

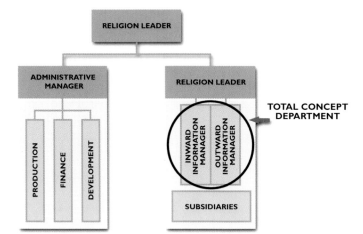

This is how the organisational structure should look. The administrative director and the information controllers are positioned below the top leader with direct lines of communication.

As shown in Figure 8.6, the subsidiaries must be anchored in a controlled organisation which runs the company's Corporate Religion. The step from the non-homogeneous to the homogeneous international company must be taken fully so that the markets become completely integrated. Everything must link up in a continuous, controlled process from the central brand centre all the way out to the customers in the markets. What remains is to set up the system and then run it as efficiently as possible.

In doing so, you may have to say farewell to employees who can't adjust to the new structure. It will be especially tough on the subsidiary bosses, and that in turn can make international top management nervous about carrying it through. In my estimation, there is only one way to implement the transition. Include the best subsidiary bosses in the religion development group and give them equivalent areas of responsibility in the new organisation. To begin with, there may be a shortage of good people, so it's all about using the resources you have across demarcations.

Include the best subsidiary bosses in the religion development group, and give them equivalent areas of responsibility in the new organisation.

Fig 8.8 The organisational structure of the future

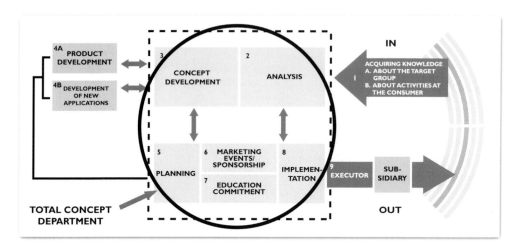

This is how the organisation of the future should look. See explanations below Figure 6.3.

10 Changing the organisation simultaneously

The new organisation must be changed simultaneously, since many of the company's resources must be released and redistributed to new functions. Obviously, that can only happen if it all occurs at the same time. This will precipitate some short-term panic, but it also stimulates a lot of dynamism. Oticon discovered this in 1990 when the company physically uprooted its headquarters and all the employees got new job descriptions. From that day, nobody had a fixed job in principle, but instead had to offer their working capacity to well-defined projects. It created some frustration and chaos for a while, but out of it came a wonderfully rejuvenated, dynamic organisation which now develops products in a focused stream and leads its field. The Oticon case shows that you can change an organisation quite drastically, if everything is planned down to the smallest detail and systems are developed by which you can run the new organisation. There may be a colossal amount of work involved in planning it, but this must never become an excuse for not carrying the transformation through.

11 The religion must be impressed on everybody right from the start

During the period of transformation the religion leader must be highly visible. Realistically speaking, he or she must set aside a full year to successfully implement the new idea. Many employees will have new tasks and priorities, which is why a comprehensive internal training programme and internal sales work is so necessary. It is important that the pace is set from the start – and preferably increased – so that the organisation experiences the new dynamic, which is in itself a success criterion. All visible results must be published in new internal media which are widely read. The sender is either the top leader or the customers, or both, so that everyone can see that the new model works. The management must communicate the new concepts, so that nothing is misunderstood, and when the first consumer surveys come in, everyone must be informed. In this way, the company suddenly becomes well structured – and that is one of its primary aims. Results and knowledge are conveyed through the entire company, so that everyone becomes strongly motivated and the company's Corporate Religion is constantly adhered to.

It is important that the pace is set from the start – and preferably increased – so that the organisation experiences the new dynamic.

12 The religion is established within a year

Within a year, it is necessary to establish close contact between all the vital markets and the central development function so that the foundation for a tightly controlled process is put into place.

Within a year, it is necessary to establish close contact between all the vital markets and the central development function.

All systems run the main system. Many resources are needed to get the process off the ground, and there will be many in the company who concentrate on nothing else from the day the Corporate Religion is introduced. At the same time it must have its own placement in the company, so that it can be implemented as shown in Figure 8.8. Most companies make the mistake of not setting aside resources for inward information which, as we have seen, is essential for proper control of the brand and ensuring that external activities are being carried through.

One of the critical factors is implementation in the individual markets, where education and control are needed to get sales pushed in the right direction. In many companies this will be the biggest hurdle of all, since sales companies are used to being sales-controlled and the salesperson is the hub of the universe. Against that background, these same corporations are now to be run through differently focused activities and with totally different goals. Their efforts will be measured in the customers' attitude to the brand, with the salespeople now cogs in a greater marketing machine where the focus in most cases will have been shifted. They will be controlled to a much greater extent. There may be strong resistance, but many will become quickly attuned to the much higher level of consumer-directed activity made possible by reductions in administrative costs. By exercising a much bigger level of activity in the market than you are used to, you can more easily lead the company in the right direction. Logistics are an essential condition of success.

This is also the case in the transitional period to becoming a religion-driven company. If the systems do not get up and running, the entire machinery will fail to function. Look at the most successful international companies and you will see that they have built some awesomely efficient systems to control the brand and the organisation. At The Coca-Cola Company and McDonald's, nothing is left to

Fig 8.9 The religion is established during the first year

Even though it is not possible to get the complete new organisation structure in place immediately, the company must quickly get into establishing the religion. From the word go, resources must be deployed for collecting and analysing data to ensure that the strategy is being implemented and that there is action in the markets.

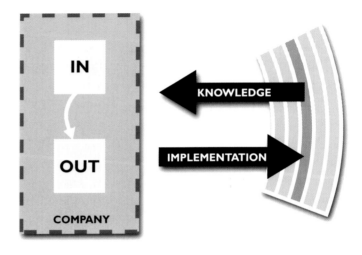

chance. They have control over absolutely everything. With full knowledge at top management level, you can control the company much more effectively.

The corporate religion driven company is always evolving

Once you have established the system, adjusted the company's Corporate Concept, and the global brand is running, you can start to reap the rewards of your strategy. The resources which have been released by considerably reducing the organisation can be reallocated to direct market adaptation, new product development and applications, and constant education of the market. The most important contribution a religion makes to a company is reducing the negative energy between the parent company and the subsidiaries. By using it in direct market adaptation, you get increased pressure on the target group and a more consistent brand, which ultimately leads to considerable economies of scale. When the company is up and running, you can start optimising the brand band and begin the search for new markets which fit the company's Corporate Religion. Now you have full control of the company again. The next aim should be to get control of the market. The company which achieves success by running the corporation with a Corporate Religion will turn its brand into a Brand Religion.

The most important contribution a religion makes to a company is the disengagement of the negative and destructive energy between the parent company and the subsidiaries.

... And the future?

During my work on this book, one thing has become clear to me. The most successful companies have, in one way or another, created a reliable platform for themselves.

These companies are consistent, and have a spiritual ethos which powers the company forward, generating much more value with consumers than their competitors. These companies believe in themselves. They utilise the attitudes and values which I believe are the basis of Corporate Religions. They influence their companies through attitudes and values rather than skills. These companies which have gained control of their qualitative attitudes are those which command most respect. They lead with dynamic energy and verve, and are constantly at the cutting edge of future development.

My message is:

> *Start work now on the qualitative parameters, both on the brand side and in the internal organisation and don't let it happen in committees. This must be the top managers' most important task.*

In the future we will see the following:

- Brands will increasingly be assessed on their non-material and emotional values.
- Brand extensions and line extensions will take on another meaning. In the future we will see extensions of non-material and emotional values, which means that such extensions will traverse more categories of products.
- More clearly focused companies.
- Knowledge based companies will surge forward in the business-to-business market.
- Subsidiaries will shift from being autonomous principalities to become co-ordinating units as a re-integrated part of the international company.
- Consumers will increasingly demand to know the attitudes of the companies they are purchasing from. Who are they? What do they stand for? What do they themselves want? What do they do well?
- Many large international companies will fail because they have split themselves up into too many different power centres.
- A change in senior management role from book-keeper to corporate commander, with resources used on the most important and the most demanding task: to lead the company safely into the future.
- A huge demand for visionary managers.
- Market orientation will be replaced by future orientation.

The winners of the future will be consistent and reliable. At the same time they will have a spiritual ethos which powers the company forward in a focused way and creates real value for the consumers, employees and shareholders. The establishment of strong Corporate Religions and Brand Religions means strong growth. But remember that religions can be powerful forces – they must be carefully controlled. That will be the next major business challenge.

CHAPTER 9

Epilogue

The first question that
will occur to you is
has the author used
Corporate Religion ideas
in his own company?
The answer is Yes!

Introduction to the Epilogue

In this book I have described how a number of
competent companies have developed a
Corporate Religion way of thinking, and how they
got it right. My purpose in offering these
descriptions is to encourage others to put these
ideas into practice for themselves.

This book was published in Denmark in April 1997 and a
year later in Sweden. In both countries, its publication led
to numerous media interviews and many presentations to
company managements. On each occasion I was always
asked the same question. Have you used Corporate
Religion ideas in the development of your own company?

*The epilogue is for those
who are interested to
know how I have used
Corporate Religion ideas
to build a market position
as the most serious-
minded marketing agency
in Denmark.*

Well, I certainly do practise what I preach. What is more,
I believe that putting Corporate Religion into practice is
one of the principal reasons why Kunde & Co. has
propelled itself from ground zero to become the largest
agency in Denmark in just 10 years. I have written this
epilogue for those who are interested to know how I have
used Corporate Religion ideas to build a market position
as the most serious-minded marketing agency in
Denmark.

To provide a comprehensive understanding of what I
have done at Kunde & Co. and why, the description
which follows is quite lengthy and reasonably thorough.
It's optional reading. The previous chapters give you the
full set of tools to grow your own Corporate Religion –
this final chapter records my personal experiences.

My experiences in building a religion-driven company which continuously strengthens its own market position.

In 1988 I opened an advertising agency in protest against the traditional agencies' obsession with creative awards – and against their lack of insight and interest in the clients they were working for. Until then, I had been working in marketing as a product manager at Tuborg (Carlsberg), and before that with the industrial company LK, where I had responsibility for sales and markets. LK produces installation materials and during the time I was there, they had a virtual monopoly of the domestic market – but were weak on exports.

Major marketing tasks

During my time in industry, I had become profoundly tired of advertising agencies which painted pretty solutions without bothering to acquaint themselves with the company's problems. My ambition was to create a seriously different marketing agency – an agency which went deeper into the customer's problems and became an expert in that area. The conventional agencies were specialists in creating advertisements and commercials, but I realised that much more was needed to solve marketing problems in practice. The prevailing dogma that agencies should be as "creative" as possible was often in diametric opposition to the most profitable solution. The fact is that marketing problems are often very complex, and you have to market yourself through many stages before a new product reaches the end-user.

My first problem in 1988 was how to explain that I had an agency with a new way of thinking. At the time, everybody thought that I wanted to start a marketing company selling consultant assistance, but my actual wish was to become a part of companies' everyday lives – a partner in their marketing work. Traditional marketing such as advertisements and commercials were to be just two of the services we sold. Nor was I content to work with isolated marketing problems.

I solved the problem of explanation by depicting the marketing problem as a hurdle race (see Figure 9.1). It turned out to be perfect for explaining our positioning as a serious agency, without losing our foothold in the normal marketing trade. Our customers were product managers and marketing managers, although my ambition was to get the whole company involved in marketing, especially top management.

Fig 9.1 The hurdle race

| Analysis | Development of concept | Development of creative solution | Marketing to subsidiaries | Marketing to the salesforce | Marketing to the retailers | Marketing to consumers |

From the very beginning Kunde & Co. has used this model to illustrate that many obstacles have to be surmounted before the customer is reached. Advertisements and commercials are just a small part of our "product range".

At that time, marketing was a subordinate discipline in most companies, and senior managers were not much occupied with it. Only the big American corporations and the most professional European companies took marketing seriously at boardroom level. I myself had been part of the management of an industrial company, and I knew how far down marketing ranked on my former colleagues' list of priorities. I was convinced that the leaders of the future would be those who considered marketing to be a decisive competition parameter, and I could see that they would be short of sparring partners because the traditional advertising agencies were solely occupied with themselves and their creativity – not the actual marketing tasks. Then again there were the management agencies which assisted in formulating big strategies based on technologies, trade structures and organisational structures.

Practical experience

Companies would soon be looking for an agency with experience in marketing. An agency that could translate this experience into marketing strategies which could become the companies' actual strategies.

Companies would soon be looking for an agency with experience in marketing – an agency that could translate this experience into marketing strategies which could become the companies' actual strategies, a marketing specialist agency. My agency. I opened it with the mission:

> "We will be the companies' agency and provide help on their behalf across the full marketing spectrum. Furthermore we will help Danish companies to go out into the world". The agency's vision was: "We want to be the leading marketing specialist in this country".

Reasons for success

It was an ambitious objective and there were few who took it seriously because, as with many young companies, we were just three men sitting in a basement office.

Looking back, I am convinced that my decision to begin with a clear mission – and build the company accordingly – constitutes one of the main reasons for our success. The original objective was by no means beyond our reach. We realised the vision in less than ten years and we gained our position as a seriously different agency much earlier. To become the marketing specialists, we had to extend the operational area. To cover the entire marketing spectrum, new competencies have to be continuously integrated into a coherent solution.

Fixed budgets

Right from the start, we always worked to fixed budgets and fought against the prevailing trend among agencies to be paid by the hour. That's the same as writing a blank cheque with no guarantee of any result. It might seem an attractive proposition to agencies in the short term, but in the long-term it's a loser. Operating with fixed budgets, our clients always knew exactly how much money they were spending, and in that way we were able to build long-term relationships. At the start of our collaboration we spent an enormous amount of time studying the customer's problem, for which we did not charge. If we did not win the account, we lost a lot of money – but it was a risk we were prepared to take.

Usually, it was money well spent. It made us a worthy sparring partner, and compared with the rest of the industry, we have always had long customer relationships. Our marketing proposals went into great depth strategically and this often took us up to the management corridor. We gained wide access inside companies because we had the right qualifications to deliver marketing solutions.

Our intention to go deeper into our customers' problems was realised. It is my belief that our account directors must see themselves as owners, managing directors and marketing executives in the companies they work for. Only in that way can we prove our value as sparring partners.

It is my belief that our account directors must see themselves as owners, managing directors and marketing executives in the companies they work for.

The international dimension

From my time in industry, I knew how much Danish companies were struggling out there in the big wide world. And I knew why. They didn't understand the importance of marketing. Instead, they developed their products and sold them through subsidiaries and agents. When the competition got hotter because lots of companies were producing the same products, it turned into a fight for market positions. It was here that companies failed because they couldn't figure out what was happening.

Our approach was the absolute opposite. We threw ourselves into a crusade to develop international concepts and run them centrally. At that time, every agency felt they had to be a member of an international chain in order to survive; but it soon became clear to me that international chains only existed for the big blue chip brands such as Coca-Cola, Procter & Gamble, Kellogg's, Gillette and so on. The vast majority of companies that were moving onto the international scene didn't have the international marketing organisations to necessitate the use of large international agencies, and it was these companies we wanted to help. What we discovered through our international concept work with them led to the writing of this book. It became clear that these companies lacked the coherent descriptions and Corporate Religions they needed to survive in the world of international competition and cope with the future.

Strong market positions

I believe it is essential for company managers, myself included, to try to describe their company so that everyone can understand where the company is in relation to the market, where it is heading, and how it is going to get there.

In the future, market position will be the company's most important asset. It will be crucial for creating a conceptual tool which can explain the influence and connections of different parameters. Acknowledging the vital importance of market position leads immediately to the next realisation – that consumers and customers are increasingly buying the whole company.

We confirmed this fact in focus groups across Europe when we tested concept development projects. The result is illustrated in Figures 3.5 and 3.7 which includes the company as a brand and shows the customers' level of brand involvement. The Corporate Concept model is useful for providing a simple and concise description of the company and its position on the market.

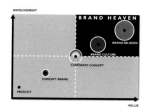

See Figure 3.5 for explanation.

When you describe a company in terms of mission, values and market position, you get a new picture which can help the management to lead the company into the future. Market position is something you own in the consciousness of your customers/end users. It is about values, and this is where the battles will take place in the future. Management must develop methods which communicate these values both internally and externally. This in turn creates the need for a Corporate Religion that will define the company in relation to the market. It makes the coherent description of the company into a power tool that unites the company and the market. It must have total credibility at whichever point you meet the company. The description must be understandable internally in relation to what the company delivers to its customers, and externally in relation to what the company does. The company must live up to the values inherent in its market position, which means that it must constantly monitor the market's opinions and expectations. All this is vital to maintaining a strong market position. Figure 9.2 shows a total model which unites the internal culture and the external positioning in one coherent description. The model has its basis in the Corporate Concept that leads to an internal religion project and an external marketing concept in which everything is coherent.

See Figure 3.6 for explanation.

The coherent company description

All these thoughts resulted in a project to unite my own company in a single total description. We had established our position as the most heavyweight marketing agency around, but as we continued to grow in size, I gradually had to accept that I couldn't reach into every single corner and include absolutely everyone. The challenge of describing the total marketing concept didn't get any easier when we ourselves opened offices in Stockholm and London.

Kunde & Co.'s religion project

The agency's religion project has lasted three years – and it will continue as an interactive process as long as the agency exists. The market must be monitored, the agency must live up to its mission, and we must also keep up with the times.

The external position

To help companies create consistent Corporate Concepts and gain strong market positions, it was obvious what the agency's mission should be: "We help companies to build strong market positions". This book 'Corporate Religion' provides a complete description of what we mean by it. We must help companies to elevate themselves in the Brand Religion model (Figure 3.5). To gain a market position they must first define who they are and what they own in the consumer's consciousness. When they have discovered it, they must then make a description of it as shown in the total model Figure 9.2, which itself leads to an internal religion project and an external marketing project.

We ourselves do not go jumping in as organisational or structural consultants, or anything else we are not qualified to do. Our role is to help with a total description of the company from a communicational point of view. It often becomes a total strategy and positioning project, because almost every company needs its position determined. International companies especially go through a change of system from unhomogeneous to homogeneous international companies (see Figure 6.2). The models in the book help us to describe our new spearhead products. When we follow the model for the Corporate Concept (Figure 3.7) and describe the product using the mission in order to help companies to build consistent market positions, we must also be consistent. Our product must be more than just a conventional advertising agency product.

Fig 9.2 The internal and external company – a total description of the company's personality

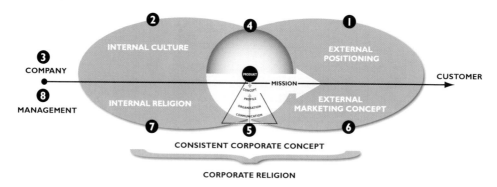

See Figure 4.7 for a detailed explanation of each phase.

Integrating specialist competencies

The trend in the advertising industry has been for large international agencies to buy up specialist agencies every time a new communication discipline appears. A traditional agency chain uses the main agency to make advertisements and film, while the specialist agencies produce designs, interactive solutions, direct marketing, PR and so on. Since specialist agencies rarely work together, that isn't going to help the customer to integrate the communication, and create a consistent picture of the company. At Kunde & Co. we have built the specialist competencies into one agency as a total concept, with a co-ordinating function to help customers integrate the communication.

From our desired market position derived from our mission, we can build the bridge from "helping companies to build strong market positions" to a "total communication agency". The explanation of our total product and its connection with our mission is shown in Figure 9.3.

Against the industry tide

Customers are used to being told how important it is to have specialists for the different disciplines, so it's important to explain why our product looks like this, and why it goes against the industry tide. We go the opposite way because we believe that it can be damaging to cultivate specialist disciplines in marketing at the expense of coherence in the communication. We believe that consistent flow, content and expression are of the utmost importance to a company.

Fig 9.3 Total communication agency

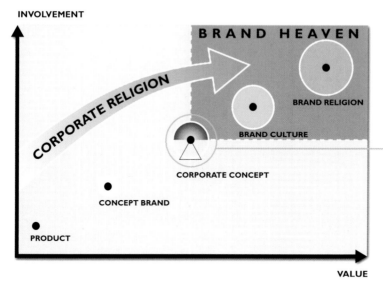

Kunde & Co's mission is to help companies build strong market positions – to help them ascend the involvement axis towards Brand Religion. It is crucial that the company has a thoroughly consistent communication. At Kunde & Co. we are able to help with every communication task and thus ensure consistency – see the wheel to the right.

This provides a unified picture for customers – from customer service (not necessarily your own), to advertisements, PR, annual reports, environmental policy, staff policy, ethics, invoicing, direct mails, brochures, Internet, TV commercials, product design and packaging design. The important issue here is to explain the company's interface with its surroundings and have a policy which enables every single element to play a useful part in building a unified expression of the company.

The total communication agency

The marked area in Figure 9.4 shows what a conventional advertising agency handles. The other boxes are typically divided into specialist agencies. The description of the "total communication agency" is the external description of Kunde & Co.'s total product. Our main competence lies here, and so we aim to work outwards from that model in relation to all our customers. Of course, we also make smaller parts of the product spectrum for customers, but the objective is the "total".

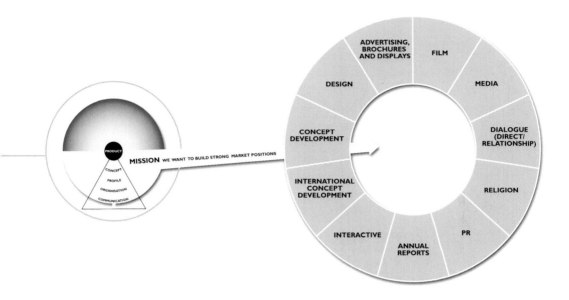

Fig 9.4 Kunde & Co's communication wheel

The marked area shows what a conventional advertising agency handles.

The profile and the communication

Kunde & Co.'s profile is that of a serious marketing agency. We do everything we can to deliver a consistent flow to the market. Recently, we have described ourselves in a corporate brochure of more than 150 pages. It explains our philosophy and how we work, while comprehensive case histories ensure that clients can relate to the results of our work. Since the agency opened we have also advertised ourselves, something that is usually considered taboo in the advertising world. We do it because we see our company as a brand which must be built – so it is natural to inform the market about who we are, what we stand for, and what we can do. Our advertisements feature our business concepts and the marketing problems we have solved for our clients.

A well dressed agency

When we advertise, we are very conscious of the business approach we take. We advertise because we have something to say. Every year we run continuous campaigns with inserts and direct mails to potential customers generated from the agency's database. We also advertise in business journals – not just in magazines for the advertising industry; and when you meet our consultants, you'll find them dressed in jacket and tie as befits a serious marketing agency. There's none of the roll-neck sweater and tennis shoes types you come across in other parts of the advertising trade.

Fig 9.5 Organising a total communication agency

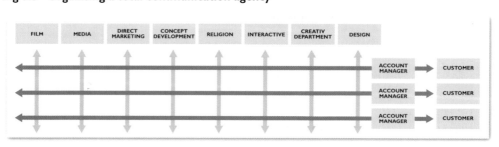

The consultants are the co-ordinating factor between the internal specialist functions and the customer.

The central consultant function

Since we want to be a total concept agency on our clients'
terms, we have built the agency up around the consultant
function. The consultant is the focal point in relation to
the customer, and carries full responsibility. It is he or she
who runs the large scale concept development projects in
which the entire agency is involved. The consultant is also
the co-ordinator for all the specialist competencies.
Individual specialist units can of course work directly with
the client, but it is the consultant who has the ultimate
responsibility for the task, and the budget.

Figure 9.5 shows how the consultants form the entry
point to the company. They are experienced people
qualified to handle Kunde & Co.'s total product concept
– not junior creatives who have just made their first
advertisement.

In major development projects such as direct marketing,
interactive and film where designers, creatives,
desktoppers and specialist departments are used, it is the
consultant's responsibility to ensure that everybody
follows the same conceptual path.

Creative chaos

At Kunde & Co. we try to maintain a flat hierarchy and a
very high chaos level – simultaneously. It encourages both
creative and total solutions for our clients. We don't want
little empires dotted around that become states with in a
state – there are more than enough of them to be found
among our customers. To create ground-breaking, total
concepts across disciplines and between departments, we
must ourselves be as fluid as possible; it requires an
enormous amount of work to achieve it.

The internal culture

The culture in Kunde & Co. has been grown by my
partner Gaute Høgh and myself. We started the agency,
and we are still there. We remain a living part of the
culture. Along with us, there is a core of key employees
who have also journeyed from a small basement
beginning to where we are now as one of Denmark's

leading agencies. They are also a valued part of setting the agenda in the company.

When we first started, the company grew at 50% a year – on the employee side. How could we know if all these new employees would suit the agency without finding out which values had brought us to our present position? The realisations that led to this book convinced me that we had to uncover what constituted our culture or religion. By doing so, we could communicate it to new employees and get them up and running more quickly. Our product is complex and goes deep, demanding that everybody is highly committed.

Our commitment to study our clients' marketing problems in great depth, rather than throwing together cheap, superficial solutions, is something we would move mountains to protect.

The practical implementation of marketing solutions involving direct contact with many of our clients' subsidiaries is a monumental task. Our commitment to study our clients' marketing problems in great depth, rather than throwing together cheap, superficial solutions, is something we would move mountains to protect.

It must be done in the right way

How do we ensure that all our new employees have the abilities and attitudes necessary to do the job in the right way? And how do we teach them to do it profitably? On billings we have always been at the top of the tree because the total product does not have any competition. And we have always generated big results for our clients. At first we tried the group approach, but it didn't work; so we held a seminar where I related the content and thoughts of my book "Corporate Religion", which would be published a couple of months later. I presented the mission and the vision, which would clearly need to be continuously updated. This is because we had already reached the first major milestone of becoming the leading marketing expert in Denmark. Later we tried to define the values and attitudes which had brought us to where we were. Again, we went into groups, where many good thoughts, ideas and explanations were put forward; but none really captured the essence of what we were seeking.

An attempt with external consultants

Immediately after the book was published, I was contacted by a research scholar from the College of Commerce in Århus, Denmark. He wanted to discuss Corporate Religion with me, as he was just in the process of finishing a dissertation on value-based management at the Institute for Organisation. The upshot of our meeting was that I hired him and his colleagues as external consultants, with the task of trying to uncover Kunde & Co.'s Corporate Religion. Since we were having such difficulties with it, I felt that an external team might be able to achieve what we could not.

You must do it yourself

It was a classic mistake, and I made it. It was the mistake of forgetting to spend time on yourself and your own organisation. There are always things that are waiting to be done, but if you want to build a strong culture you have to make it a priority, and make time for it.

It was a classic mistake, and I made it. It was the mistake of forgetting to spend time on yourself and your own organisation.

One of the first initiatives our external consultants took was to ask us to write an essay during the summer holiday, just like we did at school. They wanted a description of what it was like to be at Kunde & Co., and what each of us thought were the important values. We on the other hand wanted to know what we were good at and how we delivered value. The exercise generated many excellent statements about who we were and why, what we should preserve, and what we shouldn't. My own contribution covered 27 A4 pages.

And you must write it yourself

It is a practice that I can recommend to all managers, and you ought to do it once a year. It is a realisation process that quickens your thoughts and sharpens your mind. Above all, it helps create a breathing space for reflection which you easily lose in the hectic bustle of everyday life. Six months previously I had employed an administration manager to systematise the agency and control the finances because it was taking up far too much of my time. By releasing myself from it, I could concentrate more on developing total concepts for our clients, and fully developing our own business concept. I also wanted to spend more time on the religion aspect of our company, so that we could grow qualitatively. I wrote down what I felt was most important at Kunde & Co., and what I wanted to preserve. Our new administration manager viewed what I had written as a personal attack on him, and duly phoned the chairman of the board. The chairman read the document and replied: "Fantastic. Now we have captured in words what we have been doing all along."

A special culture

The administration manager resigned some months later when he realised that we didn't want change, but to increase our success.

We wanted to preserve a special culture, not change it because there were people joining us with different attitudes on what constitutes good management. What use would that be? We were a big success – it was about getting it described so that it could be copied. The administration manager resigned some months later when he realised that we didn't want to change, but to increase our success.

At about this time, our external consultants embarked on a big round of employee interviews. The report they subsequently delivered appalled me. It said that we were lacking in structure, lacking in leaders, and lacking in professional management (whatever that means). The employees wanted to be supervised and led, the report stated. I just didn't understand it. This was not the company I had built, nor did it reflect the attitudes of the people who had been a part of building it. Something was very wrong here, but what? To get the answer, I sat down with the pile of essays from the summer holidays and read through them again, one by one.

A marked difference

There was a marked difference in which attitudes were seen as important in Kunde & Co., and how the company should be run. The difference came from whether you were a long-serving Kunde & Co. key employee, or a newcomer. With the enormous growth we had experienced, there were many new faces around. In one year, we doubled our workforce from 60 to 120.

Safety deception

We were very close to making what would have been the biggest blunder in the history of Kunde & Co. – if we had described the company on the basis of new employees' vague ideas about their need to feel safe. I call it safety deception. You are lulled into a false sense of security and your initiative disappears because you want to be told what to do. We wanted the exact opposite. We wanted independent-spirited employees who work together because they like it, because they share the same ideas about how things should be done, and because they want to work for an agency that wants not to just be there – but to be the best.

The representative group

We needed to form a group of key employees from the different departments in the agency so that all the important working functions were represented. The main criterion for inclusion in the group was length of service, but we did however include two more recent employees who were widely respected and considered able representatives.

That representative group was so named because it represented each separate discipline in the company. The individual members of the group held regular meetings with the colleagues they represented and discussed proposals on attitudes and values. The representative group then presented an overall proposal for Kunde & Co.'s Corporate Religion on the basis of these discussions. I also participated actively in debating how we should describe the religion. I particularly remember one occasion when the group took exception to something that I had written:

The original formulation from my "expercise"

"Elite Company: We are an élite company. We set ourselves ambitious objectives, and the company expects a lot from its employees etc, etc ."

A female account executive in the representative group had discussed this with her colleagues. They didn't like the word élite, and she didn't like it either. At first, I thought they were opposed to saying that we wanted to be the best. I wondered if it was a female attitude to things, but I was completely wrong. They did want to be the best, that was why they were with Kunde & Co. The problem was that to them, élite had the unfavourable sound of élitist. That experience taught me that choice of words is extremely important. They must convey exactly the right meaning to new employees, so that they can correctly interpret statements on religion and other important issues.

> **The final formulation from "Attitude" was like this:**
>
> *"We are bringing together people with a high level of commitment and drive. Kunde & Co. is a hard working culture. Each contributes in his or her own way. We share the common characteristic of a passion for our work. We want to get something special out of it. If you don't want that, you're in the wrong place. We demand more than other companies, because we want to be better than the rest. That is hard work."*

The book "Attitude" helps us to employ the right people.

Religion delivers results

As a result of our major religion exercise, the representative group developed a booklet simply called "Attitude". It explains our mission and vision, and describes the attitudes and values we hold in high regard. When screening potential new employees, we give them the booklet, ask them to read it carefully and then come back and tell us what they think about our attitudes and values. The intention with the booklet is to help us employ the right people for Kunde & Co., and to turn away the rest.

Resurrecting past beliefs

We have clarified and developed our Corporate Religion, and use it in every connection. An offshoot from the project was that we reaffirmed some ideas we previously held. At one time, we let potential employees talk to many different people in the organisation before deciding whether to employ them. This is because in our organisation you have to be able to co-operate extensively with many different functions. If just one of us thought that there could be problems with a candidate fitting in, he or she was not employed. It was simply too risky for both the individual – and the whole organisation.

Caring for chaos

We aim to maintain as much chaos as possible in order to encourage the creative development process. But it is a highly volatile substance, and not many accidental sparks are needed before it explodes. We made an important discovery during the representative group work. Several of the discussion groups could not relate our mission to their actual work. For example, a number of creatives could not see how "building strong market positions for our clients" translated into their own activities; so I wrote a specific description which fully explained the importance of their work to fulfilling our mission, and the criteria for success. The Attitude booklet is just one part of our religion work. We also decided to develop a description of our work flow, which could be incorporated into a total description of Attitude and Action in Kunde & Co. This project is not yet completed.

The Overall Mission:

MISSION FOR KUNDE & CO.
"WE HELP COMPANIES TO BUILD STRONG MARKET POSITIONS"

Component Mission for a Department:

MISSION – CREATIVES

To build strong market positions for our clients requires that creatives can express a thorough and well-prepared strategy in a closely reasoned, relevant and impactful creative solution. We do not develop our solutions from isolated flights of fancy or crazy ideas. Other agencies can use those playpens. We communicate the company's soul and position. That is one major responsibility! We give the company strong exposure and draw the consumer towards it. Our creative solution must impress the consumer and contribute strongly to making the consumer choose the company's product.

That we work within carefully determined limits makes the creative task more difficult. It narrows the possibilities and requires that we are even more imaginative. A solution has got to be found – and it must have the optimum creative quality. This means creatives have an obligation to keep up with the times and keep themselves well informed – so the way we express the company's communication is always at the leading edge of development.

All employees must be able to relate their work to the overall mission, so the booklet "Attitude" describes component missions for each department. The example shows the component mission for the creative department.

Look up to the employee

To the employees, it matters very much what the management thinks – where the company is going, and where it is supposed to be going. In many places, employees are not properly informed about these things, so they spend a lot of time wondering. In my opinion, this should not be allowed to occur. Employees must never be left guessing at management's intentions. They live and breathe for the company. If you want to manage a value-driven company, there must be clear objectives and clear lines of communication. If there are changes in thinking or direction, the employees must be the first to know about it.

What we want in the future

Our religion project made it clear that we had to make up our minds about the future. How big would we become? How big did we want to become? Should we expand across borders? The original vision of becoming the most serious marketing agency had been achieved a long time ago, so we had to set new targets to advance further. We defined a larger vision – to be the most serious marketing agency in Scandinavia. It seemed a logical ambition, since we already had important clients in Sweden, Finland and Norway. But it quickly proved to be too narrow. Our real vision was to be the most serious agency in Europe – at the end of 1998 we opened an office in London. In the Attitude booklet, this vision is fully described and explained. For example, it does not mean that we will open offices in every European country, but rather that we want balanced growth. Offices will open when we find the right people, and have the capacity and surplus to train and manage these units. At the same time, it has been made clear that our main priorities are Scandinavia and Northern Europe.

Finding the future in the past

Over the last two years, we have carried out religion projects for several companies, and we have learned the importance of uncovering history in order to understand who they are, and why their culture is the way it is. The seeds of a company's religion, it frequently transpires, are

To mark Kunde & Co.'s 10th anniversary, I wrote a book (The Hurdle Race) which was distributed to all employees – and only to them!

to be found in historical events. Most companies come into existence on the back of an idea. Development can be seen as a refinement of that idea while a larger marketing system is being created. By going back to the origin, a clear picture emerges of the company and the values and the attitudes which lie behind their success. This is what I have done with my own company.

So why did I open Kunde & Co.? And how had it gone so far? My book was later distributed to every employee at the time of the company's 10th anniversary. My main purpose with the book was to provide the background for the Attitude booklet. I end the book with my view of the future – and what I think will be the most important challenges the company will face. The book has been written specifically for internal use. Many people have asked whether I'm making too much of the whole thing, but my answer is a categorical no. You can never go too far in cultivating clarity and understanding of the company you are part of.

The total description

At Kunde & Co. we believe that we can describe our company both externally and internally. Figure 9.6 shows the tools that describe the company. From left to right, The Hurdle Race illustrates the idea on which the company was founded, and the first 10 years that laid the foundation.

This is followed by an internal description of the business concept in relation to attitudes and action.

In the centre of the Figure there is a concept brochure which describes to the outside world what Kunde & Co.'s business concept is all about, comprehensively illustrated with case histories. Then come the advertisements for the company's external communication. The most important feature of the total description is that all the individual elements fit together coherently and support each other.

In building total business concepts for our clients, we have worked hard to set their individual specialist areas in the context of a total overall objective. The more easily

employees can gain an overview the entire company in
which they work, the more motivated and effective they
will be in their jobs.

Fig 9.6   Tools for describing the integrated company Kunde & Co.

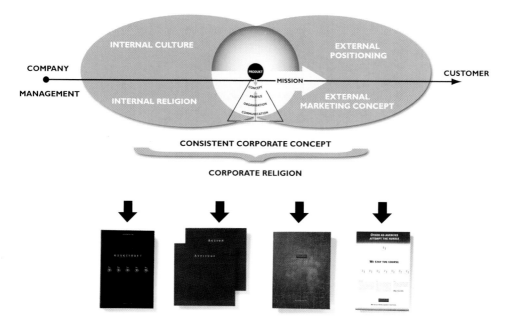

*For a description of the internal and external aspects of the company, the following tools are used:
The Hurdle Race (the first 10 years of Kunde & Co's history), Attitude (vision, mission, attitudes and
values), Action (workflow and work distribution), Kunde Report (concept description and cases) and
Advertisements (business concepts and cases).*

Nurture your Corporate Religion

Figure 9.6 illustrates how both the internal and external
elements describe the Total Corporate Religion. Other
essential aspects are the employees' abilities in relation to
the company's concept, and their attitudes to its
implementation. Our experience shows that it is not
enough just to describe it in books and booklets – it is
only when it is deeply ingrained in the company that it
begins to flow by itself. We decided to set up an internal
Kunde & Co. University to develop the abilities and
attitudes of the organisation, using internal teachers with
key competencies in their own specialist areas. Their task
is to ensure that competence in the agency as a whole is

*Employees being taught at
Kunde & Co. University.*

as high as possible. Courses are offered on the history of the agency, the company's corporate religion, and work flow in administration and all specialist areas. Not surprisingly, it has turned out to require considerable organisational resources to establish this university, because those who run it are busy people to start with. But it works.

Take care of the family

One of the most controversial points in the whole religion development course was the concept of "the company as a family". The "old guard" employees, who had experienced our development from a small unit to a company with 150 employees, felt it was difficult to form close-knit relationships with so many people. New employees, on the other hand, considered the word family far too intimate to describe a work place. One of the reasons why I started my own company was to create a more vibrant and enlivened environment, somewhere that was more than just the place where you work. My ambition was to bring together people who really wanted to get something out of their work. Their efforts would not be frustrated by negative-minded bureaucrats, which is almost always the case in large companies. Having been in major industrial groups myself, I knew only too well the alienation and indifference from the top management that employees suffer. I could do a lot better than that.

My ambition was to bring together people who really wanted to get something out of their work.

The electricity of chaos

I saw the agency as one big family, which could cope with large oscillations as a result of the strong bonds holding us together. The family concept had no problems in the early days, when new employees started as colleagues and quickly became friends. The company's growth changed this pattern, but I refused to accept that our larger size would necessitate systems and hierarchies. Our most important asset is chaos, which generates an amazing electricity and which, in turn, gives us the energy and desire to push the boundaries for our clients. I saw that if we became stiff and stereotyped, we would be unable to think in a free and expansive way. I have regularly introduced new initiatives to encourage family ties and togetherness in the agency because I believe they are essential for maintaining a high energy level. We are dependent on explosions for our development. We must like each other, and that only happens with continuous investment.

Culture Club

We held parties to develop our spirit of togetherness and always invited partners so that they could understand what we were all about. Christmas lunches were major events to which partners were again invited. These events became grander in scale as the need grew. Day trips to Paris, Prague, Rome and Barcelona in the run-up to Christmas are some of the investments we have made in being together and getting to know each other. One year, we organised a three-day trip to Verbier in Switzerland, with blue ski suits provided for everyone, so that we could recognise colleagues and partners out on the piste. Every single trip pumped up the culture by 50%. Whenever we want to give ourselves a boost, we do something new.

Parent's Day

Another initiative we have developed to remove the traditional boundaries between work and family is Parents' Day. That doesn't mean you bring your children with you – it means you bring your parents. We have many young people employed here, and in the creative areas of the company especially, the parents do not understand what their offspring are doing. So we ask a client to brief us on a real task and divide all the parents and employees into groups, which are then given two hours to complete the task. For example, it might be a brief to develop a marketing concept for a new mobile phone. The proposals are presented by the parents and the client chooses the best solution. It's followed by a giant party.

Everyone wants the support of family and friends in what they do – and at Kunde & Co. employees get a brilliant opportunity to have this. You can think of it as internal marketing. The most important thing is to find what makes you unique and cultivate it, to do things that strengthen your uniqueness and make people proud of their working place. The company must also do things to make the individual feel valued. I've heard the argument many times that we are too big to make it happen. My answer is: Then go and find a way to make it happen. Just as the company continuously invests in desks and chairs and computers, so we must do the same for our internal culture.

Index